# Interest and Alternative Remedies in International Arbitration

Edited by Filip De Ly and Laurent Lévy

DOSSIERS
ICC Institute of World Business Law

**ICC Services**
**Publications Department**
38 Cours Albert 1er
75008 Paris – France
**www.iccbooks.com**

**ICC Publication No. 684**
ISBN: 978-92-842-0033-7

# Contents

# Foreword

### By **Serge Lazareff**
*Member of the Paris Bar*
*Chairman, ICC Institute of World Business Law*

Once again, the ICC Institute of World Business Law held its Annual Meeting on a topic that concerns business the most: the bottom line.

During arbitral procedures, lawyers enjoy submitting sophisticated briefs, raising incidents on language, jurisdiction, challenge of arbitrators and so forth, followed by long hearings and, sometimes, interminable oral presentations. Under the auspices of the ICC International Court of Arbitration, a great effort has recently been made to reduce the duration and costs of arbitral proceedings, and the Institute contributes towards moving even faster in this direction, particularly through the training programmes it conducts.

Nevertheless, it is striking to note that, while no legal stone remains unturned in procedures, when it comes to calculating damages and auxiliary financial matters such as interest, liquidated damages, judicial penalties and, more globally, the amounts claimed, the arbitrator is at a loss most of the time because these issues, as important as they may be, often remain neglected.

This is quite regrettable, as auxiliary financial claims often represent huge sums. It is therefore essential to have a clear approach for rightly assessing the time value of money so as to adjust the amount of the damage suffered to reflect present-day monetary values. There are many facets to this evaluation – and the purpose of the present Dossier of the Institute is to cover as many as possible.

How far does the authority of the arbitrator go to control the amount of the damage and its full compensation? Add to this the sometimes emotional approach to interest and the interference of religious and social factors, which in certain cases are centuries old and deeply routed in various cultures. Approaches for awarding damages, in particular interest, may vary not only from one law to another but also depending on the background and the personal approaches of the arbitrator.

It is therefore essential to firmly establish the principles in this field and to study each item that needs to be taken into consideration when calculating and awarding interest, auxiliary and alternative remedies.

This is the ambition of this new Dossier, which forms the fifth volume of our series.

Welcome to our readers, who will, I hope, enjoy this book as much as I had the pleasure (and interest!) in listening to the speakers at our Annual Meeting, each a renowned specialist in his or her field.

# Introduction

### *By* **Laurent Lévy**
### *Co-Editor*

*"Justice delayed is justice denied" (Gladstone)*

*"Jura vigilantibus non dormientibus prosunt / jura vigilantibus tarde venintibus ossa"*

*"A party who knows that any provision of, or requirement under, these Rules has not been complied with and yet proceeds with the arbitration without promptly stating his objection to such non-compliance, shall be deemed to have waived his right to object." (UNCITRAL Arbitration Rules Article 30)[1]*

How long a "reasonable time" ought to be is not defined in law, but is left to the discretion of the judges (Black's Law Dictionary *ad* time, "reasonable time" quote from a US court decision).

Time is among the most elusive dimensions in human life. Even more than the sense of direction and space geometry, time consciousness pervades every aspect of human existence. As is well known, in addition to length, width and height, time may be identified as the fourth dimension, at least according to the Theory of Relativity, and this theory is beyond the understanding of the layman, especially the lawyer.

As the preceding quotations show, the law cannot avoid taking the time factor into consideration.

In fact, time will permeate every aspect of the law, including contracts, torts, procedures, enforcement and so forth.

In general, time saved is always beneficial, especially since "time is money".[2] Time efficiency is a factor in arbitration. Rightly or wrongly, speed is frequently mentioned as one of the advantages of arbitration. Numerous conferences, writings and court decisions address the issue of time in arbitration. More often than not, they take issue with efficient case management and address, for instance, such matters as parties' dilatory tactics, arbitrators' pro-active conduct of the proceedings and the role of institutions in controlling the lapse of time. However, should the time concern be restricted to the period between the initiation of an arbitration and the award? Should it not encompass the period from the occurrence of the damage until the actual discharge of the award, in other words the compensation?

This book deals with efficiency and time.

However, its approach is different in that it is less procedural and more substantive than usually the case in arbitration publications.

The initial step is an axiom. With great uniformity, everyone seems to accept that:

> *"The nature of liability is to re-establish as exactly as possible the equilibrium that the damage destroyed and to have the aggrieved party into the same situation that would have been his if the damaging event had not occurred."[3]*

> *"Le propre de la responsabilité civile est de replacer la victime dans la situation où elle se serait trouvée si l'acte dommageable ne s'était pas produit."* (Cour de cassation, Deuxième chambre civile, July 9, 1981, *Bulletin civil des arrêts de la Cour de cassation II, No. 1561*)

It would be impossible to cite the multitude of decisions (whether of municipal, international or arbitral courts) calling for full and adequate compensation of damage. Practically all point to the need for such compensation to be "prompt" in order to be adequate.[4]

This book is an attempt at finding how the parties to a contract or to an arbitration, as well as the arbitrators themselves, should proceed efficiently to ensure the timeliness of the compensation or to find a remedy for the lack of such timeliness.

It is not unusual – quite the contrary – to find writings, symposia and guidelines dealing with the efficiency of the arbitration process itself.[5] What has attracted less attention, however, is how the parties and the arbitrators may find alternative remedies to address those very issues of time and efficiency.

The parties themselves may forestall the arbitration process and endeavour to find contractual remedies. They may either think of ways to avoid time elapsed or endeavour to facilitate the reaction to any time loss. Monetary penalties and liquidated damages clauses are some examples of such anticipatory thinking. Antonias Dimolitsa addresses such contractual remedies.

In principle, between the occurrence of the damage and the actual compensation, there is a time period with which the arbitrators do not concern themselves. This is the period of the enforcement of the award, since the arbitrators do not have any *imperium*. Should efficient arbitrators totally disregard the time factor after the handing down of this award? Do the early 21st century arbitrators still think that *lata sententia arbiter desinit esse arbiter*? Not necessarily, if they may resort to such relief as a judicial penalty.

Judicial penalties may be a way of ensuring the actual and timely enforcement of awards ordering specific performance. Is specific performance the "ultimate remedy"? In theory, the answer is obviously yes, provided, however, that specific performance is admissible under the applicable laws and actually carried out. Even if it is admissible, specific performance will in practice raise considerable difficulties, both during the arbitration process to grant it and subsequently at the enforcement stage. Alexis Mourre and V.V. Veeder will expound on such questions.

Last but not least, this book would not be complete if it left out the more classical way of efficiently addressing the time factor in arbitration, namely interim relief. On this issue, see the contribution of John Beechey and Gareth Kenny.

As is now clear, the first part of this book looks for "alternative" remedies seeking to avoid the rise of any injury due to time lapsing after the occurrence of the damage.

However, should the parties and the arbitrators not (totally) achieve this objective, then it will become necessary to compensate the aggrieved party for such further damages. This is also known as interest, which forms the subject of the second part of this book.

To be precise, interest is, among other things, compensation allowed by law or contract for the use, forbearance or deprivation of money. In fact, interest is a way to take into consideration the lapse of time prior to, during and after the proceedings.

John Gotanda studies the nature of and the general rules applicable to the various kinds of interest. Andrea Giardina focuses on some peculiar rules that frequently apply to the allocation of interest in international arbitration and, given the general scope of this book, adopts a substantive rather than procedural approach to such matters. When it comes to the matter of interest, a book would not be complete without addressing the specifics of Islamic law, which Tarek Riad does (with some additional comments from Hamayoon Arfazadeh). Finally, Thierry Sénéchal gives a short review of some economic aspects of interest and deprivation of money.

In summary, arbitrators must navigate between two dangerous reefs.

Should they wish to be extremely efficient, they may endeavour to rush for their award or resort to alternative remedies that are to a certain extent *terra incognita*. This may result in a less than stalwart award. Should they prefer to be (over-)prudent, they might disregard the time factor and hand down an award of diminished actual economic value. The first aim of this book and of the authors is to locate the happy medium between these two preoccupations. Its second and foremost aim is to supply material for courageous arbitrators who prefer the first risk, thus contributing to the progress of efficiency in international arbitration.

## END NOTES

[1]  Cf. Art. 33 – Waiver of the ICC Arbitration Rules; Y. Derains and E.A. Schwartz, *A Guide to the ICC Rules of Arbitration*, 2nd edn. (2005) p. 379.

[2]  And one might add "and vice versa". See the contribution of Thierry Sénéchal in this volume, entitled: 'Present-Day Valuation in International Arbitration: A Conceptual Framework for Awarding Interest'.

[3]  *Chorzow Factory* case, Merits, PCIJ, Series A, No. 17, 1928, at 47-48.

[4]  However, the profusion and repetition of such decisions point to an ever-occurring difficulty that is never remedied.

[5]  J. Gotanda, 'Damages in Private International Law', *Recueil des Cours*, Vol. 326 (2007) p. 73 et seq.

# 1

## Contractual remedies:
## *clauses pénales* and liquidated damages clauses

*By* **Antonias Dimolitsa**

*Partner, A. Dimolitsa & Associates*
*Council Member of the ICC Institute of World Business Law*
*Vice-President of the ICC Commission on Arbitration*

### I. COMMON FEATURES

The *clauses pénales* and liquidated damages clauses are contractual remedies – meant for the purposes of the present study only as monetary remedies, i.e. as accessory obligations to pay a sum of money – for non-performance or breach of an obligation. Without disregarding terminology, in particular the hybrid character of *clauses pénales*, and specific questions that may arise at the stage of their enforcement depending on the different applicable rules of law, one can assert that in normal practice:

- First, they both regulate in advance, in an agreed and certain manner, the assessment of damages in the event of breach of an obligation.

- Second, they reinforce the contractual obligations to which they refer and constitute a deterrent to breach – this word *per se* does not imply a penal sanction – due to the foreseeability and the apparent certainty of the amount of damages to be paid in case of breach.

- Third, if a dispute is not avoided, the non-defaulting party does not need to prove its actual damages, if any.

- Fourth, regarding international arbitration, which aims to be the specific angle of the present study, if arbitration is not avoided, as there will be no need to prove actual damages, the arbitration proceedings will be more efficient in terms of both time and cost.

## II.   THE CONTRACTUAL CLAUSES

Both *clauses pénales* and liquidated damages clauses are very frequent in practice; they are in fact used interchangeably or indiscriminately in different kinds of international contracts (sales contracts, construction contracts, loan agreements, licensing agreements, etc.) and refer to different types of breached obligations (late performance, failure to supply, inadequate performance, etc.).

The study of the contractual clauses reveals a great diversity in their drafting,[1] often ambiguity as to their real nature as compensatory or punitive and sometimes a marked similarity to clauses with a different legal function.[2] The contracting parties are invited to pay specific attention to different aspects when drafting such clauses, as to the granting of grace periods, the fixing of a maximum amount, the possible reduction of penalties, but also – more importantly – the limitative, cumulative or optional character of the clause.[3] They must especially make clear in the clause, when it is anticipated that its enforcement may be sought under the common law system, that their intention is to assess future damages for breach.

## III.   OVERVIEW IN COMPARATIVE LAW

The legal function of *clauses pénales* and liquidated damages clauses is one of the most discussed issues in comparative law; one may easily find a series of scholarly writings on the solutions adopted under the different national laws as well as many comparative studies. Be this as it may, the main, recurring topic in comparative law is the theoretical divergence between common law and civil law countries regarding the enforcement of these clauses.

In civil law countries,[4] the *clauses pénales* are an assessment in advance of the amount of damages to be paid in the event of breach of an obligation; this amount may sometimes include an extra-compensatory element, which constitutes the penalty, but the courts never evaluate the intent behind the clause since the clause is always enforceable. Yet, the courts have the power to reduce the amount of the clause if it is considered grossly excessive on the basis of different criteria; the relevant provision is mandatory in most national laws.[5] The courts also have the power to increase the amount of the clause or award additional damages, but the conditions for the exercise of this power differ under the national legislations of the civil law countries.[6]

In common law, a liquidated damages clause will be enforced if it is a reasonable pre-estimate of actual damages to be recovered by the non-defaulting party in case of breach by the other party.[7] It will not matter that the contract uses the word "penalty" if this sum is in reality a pre-estimate of damages or is intended as a limitation of damages and not *in terrorem*,[8] or, in a more modern sense, not excessive. The decision as to whether a sum represents liquidated damages or a penalty depends on the terms of the contract and the intention of the parties at the time of concluding the contract. If the sum is held to be a penalty, the clause becomes unenforceable. On the other hand, if it is held to be liquidated damages, the aggrieved party will be entitled to the stipulated sum whether its actual damages are greater, less or non-existent.[9]

However, some different approaches in the construction of the clauses in order to qualify them as excessive, and thus as a penalty, or as a genuine pre-estimate of damages do exist in common law countries. For instance, while English courts always have regard to the range of losses that could reasonably be anticipated at the time the contract was entered into,[10] US courts consider not only what could be anticipated as loss flowing from the breach at the time the parties concluded their contract but also the actual loss caused by the breach at the time that the breach took place.[11]

## IV. THE INTERNATIONAL EFFORTS TO HARMONIZE NATIONAL LAWS

It has to be stressed that, in all international harmonized rules regarding *clauses pénales* and liquidated damages clauses, the civil law approach has prevailed. Reference is made to (i) the Uniform Rules on Contract Clauses for an Agreed Sum Due upon Failure of Performance,[12] adopted by UNCITRAL in December 1983, with the recommendation that states implement them in the form of either a Model Law or a Convention;[13] (ii) Article 7.4.13 of the UNIDROIT Principles; and (iii) Article 9:509 of the Principles of European Contract Law.

Indeed, all the above harmonized rules apply to agreements on liquidated damages, penalties or hybrid clauses. The only difference is that whereas Article 7.4.13 of the UNIDROIT Principles[14] and Article 9:509 of the European Principles[15] – which, in essence, are identical in their wording – use a broad definition of the agreements to which they apply ("to pay a specified sum to the aggrieved party for such non-performance"), Article 1 of the UNCITRAL Uniform Rules[16] specifies that the non-defaulting party is entitled to the agreed sum "whether as a penalty or as compensation".

All three international harmonized rules provide further that the agreed sum may be reduced by a court, if it is "grossly excessive" (UNIDROIT and European Principles) or "substantially disproportionate" (Article 8 of the UNCITRAL Uniform Rules[17]) in relation to "the loss that has been suffered" and (UNIDROIT and European Principles) "to the other circumstances"; this power of the court exists, according to all three rules, despite any agreement of the parties to the contrary.

But it is only the UNCITRAL Uniform Rules that provide[18] the possibility of a claim for additional damages by the aggrieved party "if the loss substantially exceeds the agreed sum".

Notwithstanding these important international efforts to harmonize national laws, national legislators did not react. As a result, the disparities in the treatment of these clauses are still apparent in comparative law. The question is whether these disparities and especially the divergence in the approach of the clauses between civil and common law systems are limited to legal theory, while *in concreto* the different courts ultimately come to similar solutions, at least with regard to upholding or reducing these clauses depending on the circumstances.

It is undoubted that all courts accord pre-eminence to the freedom of contract and wish to validate the certainty of commercial transactions, on the grounds that "what the parties have agreed should normally be upheld".[19] The drafting of these clauses is obviously of the utmost importance. If the question now arises whether the agreed sum is excessive or not when considering the contractual clause, courts will balance justice, certainty and freedom of contract by referring to different criteria under the two law systems.

Under the civil law system, courts will resort to the concepts of good faith and morality in relation to the time of the breach, while, under the common law system, courts will consider primarily the bargaining powers of the parties at the time of the conclusion of the contract. But is the common law courts' approach not actually a disguised application of the same civil law concepts, albeit with reference to a different critical time? The court decision to uphold the clause would therefore arguably be the same under both systems, notwithstanding the difference in the reference period, as the threshold imposed by *Dunlop*[20] for the charac-terization of the sum as a penalty is extremely high – it must be "extravagant and unconscionable" in relation to the "greatest possible loss" that could be anticipated. And the civil law decision to reduce the agreed sum because it is grossly excessive would not differ substantially in terms of the finally payable amount from the common law decision characterizing the clause as a penalty and assessing *in lieu*[21] the actual damages, except if we consider that an important extra-compensatory/penal element would be retained in the reduced amount by the civil law court.[22]

In contrast, similar solutions of the courts under the two law systems in cases where the actual loss is more than the *clause pénale* or the liquidated damages clause seem improbable. Because common law courts will traditionally consider that the clause acts as a limitation on recoverable damages, while civil law courts, though respecting the agreement of the parties in principle, may exercise their power to award additional damages under the conditions provided in the applicable national law. Moreover, these conditions differ fundamentally in the civil law countries. This is all the more so, as civil law courts may often not accept a limitation on recoverable damages if the clause is considered to be a limited liability clause and there is evidence of fraud, wilful misconduct or gross negligence by the defaulting party.

## V. THE ATTITUDE OF THE ARBITRAL TRIBUNALS

The attitude of the international arbitral tribunals towards such clauses aims to be the real focus of the present study. The question is to what extent international arbitral tribunals tend to apply the harmonized rules or at least avoid to analyze the purposes of the clause in a reasoning "penalty versus genuine pre-estimate of damages".

There are a limited number of published arbitral awards dealing with *clauses pénales* or liquidated damages clauses; the 30 awards summarized in the Annex to the present study are the result of specific research in this respect. Most of them are not really indicative of a tendency of the arbitrators to search for and apply international rules; they are rather confined to the interpretation of the relevant contractual clauses and to considerations related to specific provisions of the applicable national law.

The arbitral awards in the Annex are assembled in three groups:
(A) awards applying national laws; (B) awards applying usages, general principles and the UNIDROIT Principles; and (C) awards applying the UN Convention on Contracts for the International Sale of Goods of 1980 (CISG). Only one of them, applying New York law,[23] involves a discussion of the purposes of the clause (penalty v. liquidated damages), concluding with its validation as a reasonable estimate of the expected loss. In all the others, the arbitral tribunals are not preoccupied with such an analysis of the clause. Interestingly enough, in one award,[24] the clause (providing for "a compensation fee") is interpreted as a real penalty and granted in addition to damages pursuant to Articles 74 and 75 CISG, without any reference to a national law.

The awards that do not refer to a national law are scarce. In one of them, an ICC award of 1979,[25] the arbitral tribunal decided to apply "the widely accepted general principles governing commercial international law". However, the arbitral tribunal then proceeded to analyze the contractually agreed payments, found that they were in the nature of damages rather than a penalty and adopted the view that, contrary to the amounts of a penalty, which may be reviewed, the amounts of liquidated damages are not subject to such a review. The arbitral tribunal in fact followed the common law approach.

Some more recent awards, however, do refer to Article 7.4.13 of the UNIDROIT Principles. These provisions are applied directly in some awards because the Principles are explicitly agreed by the parties or because they are considered applicable in the absence of an explicit choice of law by the parties.[26] In some other awards, they are applied indirectly because the applicable rules of law refer to international trade usages.[27]

In yet some other awards, finally, these provisions are simply applied with a view to corroborating the contents of the applicable national provisions.[28]

The CISG does not address the issue of *clauses pénales* and liquidated damages clauses. By stipulating such a clause in their contract and depending on its drafting, parties may be held as having tacitly derogated from the application of Articles 74-76 of the Convention, pursuant to Article 6 CISG. When interpreting and applying such contractually agreed clauses, arbitral tribunals have two possibilities pursuant to Article 7(2) CISG: either to resort to the general principles on which the Convention is based (first limb) or to apply a national law by virtue of a conflict of laws system (second limb).

A recourse to the general principles of the Convention may arguably lead to a rule like Article 7.4.13 of the UNIDROIT Principles, after due consideration and balancing of the principle of the freedom of the parties (Articles 6 and 45(2) CISG) and the principle of full compensation of damages (Article 74 CISG). Conversely, the application of the UNIDROIT Principles by reference to Article 9(2) CISG, which considers them to be usages,[29] is deemed a theoretically wrong process notwithstanding its welcome purpose.

However, most of the awards applying the CISG and summarized in the Annex have had recourse to a national law when addressing the issue of *clauses pénales*/liquidated damages clauses. As to the solutions on the merits, the general impression that one may obtain from these awards is that contractual penalties for delay, in addition to payment of the price due for delivered goods or reimbursement of payment for undelivered goods, are granted to the extent that they are not excessive.

It would be presumptuous to posit on the basis of the awards referring to the UNIDROIT Principles, which, moreover, are only known through abstracts, that there is currently a trend of international arbitral tribunals to apply – or create – transnational rules with regard to clauses on agreed sums for non-performance or breach of an obligation. Quite the opposite, arbitral tribunals apparently seek the security of the provisions of a national law. However, in actual fact, their attitude is in line with the provisions of Article 7.4.13 of the UNIDROIT Principles and thus leaves leeway for some general propositions.

First, international arbitral tribunals should be inclined to uphold the agreed *clause pénale* or liquidated damages clause, irrespective of the actual loss – if any – and of its extra-compensatory/penal element, not only on the basis of the principles of the parties' will and *pacta sunt servanda* but also in view of the efficiency of the arbitration proceedings, which is normally wished by the parties through the inclusion of such a clause in their contract. Indeed, by enforcing such clauses, a long and costly evidentiary procedure on the existence of damages, the identification of the compensable ones and their quantification is avoided, and issues such as the remoteness in the causal link between the breach and the damages or the obligation to mitigate damages will not arise. Moreover, international arbitral tribunals apparently need not be preoccupied by international public policy enquiries, as provisions of national laws prohibiting agreements for lump-sum damages in some cases,[30] or penalty clauses proper,[31] do not seem to be matters of international public policy or to preclude enforcement of the award, at least when they are not excessive.

Second, irrespective of the stipulations of the clause and the provisions of the applicable law, international arbitral tribunals, should acknowledge their discretion to reduce[32] rather than invalidate – for the same reason of efficiency of the proceedings[33] – such clauses but should proceed with such a reduction only exceptionally, in cases where the agreed amount is grossly excessive in relation to the loss actually suffered by the non-defaulting party.[34] Considerations of other relevant circumstances, like the gravity of the fault, the bargaining power of the parties,[35] their financial situation[36] or the benefit that is likely to result from the breach for the aggrieved party, may also enter into play. As to the obligation of the aggrieved party to mitigate its damages, it is doubtful whether such a consideration can effectively influence the decision on the reduction.

Third, the arbitrators should not use their discretionary power to reduce the agreed amount of damages in the same way as when they apply the principle of full compensation of damages in the absence of a *clause pénale* or liquidated damages clause. When a *clause pénale* or liquidated damages clause is present, the arbitrators cannot ignore that they intervene against the parties' will and that it is only the excessive character of the agreed amount that is to be redressed. Arguably, their *pouvoir souverain d'appréciation* regarding the reduction operates irrespective of the degree of certainty of the established actual loss (Article 7.4.3 of the UNIDROIT Principles) and the reduced sum may well exceed the foreseeable (Article 7.4.4 of the UNIDROIT Principles) or actual loss.[37]

As regards the possibility to award additional damages over and above the agreed amount, there is no room for an argument on the existence of a principle in this respect – as in the case of reduction – due to the great variety of the relevant national provisions and the silence of the UNIDROIT Principles. It has proved impossible to find any award on additional damages among those published, which would be based only on the finding that the actual loss substantially exceeded the agreed amount, without any reference to the contract or a national law. However, notwithstanding the stipulations of the clause and the relevant provisions of the applicable national law precluding *ex hypothesi* additional damages, one may assume that, in exceptional circumstances, when the agreed amount is indeed derisory in relation to the actual loss, other legal concepts or general principles are likely to enter into play and invalidate the clause or ground the payment of additional damages, such as abuse of rights and good faith, morality and unconscionability or *rebus sic stantibus* and frustration of the contract, as well as – possibly – considerations of international public policy.

To conclude, in an effort to make things if not simpler then at least theoretically more precise, the trend in international arbitration should be towards the creation of self-sufficient rules, in the spirit of the provisions of Article 1152 of the French Civil Code.[38] The needs of international arbitration would be effectively met by the general principle of upholding the clause but also by the discretion left to the arbitral tribunals to intervene in both directions, i.e. to reduce or increase the agreed sum, in exceptional cases. In this way, predictability and parties' legitimate expectations would be satisfied, while flexibility in international arbitration and morality in international trade would at the same time be protected.

The pragmatic conclusion of this study, however, is limited to the finding that the published awards do not reveal any new transnational approach in the legal treatment of *clauses pénales* and liquidated damages clauses. The scope and function of such clauses actually depend on their drafting and the applicable rules of law. However, they do further the efficiency of the proceedings, irrespective of the applicable rules of law – be they national provisions of civil or common law systems or international rules – since they are upheld in principle and damages need not be proven.

---

## END NOTES

[1] See the two reports of UNCITRAL on liquidated damages and penalty clauses: A/CN.9/161 dated 25 April 1979 and A/CN.9/WG.2/WP.33 dated 12 February 1981. See further Marcel Fontaine and Filip De Ly, *Drafting International Contracts* (Transnational Publishers, 2006) Chapter 6: 'Penalty Clauses', based on the study of numerous varying clauses.

[2] Such as withdrawal payments (*clauses de dédit*), price adjustment clauses and, especially, clauses limiting liability.

[3] See *ICC Guide on Penalty and Liquidated Damages Clauses*, Publication No. 478 (1990); and Fontaine and De Ly, *supra* note 1.

[4] With the striking exception of Belgian law (Arts. 1226 and 1231 of the Belgian Civil Code, as modified by the Law of November 23, 1998), which prohibits penalty clauses. Regarding liquidated damages, however, it does empower the courts to reduce amounts that are excessive in relation to the foreseeable damages.

[5] See, for instance, Art. 1152.2 of the French Civil Code, Art. 1384 of the Italian Civil Code and Art. 409 of the Greek Civil Code.

[6] See, for instance, Art. 1152.2 of the French Civil Code (*même d'office*), Art. 161.2 of the Swiss Code of Obligations (upon request of the creditor who must prove a fault of the debtor), Art. 1382 of the Italian Civil Code (only if the possibility to claim further damages has been agreed upon by the parties) and Art. 407 of the Greek Civil Code (upon request of a party, only if the *clause pénale* is agreed for defective performance or delay).

[7] *Black's Law Dictionary*, 8th edn.

[8] See, *Dunlop Pneumatic Tyre Co. Ltd.* v. *New Garage & Motor Co. Ltd.* [1915] A.C. 79 at p. 86: "The essence of a penalty is a payment of money stipulated as *in terrorem* of the offending party; the essence of liquidated damages is a genuine covenanted pre-estimate of damage".

[9] *Hudson's Building and Engineering Contracts*, Vol. 2 (Sweet & Maxwell, 1995) p. 1131 et seq.

[10] The traditional position of the English courts from *Dunlop Pneumatic Tyre Co. Ltd.* v. *New Garage & Motor Co. Ltd.* onwards. See, *inter alia, Alfred McAlpine Capital Projects Ltd.* v. *Tilebox Ltd.* [2005] EWHC 281 (TCC). Four tests were suggested by Lord Dunedin in *Dunlop* for the construction of the clause with a view to distinguishing between liquidated damages and a penalty:

> *"(a) It will be held to be a penalty if the sum stipulated for is extravagant and unconscionable in amount in comparison with the greatest loss that could conceivably be proved to have followed from the breach.*
>
> *(b) It will be held to be a penalty if the breach consists only in not paying a sum of money, and the sum stipulated is a sum greater than the sum which ought to have been paid. This, though one of the most ancient instances, is truly a corollary to the last test.*
>
> *(c) There is a presumption (but no more) that it is a penalty when 'a single sum is made payable by way of compensation, on the occurrence of one or more or all of several events, some of which may occasion serious and others but trifling damages'.*
>
> *(d) It is no obstacle to the sum stipulated being a genuine pre-estimate of damage that the consequences of the breach are such as to make precise pre-estimation almost an impossibility. On the contrary, that is just the situation when it is probable the pre-estimated damage was the true bargain between the parties."*

---

[11] See Restatement (Second) of Contracts, § 356(1): "Damages for breach by either party may be liquidated in the agreement but only at an amount that is reasonable in the light of the anticipated or actual loss caused by the breach and the difficulties of proof of loss. A term fixing unreasonably large liquidated damages is unenforceable on grounds of public policy as a penalty." See also Uniform Commercial Code § 2-718(1): "Damages for breach by either party may be liquidated in the agreement but only at an amount which is reasonable in the light of the anticipated or actual harm caused by the breach, the difficulties of proof of loss, and the inconvenience or non-feasibility of otherwise obtaining an adequate remedy…".

[12] See *Official Records of the General Assembly*, 38th Session, Supplement No. 17 (A/38/17, Annex I).

[13] See Resolution No. 38/135 of the 101st plenary meeting of December 19, 1983 (A/RES/38/135), available at: <http://www.uncitral.org/uncitral/en/GA/resolutions.html>.

[14] Art. 7.4.13 of the UNIDROIT Principles:

"*(1) Where the contract provides that a party who does not perform is to pay a specified sum to the aggrieved party for such non-performance, the aggrieved party is entitled to that sum irrespective of its actual harm.*

*(2) However, notwithstanding any agreement to the contrary the specified sum may be reduced to a reasonable amount where it is grossly excessive in relation to the harm resulting from the non-performance and to the other circumstances.*"

[15] Art. 9:509 of the European Principles:

"*(1) Where the contract provides that a party who fails to perform is to pay a specified sum to the aggrieved party for such non-performance, the aggrieved party shall be awarded that sum irrespective of its actual harm.*

*(2) However, despite any agreement to the contrary the specified sum may be reduced to a reasonable amount where it is grossly excessive in relation to the loss resulting from the non-performance and the other circumstances.*"

[16] Art. 1 of the UNCITRAL Uniform Rules: "These Rules apply to international contracts in which the parties have agreed that, upon a failure of performance by one party (the obligor), the other party (the obligee) is entitled to an agreed sum from the obligor, whether as a penalty or as compensation."

[17] Art. 8 of the UNCITRAL Uniform Rules: "The agreed sum shall not be reduced by a court or arbitral tribunal unless the agreed sum is substantially disproportionate in relation to the loss that has been suffered by the obligee."

[18] Art. 7 of the UNCITRAL Uniform Rules: "If the obligee is entitled to the agreed sum, he may not claim damages to the extent of the loss covered by the agreed sum. Nevertheless, he may claim damages to the extent of the loss not covered by the agreed sum if the loss substantially exceeds the agreed sum."

[19] See *Philips Hon Kong v. A-G of Hong Kong* [1993] 61 Build LR 41, at 59.

[20] See *supra* note 10.

[21] See, however, *Jobson v. Johnson* [1989] 1 WLR 1023, where the clause was held to be a penalty. Interestingly enough, however, instead of being "wholly disregarded" it has been scaled down, which in essence means a reduction of the clause.

[22] On such an attempt to downplay the differences in the approach of the clauses, see two recent articles: Lucinda Miller, 'Penalty Clauses in England and France: A Comparative Study', 53(1) *International and Comparative Law Quarterly* (2004) pp. 79-106; and Charles R. Calleros, 'Punitive Damages, Liquidated Damages, and Clauses Pénale in Contract Actions: A Comparative Analysis of the American Common Law and the French Code Civil', *bepress Legal Series*, Working Paper 1180 (2006), available at: <http://law.bepress.com/expresso/eps/1180>. The proposition that a certain, not necessarily important extra-compensatory element may be retained by civil law courts is strengthened by the latter article and the interview of French magistrates by its author (p. 57).

[23] ICC Case No. 9839/1999, summarized in the Annex under No. 7.

[24] ICC Case No. 7585/1992, summarized in the Annex under No. 20.

[25] ICC Case No. 3267/1979, summarized in the Annex under No. 9.

[26] See awards summarized in the Annex under Nos. 11, 12, 14 and 17.

[27] See award summarized in the Annex under No. 10.

[28] See awards summarized in the Annex under Nos. 13 and 16.

[29] For such an application of Art. 7.4.13, see Arbitral Award 229/1996 of June 5, 1997 of the International Arbitration Court of the Chamber of Commerce and Industry of the Russian Federation, summarized in the Annex under No. 10.

[30] See Oberlandsgericht [Court of Appeal] Dresden, January 13, 1999, *YB Com. Arb.* (2004) p. 679, which upheld an ICC award although agreements for lump-sum damages in general conditions of sale are prohibited under German law.

[31] See Supreme Court of the United States, *Mastrobuono* v. *Shearson Lehman Hutton Inc.*, *YB Com. Arb.* (1996) p. 181, followed by numerous other court decisions. If enforcement of punitive damages awarded in arbitration is not contrary to US public policy, the same must hold true, all the more so, for penalty clauses. The position of English courts apparently does not differ, see Fontaine and De Ly, *supra* note 1, at p. 343 and *Godard* v. *Grey* [1870] L.R. 6 Q.B. 139.

[32] This proposition goes counter to the decision in ICC Case No. 3267/1979, which is, however, an old one. It is mentioned above and summarized in the Annex under No. 9.

[33] Full proof of the actual damages is not indispensable for the exercise by the arbitrators of their power to reduce the agreed amount; in this respect, see ICC Case No. 4462/1987, summarized in the Annex under No. 3.

[34] In one case, summarized in the Annex under No. 15, the arbitral tribunal awarded the interest at the agreed LIBOR rate for the delay in the payment of the price and, applying Art. 7.4.13(2), even decided to reject the claim for the agreed penalty. With regard to this possibly problematic relationship between penalty and interest, it is noted that in another case, summarized in the Annex under No. 12, by virtue of Art. 7.4.13(1), the arbitral tribunal upheld the rate of interest agreed for the delay in the payment of specific debts, which exceeded the applicable statutory rate, considering it as a penalty.

[35] This criterion is specifically mentioned in the Swedish law, S. Com. S. 36(2).

[36] See ICC Case No. 4629/1989, summarized in the Annex under No. 4.

[37] Interestingly enough, in a recent arbitral award, summarized in the Annex under No. 17, reference to Art. 7.4.3(3) of the UNIDROIT Principles was made because the amount of the penalty *per se* could not be established with a sufficient degree of certainty.

[38] Art. 1152 of the French Civil Code reads:

*"Lorsque la convention porte que celui qui manquera de l'exécuter payera une certaine somme à titre de dommages-intérêts, il ne peut être alloué à l'autre partie une somme plus forte, ni moindre.*

*Néanmoins, le juge peut, même d'office, modérer ou augmenter la peine qui avait été convenue, si elle est manifestement excessive ou dérisoire. Toute stipulation contraire sera réputée non écrite."*

# Annex:
## Published Arbitral Awards on *Clauses Pénales* and Liquidated Damages Clauses

A. ARBITRAL AWARDS APPLYING NATIONAL LAWS

1. **Award of October 4, 1979 of the Arbitration Court of the Chamber of Commerce and Industry of Czechoslovakia (*Yearbook of Commercial Arbitration* (1986) p. 101)**

   The sale contract between the Yugoslav seller and the Czechoslovak buyer provided that in case of delay in the delivery of the goods exceeding 15 days, the seller should pay liquidated damages at the rate of 10% of the value of the goods delayed or not delivered.

   Application of Czechoslovak substantive law (International Trade Code).

   The cause of non-delivery of the goods by the seller was due to an event of *force majeure*, i.e. floods and restrictions in water supplies, which caused the temporary interruption of the seller's plant.

   The Arbitral Tribunal held that the right to claim liquidated damages arises upon the occurrence of the event, i.e. the failure to perform under the obligation secured by the liquidated damages, irrespective of the cause of the failure. It exercised its power to reduce the liquidated damages, as it found that the liquidated damages were in obvious excess of the actual loss, by applying Article 194 of the International Trade Code, also taking into consideration the event that had caused the delay. The Arbitral Tribunal reduced the sum to be paid so as to cover the actual loss (the difference between the price to be paid to the seller and the higher price paid to a third supplier).

2. **ICC Case No. 4237/1984 (*Yearbook of Commercial Arbitration* (1985) p. 52)**

   Sale contract between a Syrian state trading organization (buyer-claimant) and a Ghanaian state enterprise (seller-defendant). Application of Ghanaian and English law.

After the establishment of a breach of contract by the defendant, the arbitrator proceeded to the determination of the damages without taking into account the contractual delay penalties, stating the following in this regard:

*"Although Claimants had repeatedly threatened to claim the delay penalty, Claimants have not claimed them in this arbitration. The Arbitrator therefore lacks competence to decide on them."*

3. **ICC Case No. 4462/1987 (*Yearbook of Commercial Arbitration* (1991) p. 54 and *Collection of ICC Arbitral Awards*, Vol. III, p. 3)**

Exploration and production sharing agreement governed by Libyan law.

Article 8.2 of the contract provided:

*"In the event that any part of the Exploration Program for any Area is not properly completed by the end of the Exploration Period applicable to such Area, [Sun Oil] shall immediately pay to [NOC] the costs of such uncompleted part at the end of such Exploration Period."*

The Arbitral Tribunal admitted the application of this article for the five-year areas but considered that the amount of money that would be payable by Sun Oil as liquidated damages under this article would be "grossly exaggerated" and should therefore be reduced in accordance with the mandatory provision of Article 227.2 of the Libyan Civil Code.[1] Making use of its "broad discretion" under this article, the Arbitral Tribunal reduced the liquidated damages and awarded to NOC an amount of USD 20 million, concluding as follows:

*"in fixing such an amount, which it considers fair and equitable, the Arbitral Tribunal is exercising its authority to make findings of fact based upon evidence and submission presented by the Parties, noting that despite repeated requests, NOC chooses not to produce any evidence as to its actual proven losses."*

4.  **ICC Case No. 4629/1989 (*Yearbook of Commercial Arbitration* (1993) p. 11 and *Collection of ICC Arbitral Awards*, Vol. III, p. 152)**

Work contract between two contractors (claimants) and the owner (defendant). Application of Swiss law.

The contract stated that the liquidated damages must be computed as follows: "10% of the sums paid or due in accordance with this contract if the defaulting party is the owner". The Arbitral Tribunal considered that the phrase "sums paid or due" cannot refer to anything else but to the total price of the contract regardless of the state of completion of the contract at the time of the termination.

The Tribunal further considered whether, under Article 163(3) Swiss CO,[2] the judge had the power to reduce *ex officio* liquidated damages that he deemed to be excessively high or whether one party must especially request the reduction. Without taking a position on this controversial issue in Swiss law, the Tribunal decided not to modify the contractually agreed liquidated damages by stating (with reference to Engel, *Traité de droit des obligations*):

> *"The parties are in a better position than the judge to estimate the amount of the liquidated damages applicable to their relations. The reduction is an exceptional remedy which must be applied only when the liquidated damages are so high that they exceed any common measure and are therefore incompatible with the idea of justice and equity".*

Having considered the various circumstances relevant in the case law, such as the disproportion between real damages and liquidated damages, the gravity of the defendant's fault and the financial situation of the parties, the Tribunal decided not to reduce the liquidated damages.

5.  **Arbitral Award in Case No. 16/1998 of the Arbitration Institute of the Stockholm Chamber of Commerce (2 *Stockholm Arbitration Report* (1999) p. 42)**

Object of the contract: trading in Russian securities.

The Arbitral Tribunal decided to determine the dispute on the basis of general principles of law as contained in Swedish law and to apply Swedish law to the issue of interest.

Article 5.2 of the contract provided that "a Party exceeding the time-limit of the financial obligations specified by this agreement must pay the other party a fine in the amount of 0.01% of the delayed sum as a forfeit for every calendar day of the delay but no more than 10%". Article 5.4 of the contract provided that "the payment of fines does not release the at-fault party from the execution of the obligations and caused loss compensation"[*sic*].

The penalty that had accrued until the date of the award was USD 10 880.

The Arbitral Tribunal concluded that

*"in view of the modest level of the penalty and of the contents of Article 5.4 of the Agreement, the Tribunal further finds that the penalty must have been intended to be payable in addition to default interest rather than in lieu thereof. Claimant is thus also entitled to interest, at a rate that exceeds by 8 percentage units the official discount rate, as fixed from time to time by the Bank of Sweden, from 12 January 1998 until payment on USD 317,000 [principal amount] and on the penalty amount from the date of this Award until payment."*

6.  **Arbitral Award in Case No. 75/97 of July 20, 1998 of the Italian Arbitration Association (*Yearbook of Commercial Arbitration* (1999) p. 189)**

Supply contract between an Italian supplier and a foreign buyer. Application of Italian law.

An article in the general purchasing conditions (GPC) provided that in the case of late delivery the buyer could either accept the delivery, in which case the seller would pay a penalty, or terminate the contract, both without prejudice to the buyer's right to claim damages. A clause in the purchase order provided for liquidated damages in the case of late delivery.

The Arbitral Tribunal analyzed the clause in the purchase order in the light of Italian law and found that the clause's aim was evidently to predetermine the damages to be paid in the case of delay when delivery was nonetheless accepted.

Hence, the clause fell under the provisions of Article 1382 of the Italian Civil Code (on the *clausola penale*).[3] Considering that there was a conflict between the clause in the purchase order and the article in the GPC, the Tribunal solved it in favour of the prevalence of the clause in the purchase order as *lex specialis*. Since there was no agreement between the parties in the purchase order that further damages could be reimbursed and such an agreement could not be found in the generic formulation of the article in GPC, the Tribunal granted the seller's claim for payment of the delivery minus the liquidated damages and dismissed the buyer's counterclaim for higher damages.

7. **ICC Case No. 9839/1999 (*Yearbook of Commercial Arbitration* (2004) p. 66)**

Representation agreement. Application of New York law.

The agreement provided that, in the event of a breach of the non-solicitation contractual clause, the affiliates of Q (Q Inc., an international mergers and acquisitions firm) shall be liable to pay to Q "by way of liquidated damages and not as a penalty the sum of ...".

The Arbitral Tribunal referred to a series of precedents on liquidated damages in New York law and applied the principles deriving therefrom. To be precise:

> *"Liquidated damages are compensatory damages that parties have agreed to pay to satisfy a breach of contract...*
>
> *In determining whether a liquidated provision clause is enforceable, it is necessary to determine whether it is a reasonable attempt to estimate the measure of compensation, in which case it is enforceable, or whether it is a penalty, in which case it is unenforceable...*
>
> *If the sum stipulated to bears no reasonable proportion to the actual loss sustained by a breach, it will be deemed a penalty...*
>
> *As a general rule when the actual damages are uncertain and difficult to prove and the contract does not give any data for their ascertainment, a stipulation to an amount, which is not unreasonable will be held to be liquidated damages...*

*If a court finds that the liquidated damages constitute an invalid penalty, however, the amount awarded will be limited to actual damages...".*

The Arbitral Tribunal found that the sum stipulated in the contract for breach of the non-solicitation clause was a reasonable estimate of the expected loss from the violation of the clause. Its finding was based mostly on the consideration of circumstances existing when the contract was entered into and not on the actual damages sustained by Q:

*"At the time the Agreement was negotiated, Q-affiliate's counsel thoroughly went over the contract and, in so doing, never questioned the sum specified in the liquidated damages clause. In addition, the stipulated sum bears a reasonable relationship to the probable loss suffered by Q-affiliate's violation of the clause. There was testimony that [the amount] has a rational relation to the amount invested in establishing the network divided by the number of Q offices."*

The Arbitral Tribunal refused to award interest on the liquidated damages by stating that "interest should not be awarded on this sum since both the parties agreed to the fixed sum as the full measure of liquidated damages".

B.   ARBITRAL AWARDS APPLYING USAGES, GENERAL PRINCIPLES AND/
     OR THE UNIDROIT PRINCIPLES

**8.   ICC Case No. 2139/1974 (*Journal du Droit International* (1975) p. 929)**

The defendant was held responsible for the non-performance of its contractual obligations. The contract did not include any stipulation on the quantification of damages in case of non-performance. The claimant had not succeeded in proving the actual damages it suffered but referred to arbitrary elements for their quantification.

The Arbitral Tribunal proceeded to calculate the claimant's damages by reference, as a basis for such calculation, to the usual penalty (*pénalisation*) encountered in practice in numerous sale contracts of raw materials of this kind (oil).

9.  ICC Case No. 3267/1979 (*Yearbook of Commercial Arbitration* (1982) p. 96 and *Collection of ICC Arbitral Awards*, Vol. I, p. 76; in French: *Journal du Droit International* (1980) p. 962 and *Collection of ICC Arbitral Awards*, Vol. I, p. 376)

The parties had not agreed on the application of a national law and had granted the Tribunal the powers of *amiables compositeurs*. The Arbitral Tribunal decided to apply "the widely accepted general principles governing commercial international law with no specific reference to a particular system of law".

According to the contract, the claimant (the subcontractor) had a choice between two remedies for the compensation of its damages following the termination of the contract due to the payment default of the defendant (contractor). The first remedy led to the calculation of actual damages, whereas the second, a "speedy remedy", consisting of the exercise of the claimant's rights under the REG (Risk Exposure Bank Guarantee), effected a liquidation of damages on the basis of a predetermined agreed figure.

The Arbitral Tribunal proceeded to analyze the payments under the REG by referring to Hudson and Black's Dictionary and found that they were in the nature of damages and not of a penalty. It concluded that:

> *"whereas, in many legal systems, the amount of a penalty may be reviewed by the Courts or by the arbitrators, the amounts of liquidated damages are not subject to such review. The Arbitral Tribunal adopts this view. It will not therefore review the amount agreed between the parties as liquidated damages."*

10. Arbitral Award in Case No. 229/1996 of June 5, 1997 of the International Arbitration Court of the Chamber of Commerce and Industry of the Russian Federation (abstract available at: http://www.unilex.info)

Sales contract between a Bulgarian party and a Russian party.

The contract provided for the payment of a penalty by the buyer in the case of a delay in the payment of the price corresponding to 0.5% of the price per day. When the buyer actually failed to make the payment in time, the seller asked for the payment of the penalty as agreed upon in the contract. The buyer objected on the grounds that the agreed sum was excessive.

The contract was governed by the UN Convention on Contracts for the International Sales of Goods (CISG). After having found that CISG was silent on the issue, the Arbitral Tribunal decided to resort to the UNIDROIT Principles in order to fill the gap. In doing so, the Tribunal invoked the Preamble of the UNIDROIT Principles, which states that they "may be used to interpret and supplement international uniform law instruments". It regarded the UNIDROIT Principles as applicable according to Article 9(2) CISG, because they reflect usages of which the parties knew or ought to have known and that are widely recognized in international trade.

The Tribunal applied Article 7.4.13(2) of the UNIDROIT Principles and found that a penalty amounting to 0.5% of the total contract price for each day of delay in the payment was indeed excessive and reduced the penalty to a reasonable amount. To be precise, the tribunal imposed a penalty in the amount of 50% of the sum requested by the seller.

## 11. ICC Case No. 8261/1996 (abstract available at: http://www.unilex.info)

An Italian company and a government agency of a Middle East country entered into a contract that did not contain any choice of law clause. The Arbitral Tribunal declared that it would base its decision on the terms of the contract, supplemented by general principles of trade as embodied in the *lex mercatoria*. It then referred without further explanation to different provisions of the UNIDROIT Principles, among which Article 7.4.13, in support of its reasoning.

No more precisions on the application of said provisions are given in the abstract.

## 12. Arbitral Award in Case No. A-1795/51 of December 1, 1996 of the *Camera Arbitrale Nazionale ed Internazionale di Milano* (abstract available at: http://www.unilex.info)

An Italian company and a US company entered into a contract of commercial agency. The principal terminated the contract due to the non-performance by the agent. The contract did not contain any choice of law clause, but at the outset of the arbitral proceedings the parties agreed that the dispute would be settled in conformity with the UNIDROIT Principles tempered by recourse to equity.

The Arbitral Tribunal applied a number of individual articles of the UNIDROIT Principles, including Article 7.4.9 to grant interest at the statutory rate fixed by the law of the state of the currency of payment and, interestingly enough, Article 7.4.13 in order to uphold a contract term providing for a higher rate of interest for the delay in the payment of certain specific debts.

13. **Arbitral Award of January 28, 1998,** *Ad hoc* **Arbitration, Helsinki (abstract available at: http://www.unilex.info)**

The shareholders of company X and company Y entered into an agreement whereby the former granted the latter the right to purchase at a fixed price within a specified period of time 51% of company X's shares. The contract, which was governed by the law of a Nordic country, provided for the payment of an amount corresponding to the purchase price in case of breach of the contract by the grantors of the option. A dispute arose between the parties regarding an alleged breach by the grantors of the option of some of their obligations arising out of the contract. Company Y asked for payment of the penalty.

The Arbitral Tribunal, though it held that the grantors of the option were liable for the alleged breaches, found that the amount of the penalty was excessively high for breaches different from that of the main obligation to sell the shares and awarded company Y only part of it. In justifying the reduction of the agreed amount of the penalty, the Arbitral Tribunal based its decision on Article 36 of the Nordic Contract Law, according to which any contract term that is unreasonable or the application of which leads to unreasonableness may be mitigated or set aside. In order to further corroborate its finding, it also referred to Article 7.4.13(2) of the UNIDROIT Principles.

14. **ICC Case No. 9797/2000 (15(8)** *Mealey's International Arbitration Report* **(2000) pp. A1-A45)**

The arbitration clause in the agreements (MFIFAs) between the two Andersen business units stipulated that "the arbitrator shall not be bound to apply the substantive law of any jurisdiction but shall be guided by the policies and considerations set forth in the Preamble of this Agreement and the Articles and Bylaws of [AWSC], taking into account general principles of equity…".

The Arbitral Tribunal declared that, pursuant to Article 17.1 of the ICC Rules, it would further apply "general principles of law and the general principles of equity commonly accepted by the legal systems of most countries". It also held that

> *"the UNIDROIT Principles of International Commercial Contracts are a reliable source of international commercial law in international arbitration for they contain in essence a restatement of those 'principes directeurs' that have enjoyed universal acceptance and, moreover, are at the heart of those most fundamental notions which have consistently been applied in arbitral practice."*

No specific reference was made to Article 7.4.13, as the Tribunal rejected the defendants' counterclaim for payment by the claimants of the penalty provided for in the MFIFAs. According to the MFIFAs, such a penalty was due only where the member firm(s) terminating the MFIFAs was (were) the party at fault; and the Tribunal found that the MFIFAs were terminated as a consequence of the second defendant's fundamental breach, while the claimants were not at fault.

**15. Arbitral Award in Case No. 88/2000 of January 25, 2001 of the International Arbitration Court of the Chamber of Commerce and Industry of the Russian Federation (abstract available at: http://www.unilex.info)**

A sales contract between a Russian party and an English party provided that, in case of delayed payment of the price, the buyer should pay a penalty in addition to interest at the LIBOR rate. When the buyer actually delayed the payment of the price, the seller asked for the payment of both the interest on the sum not paid in time and the agreed penalty.

The Arbitral Tribunal awarded the interest at the agreed LIBOR rate and rejected the claim for the payment of the penalty. In doing so, it referred to Article 7.4.13(2) of the UNIDROIT Principles.

16. **Arbitral Award in Case No. 134/2002 of April 4, 2003 of the International Arbitration Court of the Chamber of Commerce and Industry of the Russian Federation (abstract available at: http://www.unilex.info)**

The dispute between Russian and German private entrepreneurs related to the untimely execution of an earlier award of an arbitral tribunal. Under the earlier award, the buyer was ordered to pay to the seller, in addition to the costs of the non-paid goods and other expenses of the seller, the contractual penalty for the delay (0.5% of the cost of the goods for each day of delay) in the payment of the goods for the period of June 29 till September 21, 1999. The buyer transferred the awarded amount to the seller only on March 1, 2002. The seller's claim was thus for the payment of the penalty for a period starting from September 21, 1999 till March 1, 2002.

The Arbitral Tribunal noted that, on the grounds of the first tribunal's award, the buyer had paid the penalty in the amount of 42% of the cost of the goods with regard to the payment delay for which the penalty was accrued. The penalty claimed in the second arbitration, taking into consideration the penalty paid earlier, would constitute 487% of the cost of the goods with regard to the payment for which the delay occurred.

The Arbitral Tribunal referred to the criteria of proportionality and conformability with the negative consequences of the breach of the obligations to the sum of the penalty claimed by the seller as these criteria are set forth in the CISG and the Civil Code of the Russian Federation. It further referred specifically to Article 7.4.13 of the UNIDROIT Principles. It found that the amount of the penalty claimed by the seller was clearly not in proportion to the consequences of the breach of the obligation with regard to the payment and that it should be reduced. As to the amount of the reduction of the penalty, the Tribunal took into consideration the cost of the property in relation to payment for which the delay occurred, losses incurred by the seller in this respect and other property and non-property rights that the seller was entitled to expect.

However, the Tribunal took into account that the seller had lodged the claim for the recovery of the penalty in complete accordance with the contract concluded by the parties and that its reduction by the Tribunal was carried out in view of reasons for which the seller was not responsible. Under such circumstances, on application of para. 10 of the Regulation on Arbitration Fees and Expenses (Specific Apportionment of Arbitration Costs and Fees), the Tribunal imposed on the buyer payment of such fees and expenses in a sum calculated on the basis of the amount of the claimed penalty.

17. **Arbitral Award of November 30, 2006 of the** *Centro de Arbitraje de México* **(abstract in English and full text in Spanish available at: http://www.unilex.info)**

The defendant, a Mexican grower, and the claimant, a US distributor, entered into a one-year exclusive agreement according to which the defendant undertook to produce quantities of specific products and to provide them to the claimant on an exclusive basis, while the claimant had to distribute the goods on the Californian market against a commission.

The parties had expressly agreed in the contract on the application of the UNIDROIT Principles.

In the arbitration, the claimant asked for termination of the contract as well as damages for the harm suffered as a result of the defendant's failure to provide the goods; it also asked for payment of the penalty stipulated in the contract in case of violation of the exclusivity clause.

By reference to Article 7.1.1 of the UNIDROIT Principles, the Arbitral Tribunal held that, although the claimant could demonstrate only one concrete case of the defendant's contracting with a third person, this was sufficient proof of breach by the defendant of the exclusivity clause. It thus awarded payment of the contractually stipulated penalty for violation of the exclusivity clause. However, since the precise amount to be paid could not be established with a sufficient degree of certainty, the Arbitral Tribunal determined it on a discretionary basis according to Article 7.4.3(3) of the UNIDROIT Principles. (The relevant clause provided that the penalty would be equivalent to 25% of the value of the sale made in violation of the exclusivity clause.)

## C. ARBITRAL AWARDS APPLYING THE 1980 UN CONVENTION ON CONTRACTS FOR THE INTERNATIONAL SALE OF GOODS (CISG)

**18.  Arbitral Award of June 13, 1989 of CIETAC (abstract available at: http://cisgw3.law.pace.edu/cases/890613c1.html)**

The claimant, a Chinese company, and the defendant, a Jordan investment company, entered into a barter contract. The contract provided that the claimant would sell 2174 tons of sesame to the defendant in exchange for 10 000 tons of urea from the latter with the equal value of sesame. According to Article 4 of an agreement concluded between the parties in relation to the contract provided that the seller of urea (the defendant) should compensate the other party in the amount of 10% of the contract price in case of non-delivery of the goods.

The dispute arose when the claimant delivered the agreed quantity of sesame while the defendant did not deliver the urea. In its submissions, the claimant requested the price difference between the contract price and the market price of the quantity of urea at the time of breach of contract on the basis of Article 76 CISG and liquidated damages amounting to 10% of the contact price.

The Arbitral Tribunal, applying the provisions of the Law of the People's Republic of China on Economic Contracts Involving Foreign Interests with reference to the CISG, dismissed the claimant's claim for the loss of price difference, considering it as an extra claim in addition to the amount of the liquidated damages stipulated in the agreement, which was able to include different possible damages. Nevertheless, taking into account that such liquidated damages were far from sufficient to compensate the actual loss suffered by the claimant, the Arbitral Tribunal adjusted the compensation to a proper amount.

**19.  ICC Case No. 7197/1992 (abstract available at: http://www.unilex.info)**

An Austrian seller and a Bulgarian buyer concluded a contract for the sale of goods produced by the former. The parties agreed that the price had to be paid by documentary credit to be opened before a certain date and that the goods had to be delivered 'DAF' at the Austrian-Hungarian border four weeks after the opening of the documentary credit. The contract contained a penalty clause whereby damages were limited to x% of the purchase price in case of non-performance by either party.

The seller commenced arbitration proceedings against the buyer, alleging that the latter did not perform its obligations to open the documentary credit either within the time period fixed in the contract or within the additional period of time granted by the seller. The seller, who had to deposit the goods in order to preserve them, claimed performance of the contract as well as damages.

The Arbitral Tribunal held that the provisions of the CISG were applicable to the merits of the dispute. Accordingly, it awarded the seller damages pursuant to Article 74 et seq. CISG. In the Arbitral Tribunal's opinion, since the CISG did not contain any provisions relating to penalty clauses, Austrian law had to be applied pursuant to Article 7(2) CISG. Applying Austrian law, the Tribunal held that the seller had the right to recover all damages suffered notwithstanding the limit fixed by the penalty clause.

20. **ICC Case No. 7585/1992 (abstract available at: http://cisgw3.law.pace.edu/ cases/927585i1.html; excerpts available at: http://www.unilex.info)**

An Italian seller and a Finnish buyer entered into a contract for the sale of a production line of foamed boards. The contract contained a clause providing that "if the agreement is terminated by fault or request of the purchaser – including *force majeure* – the seller is entitled to a compensation fee of 30% of the price".

The seller filed a request for arbitration against the buyer claiming damages and interest, as the latter had failed to make the third down payment to the seller and to notify the relevant letters of credit on the required date.

On the basis of the relevant CISG provisions, the Arbitral Tribunal held that

> *"the wording 'compensation fee' has to be interpreted as an amount of money payable in consideration of the termination of the contract independently of any damages suffered by Seller. It has to be paid independently of any contractual liability on behalf of Buyer. It is expressly stated in Article 19.3 of the contract that the compensation fee is due even in a 'force majeure' situation. According to Article 79 of the CISG, a party has not to pay damages 'if he proves that the failure was to due to an impediment beyond his control'.*

*The mere fact that the compensation fee has to be paid in such a situation evidences that it has a nature different from damages in compensation of a loss. The conclusion is that Defendant has to pay the provided 'compensation fee' (30% of the price) added to the damages."*

The Arbitral Tribunal granted the seller damages on application of Articles 74 and 75 CISG, as well as the "compensation fee" as the agreed penalty, without having recourse to a national law but on application of Article 7(2) CISG (i.e. in conformity with the general principles on which the CISG is based).

21. **Arbitral Award in Case No. 251/93 of November 23, 1994 of the International Arbitration Court of Commerce and Industry of the Russian Federation (abstract available at: http://www.unilex.info)**

The seller was to deliver certain goods for a sum that had been paid by the buyer in advance. The buyer, after receiving a smaller quantity of goods than what had been agreed, filed a request for arbitration against the seller in which it requested the Arbitral Tribunal:

● to order the seller to pay back the price of the undelivered goods; and

● to award the buyer an amount covering the damages suffered by it and resulting from the seller's breach of contract, in accordance with Article 74 CISG.

The Arbitral Tribunal held that the buyer was entitled to be reimbursed the amount it had paid for the undelivered goods. As regards the claim for damages, the Arbitral Tribunal came to the conclusion that the clause in the contract that stipulated the payment of a penalty in case of a delay in delivery was of an exclusive nature and did not provide for payment of damages in excess of the sum due in accordance with the clause. Accordingly, the Arbitral Tribunal decided to award damages for the delay only up to the limited amount indicated in the penalty clause and dismissed the buyer's claims as to damages relating to the poor quality of the goods, since the latter had not been able to prove the amount of the relevant loss.

22. **Arbitral Award in Case No. 40/1995 of January 22, 1996 of the International Arbitration Court of Commerce and Industry of the Russian Federation (abstract available at: http://cisgw3.law.pace.edu/cases/960122r1.html)**

The seller, a Russian company, entered into a sales contract with the buyer, an English company. The dispute arose when the seller handed over the goods at the agreed place, while the buyer did not comply with its obligation to pay the purchase price.

According to clause 7 of the contract,

> *"if the terms of the contract as to payment agreed upon in advance are not performed, then the buyer will pay the seller damages which were estimated and agreed, in the amount of 0.1% of the whole price of the contract for each day of delay of the payment, but not exceeding 10% of the whole price of the contract."*

The seller's claims before the Arbitral Tribunal included recovery of:

● the price for the goods delivered to the buyer under the contract; and

● the liquidated damages due to the buyer's failure to perform its obligation to pay for the goods in the amount agreed upon and estimated in advance in the contract.

The Arbitral Tribunal applied the CISG provisions (since they are part of Russian substantive law) and granted the seller payment of the price for the delivered goods; it further granted payment of the total amount of liquidated damages (i.e. 10% of the price for delivered but unpaid goods).

23. **ICC Case No. 8247/1996 (abstract available at: http://www.unilex.info)**

The claimant (seller) and the defendant (buyer) entered into a contract for the sale of chemical goods that were to be paid for within ten days of transmission of the shipping documents, failing which a penalty payment would be added to the amount due. Following delivery, the defendant refused to pay, alleging that the delivered goods were of poor quality. The claimant was opposed to such refusal and insisted on the agreed payment. The defendant finally made a partial payment and offered a further sum that was unacceptable to the claimant.

In its request for arbitration, the claimant requested the Arbitral Tribunal to hold that the defendant had breached the contract by failing to pay the price within the time limit contractually set. Moreover, the claimant requested the Arbitral Tribunal to hold that the defendant caused important damages to it, and claimed not only the balance of the price due but also part of the penalty that was established by item 7 of the contract (0.5% of the contract value for each day of delay).

On the basis of the CISG provisions, the Arbitral Tribunal held that

> *"[c]onsistently with the conclusion [that the failure by the defendant to make the payment provided by the contract is not justified] and in view also of the provisions laid down by the Convention in its Art. 53 (confirming the obligation by the purchaser to pay the price for the goods)... under the conditions provided by the contract and in other relevant Articles concerning the default by the purchaser, the Arbitrator deems that the subject request [of the claimant, that its damages related to the balance of the price due as well as related to the penalty clause] should be granted."*

## 24. ICC Case No. 9978/1999 (abstract available at: http://www.cisg-online.ch/cisg/urteile/708.html)

A dispute arose as a result of non-delivery of the goods provided for by a sales contract between the claimant (buyer) and the defendant (seller). The contract contained a special clause providing that, in the event of non-delivery by the seller, the buyer would be entitled to recover from the seller a penalty of 2% of the contract value in full and final settlement. The goods were to be paid for by letter of credit (L/C) upon presentation of certain documents, including a forwarder's certificate of receipt. Though the documents were presented and payment was made, the goods were not delivered to the buyer. Accordingly, negotiations were undertaken for the sum paid to be refunded. An initial amount was repaid and an agreement made for the transfer to the claimant of sums purported to be owed to the defendant by a third party.

The buyer subsequently initiated arbitration proceedings claiming, on the basis of Articles 45(1)(b) and 74 CISG, the refund of the amounts paid under the L/C plus interest, bank interest paid in connection with the L/C, detention charges, dead freight and the penalty for non-delivery provided for in the contract. Alternatively, it claimed repayment asserting that it had voided the contract in accordance with the relevant CISG provisions and arguing that it was entitled to damages on that basis as well. In addition, it considered its claim for damages not to be barred by the penalty clause contained in the contract, since such damages were claimed not on the grounds of non-delivery but on the grounds of the breach by the defendant of an obligation arising under the CISG. The defendant rebutted the claimant's arguments invoking, *inter alia*, exemption from any liability whatsoever in excess of the 2% contractual penalty.

As far as the law applicable to the contract is concerned, the Arbitral Tribunal held that the CISG provisions would apply as being part of the applicable German law, while German contract law provisions would apply to the penalty clause. According to the Arbitral Tribunal, pursuant to Article 6 CISG, the parties to an international sales contract may derogate from the provisions on damages of Article 45(1)(b) CISG through inclusion of a penalty/liquidated damages clause. In the Arbitral Tribunal's view, the agreed penalty clause was valid under the applicable German law and precluded any further damage claims for non-performance that the claimant might bring against the defendant.

Thus, the Arbitral Tribunal found that the claimant's claim for damages under Articles 45(1) and 74 CISG triggered by the defendant's fundamental breach of contract was precluded by the special condition for non-delivery contained in the contract (i.e. the penalty clause). Consequently, the Arbitral Tribunal held that the claimant was entitled to recover:

- a penalty of 2% of the contract value under the terms of the contract; plus

- 5% interest upon the penalty according to German contract law provisions.

25. **Arbitral Award in Case No. 302/1996 of July 27, 1999 of the International Arbitration Court of Commerce and Industry of the Russian Federation (abstract available at: http://cisgw3.law.pace.edu/cases/990727r1.html)**

The buyer, a Russian company, and the seller, a Swiss company, entered into a contract for the international sale of goods in July 1993, providing for delivery to be made no later than the end of October 1993 in a few instalments on FOB terms. The buyer brought its claims against the seller when the seller delivered only one lot of the goods (20% of the total quantity required by the contract).

The Arbitral Tribune applied the CISG, on the basis of the parties' agreement reached during the hearings of the case, and for issues not covered by the CISG the Russian substantive law. It also referred to the *lex mercatoria*, the UNIDROIT Principles, international trade usages and principles of foreign law (Anglo-American and German law) used in international arbitration practice.

The Arbitral Tribunal found that following non-performance by the seller of its obligations to ship the goods, the buyer was entitled to recover from the seller its lost profit, which was considered reasonable and foreseeable. The amount of the loss of profit was not contested by the seller. With regard to the claim of the sum of the penalties that the buyer should pay for late delivery to the final purchaser, the Arbitral Tribunal found unproven the possibility to grant to the buyer the performance bond penalties for total non-delivery of the goods (10%) and, at the same time, the penalties for late delivery (5%). According to the Arbitral Tribunal, this possibility neither resulted from the contractual terms nor did it find any reasonable basis in other legal sources. An *ad verbum* interpretation of the language of the contract led the Arbitral Tribunal to the conclusion that the penalties for late delivery could not be applied in the case of non-delivery. In any event, in the Arbitral Tribunal's view, this consequence of the breach of contract neither could nor should have been foreseen by the seller at the time of the conclusion of the contract.

**26. Arbitral Award in Case No. 65/1997 of 10.1.1998 of the International Arbitration Court of Commerce and Industry of the Russian Federation (abstract available at: http://cisgw3.law.pace.edu/cases/980110r1.html)**

The buyer, an Austrian company, paid only part of the price for goods delivered to it by the seller, a Russian company, under a contract concluded between the parties in October 1995. The seller claimed before the Arbitral Tribunal recovery of the debt as well as recovery of a penalty for delay in payment calculated in accordance with the contractual provisions.

In the absence of a clause determining the applicable law, the Arbitral Tribunal found that the CISG provisions were applicable to the merits of the dispute, save where there were issues not dealt with by the CISG. In that case, the Arbitral Tribunal should apply the rules of the Russian Federation's Civil Code.

On the merits, the Arbitral Tribunal found that, pursuant to Articles 53 and 62 CISG, the buyer should pay the seller the unpaid sum for the delivered goods. As to the seller's claim to recover from the buyer the penalty for delay in payment of the purchase price of the goods, this claim complied, according to the Arbitral Tribunal, with the provisions of the contract, which did not limit the total amount of the penalty. However, considering that the amount of penalty exceeded the sum of the buyer's debt for delivered goods by a factor of three, the Arbitral Tribunal concluded that such a penalty was disproportionate in comparison to the actual loss suffered by the seller. Therefore, on the basis of Articles 333(1) and 10(2)(1) of the Russian Federation's Civil Code, the Tribunal decreased the amount of the penalty granted in favour of the seller.

**27. Arbitral Award in Case No. 165/2001 of February 18, 2002 of the International Arbitration Court of Commerce and Industry of the Russian Federation (abstract available at: http://cisgw3.law.pace.edu/cases/020218r1.html)**

A Russian company (seller) entered into an international sales contract with a US company (buyer) on January 19, 2001. According to clause 12 of the contract, in the case of non-payment of the purchase price within the time limit set forth in the contract, the buyer should pay a penalty to the seller amounting to 0.1% of the sum of the debt for each day of delay. In any case, such penalty should not exceed an amount of 8% of the price of the unpaid goods.

The seller filed a request for arbitration against the buyer following the partial payment by the latter for goods delivered by the former under the contract. In its request, the seller claimed recovery of the principal debt, recovery of contractual penalties for delay in payment as well as compensation for losses suffered by it due to the use of a loan issued by a bank.

In the absence of an agreement between the parties on the law applicable to the dispute, the Arbitral Tribunal decided that it would apply the CISG and the rules of the Russian Federation's Civil Code.

The Arbitral Tribunal granted in full to the seller the principal debt as well as the contractual penalty but dismissed the latter's claim to recover from the buyer the loss resulting from the payment to the bank of interest on a loan used by the seller during the delay in payment by the buyer. In so doing, the Arbitral Tribunal took into account:

- that the relations of the parties in connection with this issue were governed by Article 394 of the Russian Federation's Civil code, which provided that the losses should be recovered only in the part not covered by penalties, save where otherwise provided by the law or the contract; and

- that the seller recovered contractual penalties from the buyer for this delay in an amount higher than the sum of the seller's losses; the seller's losses were thus already compensated by the sum of the recovered penalties.

**28. Arbitral Award in Case No. 99/2002 of April 16, 2003 of the International Arbitration Court of Commerce and Industry of the Russian Federation (abstract available at: http://cisgw3.law.pace.edu/cases/030416r1.html)**

The buyer, a Russian company, brought claims against the seller, a Ukrainian company, following the failure of the latter to perform its obligation to deliver the goods purchased under the international sales contract entered into by the parties. Clause 5.1 of the contract set forth that the rate of penalties in case of late delivery should be 0.2% of the price of the non-delivered goods.

Both parties agreed that the dispute should be settled on the basis of the CISG as well as the rules of the Russian Federation's Civil Code.

On application of Article 45(2) CISG and Article 330 of the Russian Federation's Civil Code, the Arbitral Tribunal accepted the buyer's claims and, in addition to the refund of the amount of the advanced payment and the interest thereon, awarded to the buyer the contractual penalties for the delay in delivery until the date of termination of the contract.

29. **Arbitral Award in Case No. 65/2003 of February 19, 2004 of the International Arbitration Court of Commerce and Industry of the Russian Federation (abstract available at: http://cisgw3.law.pace.edu/cases/040219r1.html)**

The seller, a US company, lodged a claim against the buyer, a company located in the British Virgin Islands, in connection with the partial non-payment by the latter for goods delivered according to the contract entered into by the parties. According to the contractual stipulations, if the payment by the buyer of the goods delivered was delayed, the latter should pay a fine amounting to 0.3% of the sum of the uncollected payments for each overdue day during the first 20 days of delay and a fine amounting to 0.5% for each subsequent overdue day.

In its submissions, the seller claimed the main sum in arrears owed by the buyer for the goods delivered and the penalty provided in the contract. However, on its own initiative, the seller reduced its claim on the basis of the penalty clause to the amount of the main sum in arrears. (The amount of the fine exceeded the sum of the main debt by a factor of 6.5.)

Following the parties' choice of Russian substantive law as the law applicable to the merits, the Arbitral Tribunal decided that the CISG provisions applied. In the case of issues not determined by the CISG provisions, Russian civil law provisions were to be applied.

The Arbitral Tribunal awarded the seller the sum in arrears for the delivered goods in full. In addition, it held that the seller's request to reduce the amount of the penalty due by the buyer to the amount of the main sum in arrears complied with Article 333 of the Russian Civil Code, which provides for the reduction of the amount of the contractual penalty if such amount is in obvious disproportion to the losses resulting from the breach of contract.

30. **Arbitral Award in Case No. 115/2003 of April 20, 2004 of the International Arbitration Court of Commerce and Industry of the Russian Federation (abstract available at: http://cisgw3.law.pace.edu/cases/040420r1.html)**

The seller, a Russian company, lodged its claim against the buyer, a Cypriot company, on the grounds of non-payment by the latter for the goods delivered under the international sale and purchase contract entered into by the parties. According to paras. 10.1 and 10.2 of the contract, in case of a delay in payment, the buyer should pay to the seller a fine in the amount of LIBOR plus 2.5% of the sum in arrears for each overdue day as of the date on which the payment was to be made under the contract.

The following relief was sought by the seller:
• payment of the sum in arrears for the goods delivered; and
• payment of the penalty stipulated by the contract.

As far as the law applicable to the merits is concerned, the Arbitral Tribunal, after taking into consideration Article 13 of the contract, which provided that Russian law was applicable, held that the CISG provisions applied, except for the issues not specified therein, which should be settled under Russian substantive law.

The Arbitral Tribunal awarded the seller not only the sum in arrears but also the contractual penalty. More specifically, the Arbitral Tribunal found that the contractual determination by the parties of the penalty in terms of interest (i.e. LIBOR plus indicated interest) did not affect the qualification of the seller's claim as a penalty, under the relevant provisions of the Russian Civil Code. In that respect, the Arbitral Tribunal's findings were the following:

> *"addressing the issue about legal qualification of the present claim, the Tribunal states that the Vienna Convention does not regulate questions on recovery of penalties; however, it does not deprive the parties to an international sale and purchase contract of the possibility to reach an agreement on payment of a contract penalty. This sort of agreement on payment of contract penalties is to be regulated by the subsidiary applicable Russian civil legislation. According to Art. 330(1) of the Russian Civil Code, a 'penalty (fine) is a monetary sum fixed by the law or contract which is to be paid by the debtor to the creditor in case of non-fulfilment or improper fulfilment of the obligations, in particular delay in fulfilment.*

*In respect to the claim for payment of the penalty creditor is not obliged to prove caused losses.' The text of the contract does not indicate directly that the sum which is to be paid by the buyer to the seller in case of payment delay is a penalty. The intent of the parties to include in the contract specifically condition [sic] about payment of the penalty is confirmed by the representatives of the seller in the course of the hearings on the case. With due account to the above, in the Tribunal's opinion, the indication of payment of the interest should be regarded as the parties' determination of the calculation procedure of the amount of the contract penalty for payment delay... Following Article 330 of Russian Civil Code, the Tribunal finds the [seller's] claim on recovery of the penalty from the [buyer] in the amount determined by the [seller] well founded and subject to satisfaction."*

## END NOTES

[1]  Article 227 of Libyan Civil Code:

*"Agreed Damages Not Due*

1.  *Damages fixed by agreement are not due if the debtor establishes that the creditor has not suffered any loss.*

2.  *The Judge may reduce the amount of these damages if the debtor establishes that the amount fixed was grossly exaggerated or that the principal obligation has been partially performed.*

3.  *Any agreement contrary to the provisions of the two preceding paragraphs is void."*

[2]  Article 163 of Swiss *Code des Obligations*:

*"1.  Les parties fixent librement le montant de la peine.*

2.  *La peine stipulée ne peut être exigée lorsqu'elle a pour but de sanctionner une obligation illicite ou immorale, ni, sauf convention contraire, lorsque l'exécution de l'obligation est devenue impossible par l'effet d'une circonstance dont le débiteur n'est pas responsable.*

3.  *Le juge doit réduire les peines qu'il estime excessives."*

[3] Article 1382 of Italian Civil Code:

*"A clause by which it is agreed that, in the case of non-performance or delay of performance (1218), one of the contracting parties is liable for a specific penalty has the effect of limiting the compensation to the promised penalty, unless compensation was agreed on for additional damages.*

*The penalty is due regardless of proof of damage."*

**2**

# Judicial penalties and specific performance in international arbitration

## *By* **Alexis Mourre**[1]

The term "judicial penalty" (or *astreinte*) defines the decision taken by a judge or an arbitrator that a party will have to pay a certain amount of money in the case of failure to comply with a given obligation. Such an amount of money generally consists of a lump sum payable for each day, week or month of delay after the date when the debtor's obligation became due and until it has been complied with or as long as the debtor is found to be in breach of that obligation.

Judicial penalties can be applied to obligations of a procedural nature (such as the obligation to produce a document or to refrain from enforcing a bank guarantee during the time of proceedings) or to a substantial obligation deriving from the contract, such as the delivery of a good or the performance of works (in which case they are referred to hereinafter as "substantial penalties"). Substantial penalties are applied to obligations to do or to refrain from certain behaviour (*obligations de faire ou de ne pas faire*) and to obligations to deliver a good (*obligations de donner*). Their admissibility is more debatable in respect to monetary obligations, as compliance with an obligation to pay an amount of money can be compelled by other means, such as attachments of bank accounts.[2] In addition, the penalty would then play the same role as interest, which in many jurisdictions has both a moratorium and comminatory function. Yet, judicial penalties may be applicable to certain monetary obligations, such as paying a certain amount to a third party or opening an escrow account.

One of the main characteristics of judicial penalties, be they procedural or substantial, is their comminatory nature. Their aim is not to compensate a loss suffered by the other party but to impose upon such party sufficient financial pressure to force it to perform its obligation without undue delay. The amount of the penalty is therefore determined by the judge in an arbitrary manner.

As judicial penalties are generally paid to the creditor, they may lead to the enrichment of the latter. As a matter of fact, judicial penalties are independent from the damages that the aggrieved party may subsequently be entitled to claim and might therefore be cumulated with said damages.[3] Judicial penalties would be deprived of most of their deterring effect[4] if they were to be treated as a sort of advance on the damages to which the creditor would be entitled in the case of a refusal to comply. From that perspective, they can to a certain extent be compared to punitive damages.

Judicial penalties should be distinguished from contractual penalties and liquidated damages.[5] Judicial penalties are ordered by judges or arbitrators in order to ensure compliance with their orders. Their aim is to punish rather than to compensate a loss. Contractual penalties and liquidated damages, on the contrary, have a compensatory nature, and their amount can in some jurisdictions be reduced by the judge or the arbitrator if found to be in excess of the loss effectively suffered by the aggrieved party.[6] Judicial penalties should also be distinguished from statutory fines (*amendes*), as the latter are paid to the state rather than to the aggrieved party. The first are a private remedy, while the second are a public sanction reserved to national courts.

Substantial penalties may have the effect of reversing the burden of evidence. In France, for example, once the performance of an obligation has been ordered under judicial penalties, it is up to the debtor of that obligation to prove that performance took place within the prescribed time limit.[7]

Judicial penalties can be provisionally ordered by the judge, in which case the final amount of the penalty has to be subsequently confirmed by the judge. Such a system, known as *astreinte provisoire* in France, is applied to substantial obligations and has the advantage of being extremely flexible and of allowing the judge to take account of all relevant circumstances, such as external causes of the delay in the performance, in order to modulate the final amount of the penalty. A judicial penalty can also be final (*astreinte définitive*), which means that the judge will not subsequently have to confirm its amount and that the debtor will have to pay it as multiplied by the number of days, weeks or months of delay in the performance. In France, unless the judge expressly decides that the penalty is final, it is in principle provisional.

Judicial penalties were introduced by French case law at the beginning of the 19th century,[8] and the availability of this remedy was confirmed in France by statute in 1972.[9] Yet, the remedy is not universally admitted. It is unknown in certain countries, like Austria and Italy,[10] but is available in others, such as the Netherlands,[11] Belgium[12] and Switzerland.[13] In other countries, comparable remedies exist to the effect of ensuring compliance with a court order. In Denmark, the *tvangsbøde* is a daily fine, the purpose of which is to force the debtor to comply with an obligation.[14] Germany allows the debtor to be compelled to specific performance by way of fines, the payment of which, however, is not made to the creditor but to the state.[15] In Finland, the *uhkasakko* is applied in order to force a party to specific performance.[16] In Greece, a party in breach of an obligation can be ordered to pay a judicial penalty.[17] In Spain, the recent Statute on Civil Proceedings of 2000 introduced the *multa coercitiva*,[18] and Portugal has the *sançao pecuniaria compulsoria*.[19] In England, the sanction of *contempt of court* can to a certain extent play a role comparable in its comminatory effects to a judicial penalty.[20]

Although it would certainly be exaggerated to submit that judicial penalties are a generally admitted remedy in comparative law, it is noteworthy that the UNIDROIT Principles (2004) include a new Article 7.2.4 to the effect that (1) a tribunal that orders a debtor to perform its obligations can also impose a penalty upon the debtor if it does not comply with the decision; and (2) the penalty is payable to the creditor, unless the mandatory provisions of the *lex fori* provide otherwise, while payment of the penalty does not prevent the creditor from claiming damages.[21]

Said provision, which applies to substantial obligations, is directly inspired by the French *astreinte* in that it clearly states that the penalty is due to the creditor and that it may be cumulated with damages. However, the inclusion of substantial penalties in the UNIDROIT Principles should not be construed as turning such a remedy into a rule of the *lex mercatoria* or as giving it the status of a general principle of law. Although it is not within the scope of this article to analyse the status of the UNIDROIT Principles,[22] it seems clear that a rule such as the new Article 7.2.4 of the UNIDROIT Principles, which relates to the judges' powers in the exercise of their jurisdictional functions and which directly touches upon the organization of the judiciary, cannot be part of the *lex mercatoria.* Yet, it is certain that the new Article 7.2.4 reveals the existence of a certain consensus on the admissibility of judicial penalties. We shall see that, on the basis of that consensus, the power to order judicial penalties is now also admitted in many jurisdictions for arbitral tribunals (section I) but that it is still subject to certain limitations (section II).

## I.   ADMISSIBILITY OF JUDICIAL PENALTIES IN INTERNATIONAL ARBITRATION

Judicial penalties may in certain circumstances be a flexible and efficient device for ensuring compliance with a court's decisions. As such, they are well suited to the needs of international arbitration, where efforts to increase the efficiency of the process have been at the heart of the arbitral community's attention in recent years.[23] As noted by Laurent Lévy, admitting arbitral penalties follows the contemporary tendency to reinforce the effectiveness of the arbitral process:

> *"a rule deprived of any sanction, in particular of any comminatory sanction, has limited efficacy: why should we blunt the sword of the arbitrator, who risks losing his sense of responsibility either by refusing the necessary measures in fear that they will not be complied with or that possible actions before the state judge will slow the arbitral proceedings or, on the contrary, by ordering said measures just to see if they will be complied with?"[24]*

It is all the more so that obtaining judicial penalties from the judge once the award has been rendered raises a number of complex questions, both as to the determination of the competent judge[25] and to his power to grant such post-award relief.[26]

Outright exclusion of the arbitral power to order judicial penalties would therefore be unwarranted. From this perspective, the comment under the new Article 7.2.4 of the UNIDROIT Principles is worth quoting:

> *"while a majority of legal systems seem to deny* [the power to order judicial penalties] *to arbitrators, some modern legislations and recent court practice have recognised it. This solution, which is in keeping with the increasingly important role of arbitration as an alternative means of dispute resolution, especially in international commerce, is endorsed by the Principles. Since the execution of a penalty imposed by arbitrators can only be effected by, or with the assistance of, a court, appropriate supervision is available to prevent any possible abuse of the arbitrators' power."[27]*

As far as substantial rights are concerned, arbitral case law has not yet brought the demonstration that the new Article 7.2.4 of the UNIDROIT Principles reflects a general practice. Only in a limited number of cases have arbitral tribunals applied judicial penalties. In ICC Case No. 6673,[28] the arbitral tribunal enjoined a party from using certain know-how, without however ordering a penalty in case of a breach of this order. A decision awarding performance in kind was also adopted in ICC Case No. 7453. In ICC Case No. 7895,[29] a party requested an order enjoining the other from selling certain products subject to a fine for each item sold in breach of the injunction. The arbitral tribunal held that the granting of such relief was *"in no way inconsistent"* with the ICC Rules of Arbitration. The arbitral tribunal further noted that

> *"in this arbitration, there is no agreement of the parties which would forbid the granting by this tribunal of an injunction coupled with a fine".*

The tribunal concluded that

> *"it has the power, under the ICC Rules, to grant an injunction coupled with a fine, unless a mandatory provision of French procedural law, the procedural law of the place of this arbitration, requires otherwise. In that regard, French courts and French legal authors have found that arbitrators have the power to grant an injunction coupled with a fine."*

According to Ali Yesilirmak,[30] another arbitral tribunal took a similar position in ICC Case No. 9301. Conversely, a request for judicial penalties seems to have been rejected in Zurich Chamber award ZHK 273/95. Although there are certainly a number of unpublished awards that also ordered penalties to enforce an order or an injunction, this limited number of arbitral decisions is certainly insufficient to conclude that judicial penalties have become common arbitral practice. Yet, a brief overview of national legislations shows that judicial penalties are nowadays frequently considered as being part of the powers of arbitral tribunals.

French case law consistently held that the power to issue injunctions and order penalties in order to ensure their enforcement is part of the jurisdictional powers of arbitral tribunals.[31] In Belgium, Article 12 of the Statute on Arbitration of May 19, 1998 introduced into Article 1709 *bis* of the Code of Judicial Procedure a provision allowing arbitrators to order judicial penalties.[32] In the Netherlands, Article 1056 of the Code of Civil Procedure grants the same powers to arbitrators. Such power also seems to be admitted in Swiss law.[33] In the United States, the Uniform Arbitration Act gives arbitrators considerable powers to enforce their procedural orders.[34]

To our knowledge, Sweden is the only jurisdiction where the power of arbitrators to order judicial penalties is excluded by the law, although this prohibition only applies to procedural orders.[35] In Italy, Article 818 of the Code of Civil Procedure excludes the power of arbitral tribunals to order provisional or conservatory measures, which therefore also applies to judicial penalties meant to enforce such measures. As to substantial judicial penalties, they would probably also have to be ruled out.[36] In most jurisdictions, however, the law is silent as to the powers of the arbitrators to order judicial penalties. In such jurisdictions, the issue is therefore whether such silence should be construed as excluding the power to order penalties. That question is particularly relevant for procedural penalties, since, as we shall see below, the power to order substantial penalties derives from the *lex causae* rather than from the law applicable to the arbitral agreement. In respect to this problem, two theories can be used: that of the inherent jurisdictional powers of the arbitral tribunal and that of the parties' implicit or explicit consent.

The inherent powers theory is based on the assumption that fulfilling a jurisdictional function necessarily implies that certain powers are conferred upon the judge or the arbitrator. Under this theory, the arbitrators' power to order judicial penalties does not derive from a construction of the arbitral agreement but from the very nature of their function. This of course does not imply that the parties would not be able to *exclude* such relief,[37] but that, in absence of such exclusion, there is no special requirement of parties' consent to enable arbitrators to resort to such a punitive remedy. The inherent powers theory was initially developed by certain common law authors[38] in order to justify the arbitrators' powers to order provisional measures.[39] Although criticized by some,[40] it has been endorsed by the French courts. In its decisions of May 24, 1991 and October 7, 2004, the Paris Court of Appeals held that the power to order judicial penalties was *"an inherent and necessary extension of the jurisdictional function"*.[41] That view is consistent with the jurisdictional conception of the arbitrator's role. According to this approach, what the arbitration agreement is all about is to entrust a third party to perform a jurisdictional activity, and the arbitration agreement therefore vests the arbitral tribunal with all the powers that are necessary to carry out said activity. Unless the parties expressly decided to exclude either powers – which should be possible provided that the excluded power can be disposed of without affecting the very nature of the jurisdictional function – it should consequently be considered that the arbitrators dispose of all the powers necessary to fulfil their mission.[42]

The other possible approach is based on an interpretation of the arbitral agreement in order to verify that the parties have consented to the arbitrators' power to order judicial penalties. Such an approach has many inconveniences. Most of the time, as a matter of fact, the arbitral agreement will be silent on the issue of judicial penalties. As far as institutional arbitration is concerned, applicable rules will generally provide for the power of arbitral tribunals to take provisional and conservatory measures, subject to the mandatory rules of the seat of the arbitration, but will be silent on judicial penalties. In addition, judicial penalties are not necessarily to be considered as a provisional or conservatory measure.

How then should a silent arbitration agreement be construed? One option would be to consider that, absent a specific provision granting arbitrators the power to order judicial penalties, the parties are deemed not to have consented to such relief. This opinion has been submitted by Jean-François Poudret and Sébastien Besson:

> "[W]e do not think that ordering an astreinte concerns the conduct of the arbitral proceedings in the meaning of Article 182(1) of the PILS, but rather that the arbitral tribunal uses a special power pertaining to its jurisdiction. Since the PILS does not confer jurisdiction in this respect on the arbitral tribunal ex lege, unlike PILS, Art. 183(1) with regard to provisional measures, such power may not simply be presumed but must result from the arbitral agreement and in consequence conform with the formal requirements of PILS, Art. 178(1)." [43]

Yet, as far as substantial penalties are concerned, the same authors add that the *lex causae* would be sufficient grounds for the arbitrators' powers to order them:

> "[A]n exception must be made where the lex causae allows an astreinte as an accessory remedy. Arbitrators can apply such lex causae in its entirety and order an astreinte, but in our opinion only to reinforce a decision on the merits, of which the astreinte is an accessory, and not a procedural order." [44]

As a consequence, judicial penalties would be excluded from the arbitrators' powers in two situations: in respect to procedural penalties, absent a special provision to this effect in the arbitration agreement, and in respect to substantial penalties, absent a substantial rule allowing them.

As far as procedural penalties are concerned, such an approach consists in returning to the old theory according to which the arbitral agreement should be construed in a restrictive manner. This theory, which has been applied in a certain number of awards,[45] has now been superseded.[46]

There is no reason, in the absence of an express provision in the arbitration agreement permitting arbitrators to order judicial penalties, to exclude such a power on a general basis. For example, it is admitted that the silence of the *lex arbitri* on the arbitrators' powers to order provisional measures should not be construed as a general exclusion of said power.[47] The same principle should apply, with the reservations analyzed below, to judicial penalties. In order to avoid the negative consequences of the restrictive approach, which has just been described, Laurent Lévy has submitted that *"a tacit consent is sufficient* [to the effect of admitting the arbitrators' power to order judicial penalties]".[48] Nevertheless, most of the time, the parties will not have considered the issue of judicial penalties when negotiating their arbitration agreement. What should then be the basis for holding that the parties implicitly consented to the arbitrators applying such a remedy, if not that such a power has not been excluded? From this perspective, the result reached by applying the implicit consent theory is very close, if not identical, to that obtained on the basis of the inherent powers theory: absent any statutory provision to the contrary, the powers of the arbitrators to order judicial penalties should be admitted unless the parties expressly agreed to exclude it.

What should be the form of an arbitral decision to order judicial penalties? As far as substantial penalties are concerned, the order should certainly be rendered in the form of an award if it applies to a final decision. As a matter of fact, by ordering a party to comply with its substantial obligations, the arbitral tribunal will decide the merits of the dispute.[49] Regarding procedural penalties and penalties relating to provisional or temporary measures, the problem is no different than in respect to other provisional decisions. As a matter of principle, judicial penalties are meant to be enforced, and, most of the time, this will entail the rendering of an award.[50] In some jurisdictions, decisions ordering provisional or temporary measures may be enforced as awards, and this may also apply to decisions ordering judicial penalties on a provisional or temporary basis.[51] In jurisdictions that provide for a mechanism of assistance by local courts to enforce provisional measures based on the new Article 17 of the UNCITRAL Model Law, however, judicial penalties relating to provisional measures may be ordered in the form of a procedural order.

Should an arbitral tribunal be allowed to order provisional penalties, that is to say, penalties the amount of which has to be confirmed by means of a subsequent decision (*astreinte provisoire*)? Such an order would certainly not be capable of being enforced, precisely because the provisional nature of the penalty implies a subsequent decision prior to any enforcement.[52] Yet, as arbitral tribunals may in certain cases modify or review provisional measures taken for the duration of the proceedings, they should also be capable of ordering penalties on a provisional basis, subject to final determination in the award of the amount due by the debtor in breach.[53] In theory, nothing should therefore prevent arbitral tribunals from ordering provisional penalties. Yet, such a possibility should be reserved for substantial obligations, as it would not make sense in respect to procedural orders. In addition, provisional penalties may in practice prove to be burdensome, as they imply a need to reconstitute the arbitral tribunal for the sole purpose of deciding the final amount of the penalty.

Even when it has been ordered in a final manner, a judicial penalty needs to be liquidated. Although the daily, weekly or monthly amount of the penalty will not be revisable, there might still be a dispute between the parties as to the date at which the obligation has finally been complied with or as to the periods of time during which compliance may have become impossible due to *force majeure*. Do such disputes fall within the jurisdiction of the arbitral tribunal? In a decision of October 11, 1991, the Paris Court of Appeals held that

> *"the competent jurisdiction to liquidate the penalty in a final manner – which issue cannot be dealt with by the arbitral tribunal as the same has no jurisdiction to deal with the enforcement of its awards – is, regardless of the jurisdiction regarding the merits of the dispute, the court of first instance, which has jurisdiction on issues relating to difficulties of enforcement."[54]*

Yet, there is no reason to consider that an arbitral tribunal should be deprived of jurisdiction to liquidate the penalty it has ordered. As a matter of fact, contrary to the reasoning of the Paris Court in the above-mentioned decision, this is not a matter that relates to the enforcement of the penalty but rather to the determination of the final amount in respect to which the creditor will be entitled to seek enforcement.

In addition, forcing the parties to resort to the competent state court of the place of enforcement to liquidate the penalty would be contrary to their legitimate expectation that their dispute be adjudicated out of national courts. It would therefore be preferable to admit that, when the arbitral tribunal is still in place or can be reconvened, the latter retains its jurisdiction to liquidate the penalty.

Finally, the issue may arise whether a state court may add to a specific performance award by ordering a party to comply with the arbitrator's decision under a penalty that the arbitral tribunal has not ordered. The solution to such a question depends on the *lex fori*. In France, the case law seems to admit such a possibility.[55]

## II.   LIMITS TO THE ARBITRATORS' POWERS TO ORDER JUDICIAL PENALTIES

Contrary to an idea that has sometimes been put forward in order to justify the purported non-arbitrability of judicial penalties, such a remedy is not a measure of enforcement. Although judicial penalties are a sanction of a party's failure to comply with an order by the judge or the arbitrator, the aggrieved party always needs to resort to enforcement procedures in order to compel the payment of the ordered fine. The judge's intervention will always be necessary to enforce the penalty. From that perspective, judicial penalties are no different from any other arbitral relief, and there is no reason to exclude their arbitrability on the basis that they relate to the award's enforcement.

Yet, there may be other limitations on the arbitral tribunal's powers to apply judicial penalties. We will first deal with the idea that judicial penalties would require an *imperium* of which arbitrators would be deprived (1). Then we will examine the limits that may be imposed on the exercise of the arbitrators' power to order judicial penalties by the *lex causae* (2), by rules of public policy (3) or by state sovereignty (4).

## 1.   The debate on the alleged lack of *imperium* of arbitral tribunals

The view has frequently been put forward that the power to order judicial penalties would imply an *imperium* of which arbitrators would be deprived, unless the parties expressly agreed to confer it on them.

In this respect, Pierre Mayer considers that

> *"the arbitrator, by rendering its award on the merit of the dispute, exercises a jurisdiction which does not include any* imperium. *Yet, this does not mean that the* imperium, *defined as the power to command the parties, would not be necessary in order to take certain preliminary decisions, and that the arbitrator would lack it in such occasions. If we admit that this* imperium *is distinct from the power to exercise a constriction, there is in theory no obstacle to the parties conferring to the arbitrator the power to give them orders. However, the only power which necessarily and directly derives from the arbitral agreement is that of resolving the dispute, in other words the jurisdiction. It is therefore to be concluded that any measure resorting from the* imperium *requires a special investigation in order to determine if the parties can be deemed to have granted the powers to take it to the arbitrator if they did not do so in an express manner, [and] if there are limits to the powers that an arbitrator can be allowed to exercise, including with the parties' consent."*[56]

According to Pierre Mayer, judicial penalties would be part of those measures resorting from the *imperium*. As a consequence, absent a statutory provision allowing the arbitrator to order them or an express consent of the parties, the arbitrator should be deemed not to have such power:

> *"Does the arbitrator dispose of the power to order a judicial penalty to ensure the enforcement of his orders? The parties may certainly agree to give him such power. Absent such an agreement, the law may provide for such arbitral relief. But in the silence of the law and of the parties' agreement, what arbitrator would dare using such a weapon? The arbitrator cannot presume that the parties tacitly consented to the arbitrator's right to punish them in case they would fail to comply with his orders."*[57]

This view, which has been expressed in similar terms by Jean-François Poudret and Sébastien Besson,[58] is in line with the traditional view according to which the arbitrator should limit itself to assessing what the parties' rights are and that it should not care about the efficacy of its decision.[59]

Yet, in a fundamental study published in 1991,[60] Charles Jarrosson has shown that the concept of *imperium* has given rise to imprecise definitions, based on a somewhat artificial distinction with the *jurisdictio*. While the *imperium* encompasses all the powers of the judiciary, the *jurisdictio* is the power to say how the law should be applied to a given situation. The *jurisdictio* can therefore be considered as part of the more general and imprecise category defined as *imperium*.[61] In other words, exercising a jurisdictional function would always mean that a certain *imperium* is given to the judge, and the same would also be true for an arbitrator. Certain powers of the judiciary, however, are not part of the *jurisdictio*: the power of enforcing orders by resorting to the public force is one such power. Charles Jarrosson correctly qualifies such a power, consisting of forcing a party to comply by exercising a constraint, either directly or through an agent of the state to which the author of the order has the authority to give instructions, as *imperium merum*.[62] Orders that qualify as such are obviously not arbitrable, because the use of force is an exclusive prerogative of the state. Most of the debate on judicial penalties seems to have been troubled by the confusion between ordering the penalty and enforcing the penalty by using a measure of constraint. In addition, it could be submitted that a judicial penalty ordered by an arbitrator does not in itself imply any measure of constraint on the debtor: only the court decision granting the *exequatur* to the arbitrator's decision, or allowing its enforcement, would imply the use of force. From this perspective, ordering a judicial penalty would not represent the exercise of a power of *imperium merum* but would be an ancillary measure meant to ensure the efficacy of a decision taken by the arbitrator in the exercise of its *jurisdictio*. In other words, it would be part of the *imperium mixtum*, and there would consequently be no reason to deny the arbitrability of such a remedy accessory to the *jurisdictio*.

## 2. Limits on substantial judicial penalties: the principle of *nemo praecise cogi potest ad factum*

As stated above, judicial penalties may apply to procedural orders (e.g. an order to produce a document) as well as to substantial decisions (e.g. an order to deliver a good pursuant to a sales contract). In the latter case, substantial penalties will be ordered in order to compel a party to comply with its contractual obligations.

Substantial penalties are therefore intrinsically linked to the possibility of ordering specific performance of such obligations, as opposed to granting damages, which are an equivalent in money of the non-performed obligation. As a consequence, if specific performance is not permitted, there will be no room for substantial penalties.

While procedural penalties depend on the law applicable to the arbitral proceedings, substantial penalties as applied in case of specific performance should be regulated by the *lex causae*. The submission of substantial penalties to the *lex causae* is justified, as demonstrated by Horatia Muir-Watt, by the fact that the effects of the contract are defined by such law. For example, if a given contract is regulated by French law, which admits specific performance and judicial penalties, it would make no sense and may be contrary to the parties' legitimate expectations to exclude such remedies because the dispute is brought before a judge whose *lex fori* does not admit them.[63]

Yet, international instruments seem to reserve a certain space to the *lex fori* as far as specific performance is concerned. The Rome Convention of 1980 provides in Article 10.1(c) that the consequences of a breach of contract are regulated by the law applicable to the contract, but within the limits imposed on the tribunal's powers by its *lex fori*. This provision, however, can be excluded as far as arbitral penalties are concerned. As a matter of fact, the Rome Convention applies to states and, by referring to tribunals, refers to the judiciary. This is of course not to say that arbitrators could not be prevented by law from ordering judicial penalties. This only means that the limitations imposed on the judiciary in respect to injunctions and penalties will not necessarily apply to arbitral tribunals and that one would have to look at prohibitions specifically imposed upon arbitrators by the applicable statutes on arbitration. In practice, the only known example of such a prohibition applies to procedural injunctions[64] and not to substantial injunctions and penalties. As far as international sales of goods are concerned, Article 28 of the Vienna Convention provides that the judge is not compelled to order specific performance if he would not do so under his own law. Here again, however, this provision can be excluded as far as international arbitration is concerned.

As a matter of fact, international arbitral tribunals have no *lex fori* and, as a consequence, no internal law of their own that could prevent them from ordering specific performance. In sum, it can be concluded that, in international arbitration, the possibility for an arbitral tribunal to award specific performance and eventually to order penalties in the case of non-compliance is regulated by the *lex causae*. If such law admits such remedies, the arbitral tribunal will be entitled to apply them.[65] If not, such a remedy will be precluded.

When faced with a request to order specific performance of a contractual obligation with a penalty in case of non-compliance, the arbitral tribunal will therefore have to inquire whether such relief is permitted by the law applicable to the contract. In this respect, there are still important differences from jurisdiction to jurisdiction. In France, Article 1184, second paragraph of the Civil Code provides that the creditor of a contractual obligation has the right, if possible, to force the debtor to comply. In addition, albeit after some hesitation – notably in respect to promises of sale[66] – the case law now admits specific performance as a relief in the case of a breach of a contractual obligation.[67] The same position seems to prevail in Belgium.[68] In the Netherlands, Article 3:296 of the Civil Code provides that the creditor of an obligation is entitled to ask the judge to order the debtor to perform it in kind. In Switzerland, Article 97 of the *Code des obligations* provides that the creditor of an obligation to do is entitled to claim performance in kind. Other civil law jurisdictions might, on the contrary, rely on the principle according to which the breach of an obligation to do or not to do only allows the aggrieved party to seek damages. In Germany, in cases where the relevant obligation can only be performed personally by the debtor, the court will, upon application by the creditor, impose a fine up to EUR 25 000 or alternatively a prison term up to two years if he fails to perform his obligation.[69] In England, the traditional view is that damages are the preferred remedy, and specific performance is ordered only on an equitable basis in cases where damages would appear not to be an appropriate remedy.[70] This is also the general solution in common law countries such as the United States, Canada and Australia, where courts are not bound to grant specific performance. In the United States, however, specific performance relief has been admitted in arbitration.[71]

Nevertheless, even in jurisdictions where specific performance is allowed as a matter of principle, there are situations in which the admissibility of such relief is subject to the condition that the obligation does not have certain characteristics. This is the case for obligations having a strong personal character. In such cases, performance in kind may be deemed contrary to the principle *nemo praecise cogi potest ad factum*. This old Roman principle means that no direct constraint is admitted on the person of the debtor of an obligation to do. The principle was initially applied to all obligations, and Article 1142 of the French Civil Code, according to which any breach of an obligation gives rise to damages, has for long been understood in France as prohibiting in a general manner specific performance as far as obligations to do were concerned. In the Netherlands, judicial penalties are excluded in respect to obligations of a strictly personal nature.[72] The rationale for such prohibitions resides in the dignity of the human being, who should not be compelled to perform an activity against his or her will.[73] The meaning of the principle has, however, evolved in many jurisdictions. In many civil law and common law systems, the prohibition of specific performance as a remedy is limited to those obligations that are of a strictly personal character.[74] An example of such an obligation of a strictly personal character is the obligation to deliver a work of art, such as a book or a painting, or any activity requiring an intellectual creation. Yet, applying such a criteria to obligations such as to perform construction works, to deliver a sold good, to allow the use of know-how or to sell an asset may in certain cases be more difficult. These are issues that need to be considered on a case-by-case basis, and the solution thereto may be different depending on each country's conceptions. Another issue is whether the relief is at all appropriate according to the circumstances of each individual case. For example, faced with the firm refusal of a party to continue a long-term cooperation agreement implying the proactive participation of the parties' personnel, such as engineers, an order for specific performance may make little sense, and rather than ordering penalties a wise arbitrator will prefer to award damages.

As rightly noted by Florence Bellivier and Ruth Sefton-Green:

> *"If, from a certain perspective, the obligation can be considered as a circulating asset, from another point of view one cannot avoid to be stricken by an ever increasing phenomenon of personalisation of the contract. We can think here to all these sophisticated agreements (for example agreements for software maintenance) which require from the parties a long-term cooperation, both at the stage of the formation of the contract and at that of its performance, obligations in respect to which the requirements of loyalty, good faith, including contractual solidarity, have been underlined. It can be submitted, without paradox, that the more a contract is personalised, the more money is an acceptable and satisfactory equivalent in case of non performance by one of the parties of its obligations. As a matter of fact, the more refined and complicated is a human relationship, the less reasonable it is to force the parties to be bound thereto against their will."*[75]

The case has been made that there exists a general incompatibility between performance in kind and international arbitration.[76] According to one author,

> *"parties to an international contract should not have the option to provide that an eventual dispute should be finally settled by an arbitral award of specific performance of the contract, and … even where parties specify that the substantive and/or procedural law of a certain state is to govern their dispute, such an election should not necessarily be construed to include acquiescence to a final remedy of specific performance, [which] should not be applied."*[77]

The basis for such a general exclusion of remedies in kind in international arbitration would be that

> *"a meaningful enforcement of an award of specific performance would effectively require conscripting one or more foreign courts to supervise the implementation of the arbitrator's decree. Such a process would, accordingly, imply a role for the enforcing court that the treaty establishing the current system [the NY Convention] did not contemplate, and a corresponding risk that national courts will engage in the sort of judicial review of arbitral decisions that so plagues the system of mutual recognition of foreign judgments."*[78]

Yet, court intervention at the award's enforcement stage does not imply any judicial review of the award itself. Even in countries where performance in kind is perceived as an equitable remedy, courts have accepted that they have no right to review the arbitrators' decision in this regard.[79] In addition, if an award of specific performance is coupled with judicial penalties, the enforcement will entail the payment of a certain amount of money, like any award for damages. Whether specific performance can be awarded is therefore an issue for the applicable law to resolve. Positing a general incompatibility of remedies in kind with international arbitration would restrict, because they opted for arbitration, the parties' rights to specific performance in cases where the applicable law would on the contrary admit such a right.

## 3. Public policy considerations

The arbitral power to order judicial penalties may be limited by statutory provisions. As we have noted, this is the case, for example, in Sweden in respect to procedural penalties. However, other considerations may also come into play. In some jurisdictions, judicial penalties may be prohibited insofar as they would lead to an undue enrichment of the creditor. Although this view has now been superseded in France, French case law used to consider that the amount of the penalty should be limited to the loss effectively suffered by the creditor.[80] This was also the case in Belgium prior to the Law of 31 January 1980.[81] In common law countries, judicial penalties are perceived as an undue advantage to the creditor, and failure to comply with an order for specific performance is sanctioned by fines or measures of physical constriction (*contrainte par corps*).[82] In Denmark, the amount of the fines that a tribunal may order to compel the debtor to specific performance is limited by statute.[83] Other jurisdictions, like Greece, cap the judicial penalties that can be ordered in the case of specific performance.[84] In Germany, judicial penalties are payable to the state, which could be taken as an exclusion of the payment of penalties to the creditor in addition to compensatory damages.[85] Other jurisdictions might prevent the creditor from receiving penalties in an amount exceeding its effective losses. In certain countries, specific performance might be precluded due to the availability of other means of satisfying the creditor's right.

Typically, that is the case when the law provides for the performance of the contract by a third party or for the release of a judicial decision having the effect of the unperformed obligation. That is the case in Italy, where Article 2932 of the Civil Code contemplates that, in the case of a promise to conclude a contract, the judge can render a decision having the same effect as the promised contract. Finally, in certain jurisdictions, like England[86] and Ireland,[87] arbitration statutes limit the arbitrators' power to order specific performance in respect to contracts relating to land. These are rules that arbitral tribunals should take into account.

Arbitral tribunals may also be faced with the difficult issue of whether judicial penalties can be applied *ex officio*. According to Laurent Lévy, applying judicial penalties *ex officio* would be an excess of powers for arbitrators sitting in Switzerland.[88] In Belgium, the Law of 31 January 1980 provides that the judge may order judicial penalties at the request of the parties,[89] which prevents arbitrators sitting in this country from applying such a remedy *proprio motu*. In France, on the contrary, the Paris Court of Appeals refused to set aside an award where the arbitral tribunal had applied judicial penalties that had not been asked for by the claimant.[90] This position can be explained by the concept according to which, as noted above, the power to order judicial penalties does not derive from the parties' consent but is an inherent and necessary part of the arbitrator's jurisdictional powers.[91] Greece also allows judicial penalties to be ordered *ex officio*. In any event, even in jurisdictions where the arbitral tribunal may apply judicial penalties of its own motion, the principle of contradiction should be respected as a matter of procedural public policy, and the parties should therefore be invited to submit their observations on the contemplated remedy.

## 4. State sovereignty

May an arbitral tribunal order specific performance, as the case may be coupled with judicial penalties, against a sovereign state? There are few examples of such decisions.[92]

In most cases, the relief has been denied as interfering with the state's sovereignty. In *BP* v. *Libya*, the arbitral tribunal held that

> "*a rule of reason therefore dictates a result which conforms both to international law, as evidenced by State practice and the law of treaties, and to the governing principle of English and American contract law. This is that, when by the exercise of sovereign power a State has committed a fundamental breach of a concession agreement by repudiating it through a nationalization of the enterprise and its assets in a manner which implies finality, the concessionaire is not entitled to call for specific performance by the Government of the agreement and reinstatement of his contractual rights, but his sole remedy is an action for damages.*"[93]

The problem has recently been dealt with by an ICSID tribunal in a decision on provisional measures.[94] The arbitral tribunal, after having recalled the decisions rendered in the Libyan cases rejecting specific performance, held that "*specific performance will ... be refused if it imposes too heavy a burden on the party against whom it is directed*" (§ 82). After having referred to Article 35 of the ILC Articles on State Responsibility, the tribunal concluded that

> "*to impose on a sovereign State reinstatement of a foreign investor in its concession, after a nationalisation or termination of a concession license or contract by the State, would constitute a reparation disproportional to its interference with the sovereignty of the State when compared to monetary compensation*" (§ 84).

Should the exclusion of specific performance relief be limited to such cases of nationalisation or termination of a concession by the state? Future case law may provide us with an answer to that question. The case could be made that, as a matter of principle, there is no real difference in nature between an award for damages and an award for specific performance combined with judicial penalties, as both entail the payment of a certain amount of money. In both cases, the defendant may be compelled to comply with the award, and, in both cases, immunity issues may arise. It could therefore be held that the *restitutio in integrum* principle, according to which reparation should as far as possible wipe out all the consequences of the illegal act and re-establish the *status quo ante*,[95] can be equally served by an award of damages or by an award of specific performance.

As noted by the Occidental tribunal:

> *"full reparation can be achieved through restitution in kind –*
> *synonymous with specific performance – but if restitution in*
> *kind is not possible, then it can be achieved through monetary*
> *compensation."* [96]

Whether the arbitral tribunal will award one or the other therefore depends on the applicable law and the suitability of either remedy in each particular case.[97] Should the remedy be excluded in treaty-based arbitration and admitted in contract-based investment disputes? It is worth noting that, in a contract-based ICSID arbitration, the arbitral tribunal recently ordered provisional measures meant to preserve the claimant's right to a specific performance decision.[98]

## END NOTES

[1] E-mail: amourre@castaldimourre.com. The author warmly thanks Laurent Lévy for his valuable comments.

[2] In Belgium, the Law of January 31, 1980 introducing judicial penalties excludes such relief in respect to monetary obligations.

[3] This is the case in France: Ph. Le Tourneau, *Droit de la responsabilité et des contrats* (Dalloz, 2004) p. 2584: "[l'astreinte] peut être prononcée contre tout débiteur récalcitrant et se cumule avec les dommages et intérêts, ce qui conduit à un enrichissement contestable du créancier." See also Cass. 1ère Civ. October 20, 1959, *D.* 1959, 537; Cass. 3ème Civ. October 23, 1974, *Bull. Civ. III*, 376; Cass. 2ème Civ. February 18, 1987, *Bull. Civ. II*, 48; Cass. 1ère Civ. February 28, 1989, *Bull. Civ. I*, 97. The same solution seems to prevail in Switzerland: L. Lévy, 'Les astreintes et l'arbitrage international en Suisse', *Bull. ASA I*, 2001, 24: "il ne s'agit nullement de réparer un dommage, peut-être inexistant: même dans le cas où le droit suisse s'appliquerait, les dispositions relatives à la responsabilité ou aux intérêts moratoires n'ont pas vocation à exclure l'astreinte qui échappe à leur domaine. Celle-ci s'ajoute le cas échéant à la réparation d'un éventuel préjudice."

[4] A good example of the deterring effects of judicial penalties is the order that TV channels would pay fines up to EUR 2500 for each second of non-compliance with a given court decision (C.E. September 21, 1988, *D.* 1989, 124, note by Ch. Debbasch; January 20, 1989, *D.* 1990, 104, note by P. Huet).

[5] The French *Cour de cassation* held that a clause included in a contract and providing for a penalty was not submitted to the regime of the *astreintes*, as "the clause at hand could not provide for a judicial penalty (*astreinte*), which measure of constriction is reserved to courts" (Cass. 1ère Civ. March 9, 1977, *Bull. Civ. III*, 150).

[6] In France, Art. 1152 of the Civil Code.

[7] Cass. Com. October 2, 2001, *Rev. Procédures* 2001, 226, note by F. Perrot.

[8] Cass. Req. January 29, 1834, *D.P.* 1834, 1, p. 129; *Grands arrêts de la jurisprudence civile*, 11th edn., Vol. 2, p. 234.

[9] Statute of July 5, 1972 on civil proceedings. The statutory rules applicable to judicial penalties were modified by a subsequent Statute of July 9, 1991. In its *Barre and Honet* decision of May 10, 1974, the French *Conseil d'Etat* held that "the possibility for judges to order judicial penalties to ensure the enforcement of both their judgements and their decisions relating to the proceedings is a general principle of law".

[10] Judicial penalties are unknown in Italian law, save in very specific cases (judicial penalties may be applied in patents and trademarks, labour law and consumer law disputes).

[11] Art. 1056 of the Code of Civil Procedure: "The arbitral tribunal has the power to impose a penalty for non-compliance in cases where the court has such power."

[12] Art. 1709 *bis* of the Judicial Code: "The arbitrator may impose a fine on a party for non-compliance".

[13] ATF 90 (1964) II 158 (163) c5. Penalties are provided in Section 76 of the Law on Civil Proceedings.

[14] Based on the 1938 Law on the Recognition and Proof of Debts (*Gaeldsbrevlov* No. 146, 13). This solution has been abandoned in practice as a legal remedy.

[15] Art. 888 of the Code of Civil Procedure (*Zivilprozessordnung*).

[16] Art. 7, para. 1-14 of the Code of Civil Procedure.

[17] Art. 946 of the Code of Civil Procedure.

[18] Art. 709.1 of Statute of January 2000 on Civil Proceedings (LEC).

[19] Decree 262 of June 16, 1983.

[20] C. J. Miller, *Contempt of Court* (Oxford, Clarendon Press, 1989).

[21] However, no reference to judicial penalties has been included in the European Principles of Contract Law.

[22] See C. Seraglini, 'Du bon usage des principes UNIDROIT dans l'arbitrage international', 4 *Rev. Arb.* (2003) p. 1101.

[23] See the *Report of the ICC Task Force on Techniques for Controlling Time and Costs in Arbitration*, chaired by Y. Derains and R. Newmark, ICC Publication No. 843; see also the recent changes in Art. 17 of the UNCITRAL Model Law.

[24] Lévy, *supra* note 3, at p. 36.

[25] In particular in view of the arbitration exception of Art. 1(2) of Regulation 44/2001 and the Lugano Convention.

[26] For a recent decision in which the French *juge de l'execution* refused to order a judicial penalty in respect to an award ordering a party to transfer certain amounts on an escrow account because the award was not yet enforceable due to pending annulment proceedings, see Cass. 1ère Civ. July 4, 2007, *Groupe Antoine Tabet* v. *Republic of Congo*, No. 05-16586.

[27] UNIDROIT Principles (2004) p. 217.

[28] *Collection of ICC Awards*, Vol. III (ICC Publishing, 1992) p. 434.

[29] 11(1) *ICC Court Bulletin* (2000) p. 66.

[30] A. Yesilirmak, 'Les mesures provisoires et conservatoires dans la pratique arbitrale de la CCI', 11(1) *ICC Court Bulletin* (2000) p. 34, footnote 22.

[31] Cass. Civ. July 25, 1882, *D.P.* 1883, 243; Rennes, September 26, 1984, *Rev. Arb.* 1986, 441, note by J.-P. Ancel; Paris, May 24, 1991, *Rev. Arb.* 1992, 638, note by Pellerin; Paris, October 7, 2004, *Otor Participations et autres* c/ *Carlyle Holdings et autres*, *JDI* 2005, 341, note by A. Mourre and P. Pedone.

[32] See G. Horsmans, 'La loi belge du 19 mai 1998 sur l'arbitrage', *Rev. Arb.* (1999) p. 529.

[33] Lévy, *supra* note 3, at p. 25.

[34] US Uniform Arbitration Act, Section 17(d): "the arbitrator may order a party to the arbitration proceeding to comply with the arbitrator's discovery-related orders, issue subpoenas for the attendance of a witness and for the production of records and other evidence at a discovery proceeding, and take action against a noncomplying party to the extent a court could if the controversy were the subject of a civil action in this State."

[35] Art. 25-3 of the Swedish Law of March 4, 1999 on arbitration provides that "the arbitrators cannot issue injunctions with judicial penalties, nor resort to means of coercion to gather evidence". In this respect, see the critical comments of S. Jarvin in 'La nouvelle loi suédoise sur l'arbitrage', *Rev. Arb.* (2000) p. 149.

[36] Art. 2930 et seq. of the Italian Civil Code relate to the performance in kind of obligations to deliver a good (Art. 2930), to do (Art. 2931), not to do (Art. 2933) and to execute a contract (Art. 2932). In the latter case, the Code provides for the power of the court to render a decision producing the effects of the contract. In the case of an obligation not to do, the Code only provides for the destruction of works realized by the party in breach. In the other cases, enforcement is remitted to the judge. Art. 612 of the Code of Civil Procedure refers, in this respect, to the possibility of having the obligation performed by a third party *in lieu* of the debtor.

[37] According to Besson, inherent powers could not be excluded by the parties, which leads to the conclusion that the theory is ill adapted to arbitration: S. Besson, 'Arbitrage international et mesures provisoires', *Etudes suisses de droit international*, Vol. 105 (Société Suisse de droit international) p. 131.

[38] Caron and Kohl, quoted by Besson, ibid., at p. 100.

[39] Ibid., at pp. 128-131.

[40] Ibid., at p. 131.

[41] Paris, October 7, 2004, *Otor Participations et autres* c/ *Carlyle Holdings et autres, JDI* 2005, 341, note by A. Mourre and P. Pedone.

[42] G. Keutgen and G.-A. Dal, *L'arbitrage en droit belge et international*, Vol. 1 (Bruylant, 2006) p. 328 , note "from a general perspective, the powers of the arbitrator are identical to those of a judge. It is only at this condition that he will be able to correctly fulfil his mission."

[43] J.-F. Poudret and S. Besson, *Comparative Law on International Arbitration* (Thomson - Sweet & Maxwell) p. 540.

[44] Ibid.

[45] ICC Case No. 2138, *JDI* 1975, 934; ICC Case No. 2321, *JDI* 1975, 938; ICC Case No. 4392, *JDI* 1983, 907.

[45] *Fouchard Gaillard Goldman on International Commercial Arbitration* (Kluwer, 1999); Besson, *supra* note 37, at p. 123.

[47] Ibid., at para. 1314; Hascher, JDI 1993, 1081.

[48] Lévy, *supra* note 3, at p. 29.

[49] See, in French law: Paris, July 1, 1999, *Société Braspetro Oil Services Company, Rev. Arb.* 1999, 834, note by Ch. Jarrosson; Paris, July 7, 1987, *Rev. Arb.* 1988, 649, note by E. Mezger; Paris, November 10, 1995, *Rev. Arb.* 1997, 596, note by J. Pellerin.

[50] Lévy, *supra* note 3, at p. 31: "the fact that an award is necessary may entail a more burdensome procedure; such inconvenience is limited, however, if compared to its advantages, namely the possibility to seek the *exequatur*, which will make the threat sufficiently deterrent to ensure that the order to which the penalty is be complied with."

[51] In France, see Paris, October 7, 2004, *Otor* v. *Carlyle*, *JDI* 2005, 341, note by A. Mourre and P. Pedone; in the United States, see U.S. Court of Appeal, 7th Circuit, March 14, 2000, *Publicis* v. *True North*, *Rev. Arb.* 2000, 657, note by Ph. Pinsolle; *Cahiers de l'arbitrage*, *Recueil*, Vol. I (2000-2001) p. 376, note by E. Ordway and B. Derains.

[52] It is noteworthy that Art. 43 of the Lugano Convention and Art. 49 of Regulation EC 44/2001 provide that provisional penalties are not capable of being enforced.

[53] In respect to the possibility for arbitrators to order provisional penalties in Belgian law, see Horsmans, *supra* note 32, at p. 531.

[54] Paris, October 11, 1991, *Rev. Arb.* 1992, 636, note by J. Pellerin.

[55] Art. 33, para. 2 of the Statute on the Enforcement of Judicial Decisions of July 9, 1991 provides that the judge may order a party under penalty to comply with a final judgment if the penalty appears to be necessary under the circumstances. As far as arbitral awards are concerned, the *Cour de cassation* held in a July 4, 2007 decision (Cass. 1ère Civ. July 4, 2007, *Republic of Congo* v. *GAT*, *Cahiers de l'arbitrage* 2007/3, 35) that "the enforcement judge can only order penalties in respect to an enforceable title, even though provisionally enforceable. In the case at hand, there was a pending challenge against the arbitral award, which was therefore not enforceable." The *Cour de cassation* therefore seems to admit that, had the award been final, the judge would have had the power to order compliance with the same under penalty.

[56] P. Mayer, 'Imperium de l'arbitre et mesures provisoires', *Etudes de procédure et d'arbitrage en l'honneur de Jean-François Poudret* (Lausanne, 1999) p. 441.

[57] Ibid., at p. 443.

[58] Poudret and Besson, *supra* note 43.

[59] J. Robert, *Arbitrage, droit interne droit international*, 5th edn. (1983) p. 175: "il faut admettre que l'arbitre ne dispose pas d'un semblable moyen de coercition. Il est en effet admis que l'astreinte n'a pas seulement un caractère comminatoire mais est constitutive d'une peine privée que le juge trouve dans son imperium le pouvoir de prononcer et liquider. Et l'arbitre dont le pouvoir est strictement contractuel et non public, ne dispose d'aucun imperium."

[60] Ch. Jarrosson, 'Réflexions sur l'imperium', *Etudes offertes à Pierre Bellet* (Paris, Litec, 1991) p. 245.

[61] F. De Martino, 'La giurisdizione nel diritto romano', quoted by Jarrosson, *supra* note 60, at p. 38.

[62] Jarrosson, *supra* note 60, at p. 279.

[63] H. Muir-Watt, 'L'exécution du contrat dans un contexte international', in M. Fontaine and G. Viney (eds.), *Les sanctions de l'inexécution des obligations contractuelles* (Bruylant, 2001) p. 799: "it seems perfectly logical to apply the law of the contract to the remedies. It is such law that defines the binding effects of the contract. To apply, instead of the law which grants its protection to the contractual relationship, a law which would as a matter of principle only admit damages, could be perceived as contrary to the expectations based on the contract."

[64] Art. 25, para. 3 of the Swedish Law of March 4, 1999 provides that "arbitrators have no power to issue injunctions under penalties, nor to resort to means of coercion in order to gather evidence".

[65] In the absence of a substantial choice of law, new Art. 7.2.4 of the UNIDROIT Principles may allow an arbitral tribunal to apply the same solution if the will of the parties to apply non-national rules is sufficiently clear.

[66] In France: Cass. 3ème Civ. December 15, 1993; Cass. 3ème Civ., October 5, 1995; Cass. 3ème Civ. June 26, 1996, *Ferry*.

[67] G. Viney, 'Exécution de l'obligation, faculté de remplacement, et réparation en nature en droit français', in M. Fontaine and G. Viney (eds.), *Les sanctions de l'inexécution des obligations contractuelles* (Bruylant, 2001) p. 167.

[68] P. Wéry, 'L'exécution en nature de l'obligation contractuelle et la réparation en nature du dommage contractuel, Rapport Belge', in M. Fontaine and G. Viney (eds.), *Les sanctions de l'inexécution des obligations contractuelles* (Bruylant, 2001) p. 205.

[69] Art. 888 of the Code of Civil Procedure (*Zivilprozessordnung*, ZPO).

[70] Although "the current view is that specific performance can be ordered ... if it is, in the circumstances, the most appropriate remedy". See G. H Treitel, *The Law of Contract*, 11th edn. (2003) p. 1020. On specific performance in English law, see F. Bellivier and R. Sefton-Green, 'Force obligatoire et execution en nature du contrat en droit français et anglais: bonnes et mauvaises surprises du comparatisme', *Le Contrat au début du XXIème siècle, Etudes offertes à J. Ghestin* (2001) p. 91. See also the doctrine quoted by T. E. Elder, 'The Case Against Arbitral Awards of Specific Performance in Transnational Commercial Disputes', 13(1) *Arbitration International* (1997) pp. 8-11.

[71] The New York Court of Appeals decided on several occasions that an arbitral tribunal has the power to award specific relief: *Staklinski* v. *Pyramid Elec. Co.*, 180 NYS 2d 20 (NY App. Div. 1958), aff'd, 160 NE 2d 78 (NY 1959); *Grayson-Robinson Stores, Inc.* v. *Iris Constr. Corp.*, 168 NE 2d 377 (NY 1960). In *Staklinski*, the Court held that, although the contract at stake was one for personal services, New York law admitted specific performance in the circumstances of the case. The Court also found that specific performance did not entail an undue limitation of the debtor's freedom to direct its affairs as it saw fit. Finally, the Court found that the applicable AAA arbitration rules enabled the arbitral tribunal to grant said relief. In *Grayson-Robinson Stores*, the Court also found that confirmation of a specific performance award did not imply a *de novo* equity suit. In respect to these decisions, see Elder, *supra* note 70, at pp. 11-15.

[72] E.H. Hondius, 'Les sanctions de l'inexécution', in M. Fontaine and G. Viney (eds.), *Les sanctions de l'inexécution des obligations contractuelles* (Bruylant, 2001) p. 848.

[73] H. Roland and L. Boyer, *Adages du droit français* p. 510.

[74] Bellivier and Sefton-Green, *supra* note 70, at p. 20 seq. See also the decision of the New York Court of Appeals in *Staklinski*, *supra* note 71, at note 55.

[75] Ibid., at p. 42.

[76] Elder, *supra* note 70.

[77] Ibid., at p. 29.

[78] Ibid., at p. 32.

[79] See the decision of the New York Court of Appeals in *Grayson-Robinson Stores*, *supra* note 71, where the Court held that the enforcement of an award of specific performance was not "an equity suit but a motion made as of a right to confirm a completely valid arbitration award conforming in all respects to the express conferral of authority on the arbitrators and meeting all statutory requirements for confirmation".

[80] Cass. Civ. November 30, 1950, *JCP* 1951 II, 6089; Cass Civ. February 27, 1953, *Bull. Civ. II*, 63.

[81] Wéry, *supra* note 68, at p. 232, quoting Cass. January 24, 1924.

[82] Bellivier and Sefton-Green, *supra* note 70, at p. 7.

[83] Section 55 of Law No. 607 of September 6, 1986.

[84] Judicial penalties are capped at EUR 5900.

[85] Arts. 883-898 of the Code of Civil Procedure.

[86] Section 48-5(b) of the Arbitration Act 1996.

[87] Section 26 of the Arbitration Act 1954.

[88] Lévy, *supra* note 3, at p. 32.

[89] Horsmans, *supra* note 32, at p. 530.

[90] Paris, May 24, 1991, *Rev. Arb.* 1992, 636, note by J. Pellerin.

[91] For a decision adopting this approach, see also Paris, October 7, 2004, *JDI* 2005, 341, note by A. Mourre and P. Pedone.

[92] Prof. R.-J. Dupuy as Sole Arbitrator granted specific performance in the context of a nationalization in *Texaco Overseas Petroleum Co. and California Asiatic Oil Co.* v. *Libyan Arab Republic*, 17 ILM 1 (1978) § 112; YCA 1979, 177; see J.-F. Lalive, 'Un grand arbitrage pétrolier entre un gouvernement et deux sociétés privées étrangères', *JDI* (1977) p. 320.

[93] *BP Exploration Company (Libya) Limited* v. *Libyan Arab Republic*, 52 ILR 297 (1974) p. 354. In *Libya American Oil Company (LIAMCO) Limited* v. *Libyan Arab Republic*, the arbitral tribunal held that "it is impossible to compel a State to make restitution, this would constitute in fact an intolerable interference in the internal sovereignty of States" (20 ILM 1 (1981) p. 63). Specific performance was also denied in *CMS Gas Transmission Company* v. *Argentina*, ICSID Case No. ARB/01/8, Award, May 12, 2005, § 406.

[94] *Occidental Petroleum Corporation and Occidental Exploration and Production Company* v. *The Republic of Ecuador*, ICSID Case No. ARB/06/11, Decision on Provisional Measures, August 17, 2007.

[95] *Chorzow Factory (Germany v. Poland)* case, PCIJ, Series A, No. 17, 1928.

[96] *Occidental Petroleum Corporation*, *supra* note 94, at § 73.

[97] As rightly noted by Broches, the reference in Art. 54 of the Washington Convention to "pecuniary obligations" is not to be construed as an exclusion of other remedies. A. Broches, 'Awards Rendered Pursuant to the ICSID Convention; Binding Force, Finality, Recognition, Enforcement, Execution', 2 *ICSID Rev.-FILJ* (1987) pp. 287, 302. Yet, ICSID awards have almost always been for pecuniary compensation.

[98] *City Oriente Ltd* v. *Petroecuador and The Republic of Ecuador*, ISCID Case No. ARB/06/21, Decision on Provisional Measures.

**3**

# Compound interest and specific performance: "Arbitral *Imperium*" and Sections 49 and 48 of the English Arbitration Act 1996

*By* **V.V. Veeder**[1]
*Essex Court Chambers, London*

In Roman law, there was a traditional distinction drawn between those who exercised judicial powers in civil disputes: the *magistratus* and the *judex*. It was from the latter than an *arbiter* was invited to act in the resolution of private disputes. The former exercised magisterial authority delegated by the state. In the words of one commentator, they "represent the law and say what the law is, and who shall have power to employ the force which the state places at the disposal of those it selects to administer justice".[2] The latter, applying not *jus* but *judicium*, performed "an inquiry … into particular facts, evidence has to be received and weighed, and an opinion formed and pronounced as to the real merits of the case".

This is, in part, the origin of the modern debate over the existence and scope of an arbitrator's *imperium*. An arbitrator exercises powers by virtue of his office, not exhaustively defined powers delegated to him under a contractual relationship with the parties. Adapting the famous words of Lord Mustill, an arbitrator is both Superman and Batman, the legal creature of both status and contract. Yet, an arbitrator is not a state judge, with the *imperium* or status of that judge. An arbitration tribunal, in accordance with the traditional language of an arbitration clause, "settles" a dispute, and its final decision is an "award", not a judgment. A tribunal can make orders binding on the disputing parties, but it cannot make orders binding on third persons, and it cannot even enforce its own orders against the parties without the further machinery of the state, available to the state judge. In Professor Jarrosson's analysis under French law, the arbitrator has *imperium mixtum* but not *imperium merum*.[3] No less significantly, unlike a state judge, an arbitrator pays VAT on his or her arbitral fees.

This limitation on arbitral *imperium* is evident from the difficulties that common law jurisdictions have experienced in enacting the 1985 UNCITRAL Model Law on Arbitration. At common law, it was historically uncertain whether an arbitration tribunal had any power to order interest or costs. In Bermuda, the Model Law was enacted with these supplementary powers expressly added to its 1993 Act. In Scotland, a power to order costs was added to its 1991 legislation; but, unfortunately, nothing as regards interest. It therefore remains impossible to obtain an award of interest in Scotland unless that power is expressly conferred by the parties on the tribunal (which neither the ICC Rules nor the UNCITRAL Arbitration Rules do).

In France, the scholarly discussion of arbitral *imperium* by Professors Mayer and Jarrosson has, curiously, been ignored in England.[4] No such discussion can be found in any of the many judgments or treatises on English arbitration. This may surprise some; but not others. The answer, as always, is more practical and mundane. The English, like Monsieur Jourdain, speak only prose. It suffices here to relate only the story of the compound interest and the "land exception" for specific performance under the English Arbitration Act 1996.

## I.    COMPOUND INTEREST

Under Section 49 of the English Arbitration Act 1996, an arbitration tribunal may award compound interest on any sum awarded (including costs) from any date to the date of final payment at such rates and with such rests as it considers meets the justice of the case. This provision is broadly stated. It was welcomed by arbitration users and commercial arbitrators, but it is not a power enjoyed by the English court. How can it be that a private arbitrator has greater *imperium* than the English court? The answer is disappointing: the UK government planned in 1996 to extend the powers of the English court by legislation promoted by the Law Commission equivalent to Section 49 of the 1996 Act. It remains an un-enacted plan. This statutory power does not therefore support the argument that an arbitrator enjoys a greater *imperium* than a judge.

II.   THE LAND EXCEPTION TO SPECIFIC PERFORMANCE

Section 48 of the English Arbitration Act 1996 contains an odd exception regarding the remedies ordinarily available to an arbitration tribunal in England: Section 48(5)(b) of the 1996 Act provides that the tribunal has the same powers as the [English] court "to order specific performance of a contract (*other than a contract relating to land*)".

This English legal remedy of "specific performance" is not an unusual or extreme form of remedy, to be equated (for example) to punitive damages, penalties, *astreintes* or even compound interest (being at once formerly both a sin and a crime in England). Specific performance is a well-established equitable and statutory remedy ordered by the English court to enforce against a defendant the duty of what that defendant has contractually undertaken to do: *pacta sunt servanda*. It evolved many centuries ago in the Chancery Courts to address, in equity, those cases where the common law remedy of damages for breach of contract was regarded as inadequate. The English court also has power to enforce its order for specific performance by further orders, including (in appropriate cases) sequestration of the defendant's assets or committal, whether by fine or imprisonment.

Specific performance generally remains an essential part of English commercial law, available in a broad category of commercial disputes. For example, it has long been possible for the buyer to obtain an order against the defaulting seller for specific performance of a contract to deliver specific or ascertained goods. In 1856, this equitable power was enlarged and confirmed by statute.[5] There is no question that an arbitration tribunal ordinarily has the power to grant that remedy, as is now expressly confirmed by Section 48 of the 1996 Act. The tribunal itself has no power to order sequestration or committal against the defaulting defendant to compel compliance with its award of specific performance. However, the claimant can enforce the tribunal's award under Section 66 of the 1996 Act as "a judgment or order of the court to the same effect", and the English court can then apply to the defendant its powers of sequestration and contempt of court to enforce an arbitral award of specific performance against not only the non-complying respondent but also any third person thwarting the court's orders.

This statutory "land exception" is therefore an oddity. A contract to buy specific land is invariably the classic case for specific performance under English law, much more so than a contract for the sale of goods. In commerce, goods will often be a mere commodity, for which there exists a ready substitute in the market, and damages are accordingly an adequate remedy permitting the purchase of equivalent goods in that market. In contrast, the buyer of land (whether farmland or a building or any form of real property) is purchasing that particular land; there can be no exact equivalent. On the seller's breach, where damages are an inadequate remedy, the obvious and natural remedy will be an order for specific performance, ordering the seller to sell and transfer title to that land from the seller to the buyer.

Nor is this oddity based upon "public policy" under English law. The "land exception" in Section 48 is not a "mandatory" provision under Section 4 and Schedule 1 of the 1996 Act, and parties may therefore agree in writing to confer such a remedial power on the tribunal. Few parties do so, possibly because this limitation is little known. (I have never yet seen any such agreement in regard to land, although the contrary exists in certain arbitration rules in regard to contracts of insurance and reinsurance.[6]) Nonetheless, parties do refer disputes over land to arbitration under the 1996 Act. It is surprising that, so far, no real controversy has arisen. For the unwary, it looks like an accident waiting to happen.

This provision in the 1996 Act is *not* new. It was reenacted from Section 15 of the Arbitration Act 1950, itself reenacting Section 7 of the Arbitration Act 1934 (adding paragraph (j) to the First Schedule to the Arbitration Act 1889). It originally provided: "the arbitrators or umpire shall have the same power as the Court to order specific performance of any contract other than a contract relating to land or any interest in land." As was made clear by the UK government's Departmental Advisory Committee on the Law of Arbitration in its *First Report*, the government in 1996 did not intend to change the law in regard to specific performance. Hence, the origin of the "land exception" must be found in the 1934 Act itself.

Before 1934, this was not a limitation known to English statutes on arbitration. The "land exception" was missing from the Arbitration Act 1889. It was likewise absent from the failed attempts to codify the law and practice of English arbitration in 1853 and 1884-1889 by Lord Brougham and Baron Bramwell, respectively. Moreover, this "land exception" would have seemed odd to these distinguished judges and experts on English arbitration.

Clause 28 of the 1853 Brougham Bill (drafted by Francis Russell, the first author of the leading arbitration work, *Russell on Arbitration*) empowered an arbitrator to deliver "possession" of land. While this remedy was not the same as specific performance, its existence is hardly consistent with the absence of any general arbitral power to order specific performance in regard to land. Later, Clause 105 of the Bramwell 1889 Bill declared that: "an award shall not pass the property in realty or personalty as to the title to which the arbitrator in his award determines. But where the title is so determined the parties to the submission shall be estopped from denying the title so determined."[7] As indicated above, this limitation is inherent in the legal fact that an award cannot, by itself, pass property in goods or land: an order for specific performance requires enforcement by the English court, as Clause 110 of the Bramwell Bill confirms. In the seventh edition of *Russell on Arbitration* of 1891, being the first edition published after the 1889 Act, the author records (with approval) the power of an arbitrator to order specific performance generally, in regard to the provision of receipts and the payment of money (p. 436). Nothing is said about any "land exception". In the United States, an arbitral power to order specific performance of land had been expressly recognized in 1829.[8]

This 1934 provision resulted from the 1927 McKinnon Committee's *Report on the Law of Arbitration*. It was then thought "at least doubtful", in the Committee's view, whether an arbitration tribunal could make an award ordering any sort of specific performance. The Committee's distinguished members (Mr Justice McKinnon, Archibald, Chitty, Martin, Merriman, Raeburn and Cotton[9]) recommended that an arbitrator "should at any rate be given the power to order the delivery of specific goods under Section 52 of the Sale of Goods Act 1893, against payment of the price".[10] The Committee did not explain the reasons for these doubts, and it is not possible today to understand their origin. More significantly, these doubts would now seem misplaced.

At this point, the following sentence appears in the McKinnon Committee's Report: "It is perhaps a matter of policy but we see no reason why he [the arbitrator] should not also be given power to order specific performance of a contract by the delivery of any property other than land or money in any case in which the Court might lawfully do so." The first part of this recommendation was pragmatically sensible: it is always better to spell out a power expressly when doubts as to its existence exist, however misplaced. The second part is clearly the origin of the "land exception". It is impossible to understand now why it was advanced at all or why it was linked to an exception relating to "money". In particular, the Committee did not explain why an arbitration tribunal, capable of being entrusted with a decision to award damages measured in millions, or specific performance of any other contract, could not be trusted to order specific performance of the most modest dwelling or the smallest sum of money.

This "land exception" was later addressed (but not then publicly) in the UK government's 1934 Notes on Clauses to Clause 8 of the Arbitration Bill, later enacted as Section 7 of the 1934 Act.[11] It was a more elaborate explanation of English law, intended as advice to the government ministers entrusted with the 1934 Bill's passage through Parliament. These Notes recorded the government's acceptance of the Committee's recommendation, but with two qualifications.

As to the first, the government implicitly rejected the McKinnon Committee's exception for money. As to the second, it accepted the McKinnon Committee's exception for land. The Notes record: "There would, in fact, seem to be little reason why contracts relating to land should be excluded from the clause. When, however, this last point was discussed with members of the Committee at the meeting referred to [this was a reference to a private meeting on March 2, 1928 between MacKinnon, Archibald, Raeburn, the Solicitor General, Shuster and Parliamentary Counsel], they were of the opinion that where a question relating to land was referred it was, on the whole, desirable that the parties should confer express authority on the arbitrator to award specific performance if they so desired. The Bill gives effect to this view." (p. 40). Again, no explanation was offered for this "opinion". Thus was the land exception introduced into the 1934 Act, later consolidated into the 1950 Act and re-enacted in the 1996 Act.

There can only be two possible explanations for the government's decision in 1934. The first can be rejected summarily. The McKinnon Committee and the government's informal, second committee in 1928 were not hostile to the practice of commercial arbitration. Indeed, Mr Justice McKinnon had been the chairman of the League of Nation's Committee of Experts responsible for drafting the 1923 Geneva Protocol on Arbitration Clauses.

The second explanation is the more likely: these specialists did not believe, 80 or so years ago, that private arbitrators had any power to order specific performance at all because none equated arbitrators with English judges. Accordingly, they wished to see, by statute, an extension of arbitral powers as to specific performance generally, akin to the powers of the English court. However, as with all law reformers, they would have been conscious of the risk of any possible parliamentary controversy frustrating the 1934 Bill entirely. They could reasonably have feared an adverse reaction from the non-arbitral community concerned at an over-extension of arbitral powers in a private form of justice by arbitrators who (in England) were predominately non-lawyers, still less lawyers publicly accountable as state judges appointed by the state. Hence the "land exception". Why was that topic more sensitive than any other? Again, the cause can now only be surmised. In 1925, Parliament had engaged in a massive reform of land law and land registration, unprecedented in English legal history and culminating in the Law of Property Act 1925 and related legislation. This was possibly not the time to equate arbitrators with judges in relation to land disputes.

III.   SPECIFIC PERFORMANCE OF ARBITRATION AGREEMENTS

There is another historical oddity, linking arbitration and specific performance, that has produced a much greater controversy: the English court's "anti-suit injunction", whereby a disputing party is prohibited from starting or maintaining legal proceedings before a foreign court in breach of an arbitration agreement.

The orthodox view under English law is that neither the English court nor any arbitration tribunal court may grant specific performance of an arbitration agreement. This view is supported by reference to a number of ancient cases.

For example, the authors of *Mustill & Boyd* state:[12]

> *"For breach of an arbitration agreement, damages may in theory be awarded, but will not normally be a useful remedy; an injunction is rarely granted, and specific performance is not available at all."*

In support of this proposition, the authors cite six cases decided between 1802 and 1911.[13] Likewise, *Halsbury's Laws of England* states that:

> *"[t]he court does not enforce the specific performance of agreements to refer to arbitration", and Snell's Equity does not distinguish between enforcement of the agreement and the appointment of an arbitrator, stating that equity will not "directly enforce an agreement to appoint an arbitrator".[14]*

Even for orthodox believers, this unanimity is impressive. Other distinguished English arbitration commentators have long expressed the same view, including Hogg and Russell. All, however, derive their opinions from the same ancient authorities, decided long before the 1958 New York Arbitration Convention. Moreover, the modern practice of the English court is to grant more easily orders for specific performance,[15] and arbitrators may now grant other equitable remedies, such as rectification and rescission for misrepresentation, both once considered beyond their powers. If, therefore, the emperor ever had any clothes, it is now legitimate to inquire whether he still has them. This is no academic question: it lies at the heart of the relationship under English law between the English court, an arbitration agreement and an arbitration tribunal with an English seat. Given the traditional absence of specific performance as a remedy to enforce a recalcitrant party's legal obligation to abide by an arbitration agreement, it has led to the different and increasingly controversial remedy of the "anti-suit" injunction by the English court.

As is well known, Article II(3) of the New York Convention provides that a state court "shall ... refer the parties to arbitration" in appropriate cases. That is the language of specific performance and positive compulsion. However, influenced by orthodoxy, Parliament enacted Article II(3), both in 1975 and 1996, whereby the English court "shall grant a stay" of the legal proceedings before the (English) court brought in breach of an arbitration agreement.

The difference is manifest: a stay of English legal proceedings does nothing positively to compel the parties to comply with their arbitration agreement and to desist from legal proceedings in England and elsewhere in violation of that agreement. Bereft of the natural remedy of specific performance of an arbitration agreement, the English court gradually applied another equitable remedy, the anti-suit injunction, to fill the gap. It is worth considering whether the world's ire, so aroused by the anti-suit injunction, would have been similarly stirred by an order for specific performance directed at a contract-breaker in language reflecting Article II(3) of the New York Convention.

In conclusion, the moral of this story is that a rose is still a rose by any other name and that, by such other name, *imperium* matters in England. It did in 1934, many centuries after the departure from English soil of the last Roman legionnaire. It mattered again in 1996 when, as regards the land exception but not compound interest, a more cautious and traditional view prevailed in Parliament, recognizing limitations on English arbitral *imperium*. It matters even more when the fate of the anti-suit injunction remains to be determined under the Brussels Regulation. It all means that arbitrators, while not mere service providers under contract with the parties, do not and can never have the powers of a state judge, as a matter of both prose and poetry.

## END NOTES

1  E-mail: vvveeder@londonarbitrators.net.

2  Sandars, *The Statutes of Justinian* (1922) p. lxiff. See also B. de Loynes de Fumichon and M. Humbert, 'L'arbitrage à Rome', *Rev. Arb.* (2003) p. 285. (I am much indebted to M. David Chekroun for this reference.)

3  Ch. Jarrosson, *Mélanges Pierre Bellet* (1991) p. 245, see also P. Mayer, *Mélanges Poudret* (1999) p. 437.

4  Contrast the lengthy discussion in T. Clay, *L'arbitre* (2001) paras. 108-111 (p. 95 ff.), with its absence in *Mustill & Boyd: Commercial Arbitration* (1989). The same contrast exists with other English scholarly texts, including Russell, Hogg, Merkin and *Halsbury's Laws of England*.

5  Section 2 of the Mercantile Law Amendment Act 1856.

6  For example, Article 14.1 of the ARIAS (UK) Arbitration Rules provides: "For the avoidance of doubt, the Tribunal shall NOT have additional equitable powers unless such powers have been specifically conferred upon them by the Parties in writing or by these Rules." This provision originates in the law and practice of New York insurance arbitrations whereby arbitrators have ordered specific performance of insurance contracts where (under English law) damages would be the appropriate remedy. In *Telia v. Hilcourt* (4 July 2003, unreported) the English Court confirmed the arbitrator's power to order refurbishment under a land lease, as a contractual obligation separate and distinct from the lease.

7  The Bramwell draft code cites no legal authority for this proposition. See (1992) *Art. Int.*, 329, 379.

8  T.E. Elder, 'The Case Against Arbitral Awards of Specific Performance', 13(1) *Arb. Int.* (1997) p. 11.

9  Mr Justice McKinnon had been the chairman of the experts committee appointed by the League of Nations to draft the 1923 Geneva Protocol on Arbitration Clauses. Merriman was later Solicitor-General.

10  Cmnd 2817: para. 28 (p. 8).

11  At pp. 3940. (This was confidential government documentation at the time, but it later became publicly available at the Public Record Office under the 30-year rule of public disclosure.)

12  *Mustill & Boyd*, 2nd ed. (1989) p. 459.

13  The six cases cited by *Mustill & Boyd* are: (1) *Street v. Rigby* (1802) 6 Ves. 815; (2) *The Purisima Concepcion* (1849) 13 Jur. 545; (3) *Gourlay v. Duke of Somerset* (1815) 19 Ves. 429; (4) *Agar v. Macklew* (1825) 4 L.J.O.S. Ch 16; (5) *Pena Copper Mines v. Rio Tinto Co.* (1911) 105 L.T. 846 at 851; and (6) *Re Smith & Service* (1890) 25 Q.B.D. 548.

14  *Halsbury's Laws of England*, Vol. 44(1) on "Specific Performance", at para. 832; and *Snell's Equity*, 31st edn. (2004) at pp. 15-24.

15  *Co-Operative Ins. v. Argyll* [1998] 1 A.C. 1; see also the earlier commentary by G. Jones and W. Goodhart, *Specific Performance*, 2nd edn. (1996) p. 5: "Recent case law demonstrates that English courts, like American courts, are now prepared to accept that specific performance should be more freely granted and to reject precedent which inhibits their discretion to do so."

# How to control the impact of time running between the occurrence of the damage and its full compensation: complementary and alternative remedies in interim relief proceedings

*By* **John Beechey and Gareth Kenny**

## I.    INTRODUCTION

The meeting at which this paper was presented focused on the question how most effectively to mitigate the effect of the lapse of time between the occurrence of loss or damage and recovery of (hopefully) full compensation. The focus of this paper is a narrower issue. A party faced with the real prospect that its opponent in imminent or pending arbitration proceedings might (or, in certain circumstances, may have to) take steps that would result in the removal from that party's reach – or the disposal – of the subject matter of the dispute or of the means of meeting any eventual award made in the claimant party's favour will be concerned to know how best to protect its interests until an award is rendered and becomes susceptible to enforcement. The purpose of this paper is to consider what options might be open to that party in terms of interim relief and to which entity (or entities) it may be possible to apply in order to obtain it.

It has long been recognized that the "universally accepted" purpose of interim remedies is to prevent aggravation of the dispute or further injury to the party seeking orders as to interim measures.[1] In the context of international arbitration, the necessity for interim remedies[2] is obvious. The constitution of a tribunal, much less the rendering of an award in a complex international dispute generally takes time. In addition, the effects of the simple passage of time may mean that, failing the grant of interim remedies, important evidence will be lost. Interim remedies are also important, therefore, to ensure that the parties to a dispute are given an equal opportunity to present their case using the best available evidence.[3]

In summary, the purpose of interim remedies is to ensure that, insofar as possible, the "circumstances of the dispute remain effectively as if the court had entered immediate judgment".[4]

Recognition of the importance of and the ability to apply for interim measures has been steadily growing. Traditionally the preserve of the courts (if they were available at all), interim remedies are now the subject of express provision in the rules of arbitration of many arbitral institutions as well as in the UNCITRAL Rules. They are, by definition, temporary in nature; they are limited in time by the length of the arbitration proceedings themselves and by the scope of the underlying dispute.[5]

Interim measures include:[6]

- *"Those that have to do with the discovery, preservation and production of evidence concerning the dispute;[7]*

- *those that have to do with preserving the subject matter of the dispute and avoiding prejudice to the rights of the parties during the pendency of the proceedings; and*

- *those that are destined to permit the effective execution of the award."*

However, the categories of interim remedy should not be regarded as in any sense closed.[8]

The question remains to whom to turn to obtain them: the arbitral tribunal, the courts or some other entity?

## II.   THE JURISDICTION AND THE POWERS OF AN ARBITRAL TRIBUNAL TO ORDER INTERIM REMEDIES

Although an arbitral tribunal lacks the coercive powers vested in a national court, orders for interim measures made by an arbitral tribunal will generally carry real weight, nonetheless.[9] Most parties will think twice before failing to comply at an interlocutory stage with the orders or directions of the arbitral tribunal before which their case is to be heard. Arbitral tribunals also have some, albeit limited, means to encourage compliance, such as costs awards and, depending on the place of arbitration, peremptory orders.[10]

Consideration is now given, first, to the nature of the relief sought by way of interim measures for which application might be made to an arbitral tribunal; second, to the basis of the arbitrator's jurisdiction to entertain such an application; and, finally, to the criteria to which, typically, an arbitral tribunal will have regard in considering whether and, if so, how to exercise its discretion to grant interim measures of relief.

## III.  THE AMBIT OF ARBITRATOR-ORDERED INTERIM MEASURES

### 1.  Preservation of the "status quo"

It has been observed that "[i]nterlocutory orders are usually intended to give all parties equal opportunity to present their cases to the tribunal, to preserve the status quo, or to permit other reasonable measures relating to performance under the contract pending final resolution of the dispute."[11] As will be seen below, the examples drawn from the various institutional rules to which reference is made in this paper do not attempt to set out exhaustively the types of interim remedies that may be granted by an arbitral tribunal. That said, some sets of rules give more guidance (or, perhaps, seek to be more prescriptive) than others. Although they have the overarching aim of ensuring that the parties' rights are preserved and that an effective award is duly rendered, the type of interim remedy that may be appropriate in a particular situation will very much depend on the circumstances of the case. For this reason, arbitral tribunals are given broad discretion as to the form and scope of any interim measure(s) that they grant. Such measures may be directed at seizing or controlling property, or a party may be required to do, or refrain from doing, a specified act.[12]

Some types of interim remedy are more common and readily accepted as being within the scope of an arbitral tribunal's, as opposed to a state court's, powers than others. Among them are those remedies directed towards the preservation of property or evidence pending the hearing and determination of the dispute. A party may be required to store the property that forms the subject of the dispute or have it moved to a better-equipped facility for its preservation. If the goods are perishable, a party may be ordered to sell them and to hold the proceeds in an escrow account, pending the tribunal's final determination of the dispute.

Alternatively, where the goods are themselves material evidence and are perishable or may be destroyed or otherwise damaged, the tribunal may order that a sample be taken and, if necessary, tested so that the evidence is not lost.

Other interim remedies, the purpose of which is to maintain the *status quo*, go beyond the mere preservation of evidence and property.[13] In a contractual dispute, one party may claim that the contract has been rightfully terminated. However, pending a final award, the arbitral tribunal may order, as an interim remedy, the continued performance of the parties' respective obligations under the contract.[14]

For instance, in one (unpublished) ICC case, the tribunal accepted that it had the authority to order the resumption of gas deliveries through a pipeline, the gas seller having suspended deliveries on the basis of an alleged failure to make payments of due invoices (pursuant to a take-or-pay clause). Ultimately, the tribunal denied the relief sought, given that (a) a decision to grant the interim relief orders sought would have required provisional findings on the factual and legal issues at the heart of the parties' claims; and (b) the proved risks were only of a monetary/financial nature. The tribunal also concluded that such an outcome would be tantamount to granting final relief on a temporary basis.

The grant of such a remedy can be problematic. A tribunal will typically require the party requesting such an interim order to give a "cross-undertaking in damages". In other words, the party in favour of which such an order is made must accept that, if it transpires that the contract had indeed been properly terminated and the party that was obliged to continue to perform it as a result of the interlocutory order has suffered loss or damage by having to forego the pursuit of other alternatives in the meantime, that party will be entitled to be compensated for the loss by the party that sought the interim order in the first place. Equally difficult is a situation in which a party to an arbitration may seek an interim remedy that the other party refrain from a particular action – such as licensing intellectual property to a third party – pending the resolution of the dispute.[15] Faced with such an application, a tribunal must consider whether it is, in fact, no more and no less than an attempt to close down a competitor or licensee, or whether it is the case that, unless an order is made, there is a real risk that the applicant will suffer irretrievable loss or damage.

## 2.   Interim payments

In construction disputes, an overriding concern is the completion of the particular project. In many cases, the contract(s) at the heart of the dispute will include provisions requiring the parties not to cease work pending the resolution of their dispute. An arbitral tribunal will strive to facilitate the progress of the project in order to minimize disruption pending resolution of the dispute. Another remedy that may be appropriate, and which is frequently sought in construction disputes, is that of interim payments. Such payments may be needed to ensure the ongoing financial viability of the claimant party until the dispute is resolved. The tribunal may order a payment on an interim basis and then take this into consideration when the final award is issued.

## 3.   Freezing orders

The extent to which an arbitral tribunal might order a freezing of assets, by making the equivalent of what are known in some jurisdictions as Mareva injunctions, is uncertain. Section 38(1) of the English Arbitration Act 1996 provides:

> *"the parties are free to agree on the powers exercisable by the arbitral tribunal for the purposes of and in relation to the proceedings."*

There follows a default list of arbitrators' powers. It has been suggested that this default list does not exclude parties from conferring on arbitrators' powers that go beyond the default list, such as the power to grant a freezing injunction over a respondent party's assets as security for any future award.[16] However, it is submitted that the likelihood of any such express power being vested in an arbitral tribunal as a matter of specific agreement between the parties, least of all if a dispute is pending, is remote.

## 4.   Security for costs

Security for costs applications are becoming more commonplace in international commercial arbitrations, despite the fact that tribunals will usually require a strong case to be made out before granting such requests. However, the ability to award security for the legal costs of an applicant party and the costs of the arbitration remains an area of contention.

The extent to which a tribunal is satisfied that such relief is acknowledged to be a matter within its power and discretion may depend on the formulation of the rules of the particular institution applicable to the arbitration (see discussion of the ICC Rules below). Some rules and arbitration statutes state specifically that security for costs is available from arbitral tribunals as an interim remedy.[17]

## 5. Anti-suit injunctions

Most controversial of all, perhaps, not least because of their use as a means to thwart or disrupt the arbitral process rather than their deployment in support of arbitrations, are anti-suit injunctions. In the intervening period between a dispute arising and the final award being issued, a party may attempt to take steps in other fora to have the claim heard in parallel proceedings notwithstanding its agreement to resolve the dispute by arbitration.

For the purposes of this paper, no attempt will be made to develop the debate about anti-suit injunctions or to embark upon the detailed analysis that a proper study of the topic would require. It is enough, for present purposes, to note that some commentators have suggested that anti-suit injunctions are available under Article 23(1) of the ICC Rules.[18] In the revised text of Article 17(2)(b) of the UNCITRAL Model Law, the language "or prejudice to the arbitral process itself" was included in the interests of clarity so as expressly to confer the power to issue anti-suit injunctions on an arbitral tribunal.[19] One commentator has concluded that in circumstances in which an arbitrator may need to order an anti-suit injunction to protect the arbitral proceedings against undue disruption, "a showing of actual fraudulent conduct is not required".[20]

## 6. The UNCITRAL list of interim remedies

In the absence of an exhaustive (and generally acknowledged) list of the interim remedies that an arbitral tribunal may grant, the UNCITRAL Working Group, in the context of its review of the Model Law, considered a variety of measures aimed at avoiding or minimizing loss or damage, for example, by preserving a certain state of affairs until a dispute is resolved by the rendering of a final award and avoiding prejudice, for instance, by preserving confidentiality:[21]

> *"(i)   orders that goods that are the subject matter of the dispute are to remain in a party's possession but be preserved, or be held by a custodian (in some legal systems referred to as sequestration);*

*(ii)* orders that the respondent hand over property to the claimant on condition that the claimant post security for the value of the property and that the respondent may execute upon the security if the claim proves to be unfounded;

*(iii)* orders for inspection at an early stage where it is clear that a given situation may change before the arbitral tribunal addresses the issue relating to it. For example, if a dispute turned upon the berthing of vessels at a port, and it is known that the port is going to become a construction zone, the arbitral tribunal may make orders for inspection of the port at an early stage;

*(iv)* orders that one party provide to the other party certain information, such as a computer access code, that would enable, for example, certain work to be continued or completed;

*(v)* orders for the sale of perishable goods with the proceeds to be held by a third person;

*(vi)* appointment of an administrator to manage income-producing assets in dispute, the cost of which is to be borne as directed by the arbitral tribunal;

*(vii)* orders that the performance of the contract in dispute be continued;

*(viii)* orders to take appropriate action to avoid the loss of a right, such as by paying the fees needed to renew a trade mark or a payment to extend a licence of software;

*(ix)* orders directing certain information be kept confidential and measures to be taken to ensure that confidentiality."

The Working Group also listed certain types of interim remedy directed towards facilitating the later enforcement of an award:[22]

*"(i)* orders which are intended to freeze assets pending determination of the dispute, as well as orders not to move assets or the subject matter of the dispute out of a jurisdiction and orders not to dispose of assets in the jurisdiction where enforcement of the award is sought;

*(ii)* orders concerning property belonging to a party to the arbitration which is under the control of a third party (e.g. to prevent a party's funds from being released by a bank);

*(iii)* *security for the amount in dispute involving, for example, an order to pay a sum of money into a specified account, the provision of specified property, or the presentation of a guarantee by a third person such as a bank or surety; or*

*(iv)* *security for costs of an arbitration which might require, for example, depositing a sum of money with the arbitral tribunal or the provision of a bond or guarantee, usually to cover the respondent's costs if the claimant is unsuccessful."*

## IV.  JURISDICTION TO GRANT INTERIM MEASURES

Most dispute resolution provisions, often negotiated long before there is any question of a dispute arising, are broadly framed. The parties may agree little more than that they will arbitrate or go to the courts of a particular jurisdiction. If they opt for arbitration, they might express a clear wish for *ad hoc* or institutional arbitration (in the latter case, nominating the institution) and they may determine the number of arbitrators, the place and language of the arbitration and the governing law.

To the extent that the tribunal is conducting proceedings under the arbitral rules of one of the various international institutions, it is to those rules that the tribunal will turn in the first instance to determine whether or not it has the power to grant interim remedies.[23] If it does have that power, it will obviously have regard to whether or not there are any limitations on the exercise of that power (or indeed, additional powers conferred on it by the parties). It should be pointed out that the power to grant interim remedies is a matter within the discretion and authority of the tribunal upon an application of a party. It is not a matter of procedure. In other words, a tribunal may not of its own volition make an order for interim relief on the basis that it is empowered to determine the rules governing the proceedings, as might be the case under such rules as Article 15.1 of the ICC Rules. Even if the tribunal does not have the power to grant interim remedies of its own volition, however, it may still recommend such measures to the parties.[24]

## V.   INSTITUTIONAL RULES

On the basis of a comparative study of the provisions relating to interim measures to be found in the rules of a number of leading arbitral institutions (and in the UNCITRAL Rules), it can be seen that provisions allowing an arbitral tribunal to grant interim remedies have become "common currency". There is, however, some variation in the language used, which arguably means that the scope to grant interim measures is broader under some rules than others. Moreover, some sets of rules provide greater detail as to the types of interim measures that may be granted and the conditions for granting them.

### 1.   ICC Rules

Article 23(1) states:

*"Unless the parties have otherwise agreed, as soon as the file has been transmitted to it, the Arbitral Tribunal may, at the request of a party, order any interim or conservatory measure it deems appropriate. The Arbitral Tribunal may make the granting of any such measure subject to appropriate security being furnished by the requesting party. Any such measure shall take the form of an order, giving reasons, or of an Award, as the Arbitral Tribunal considers appropriate."*

When the ICC Rules were updated in 1998, specific provision was made for the grant of interim remedies. Article 23(1) vests an express power to grant interim remedies in the arbitral tribunal, absent the parties' agreement to the contrary. A broad discretion is afforded to the arbitral tribunal to grant any interim or conservatory measure it deems appropriate.

However, the expression "interim or conservatory measures" is not defined with any degree of particularity. Accordingly, the arbitral tribunal is in a position to construe those words in a broad manner, depending on the circumstances of the case.[25] Nor is there any restriction upon the application of the interim measure sought (or ordered) to the "subject matter of the dispute", a phrase that appears most notably in the UNCITRAL Rules. Provided there is sufficient connection with the arbitration, the tribunal's authority may extend to other matters of an interim or conservatory nature. In common with many other arbitration rules, the ICC Rules anticipate that the grant of an interim measure may be conditioned on the provision of security by the applicant.

Although not specifically stated, the power to grant interim measures under the Rules is subject to any mandatory provisions of law to the contrary applicable to the arbitral proceedings.

It has been suggested that the arbitral tribunal has a duty to find an equitable and commercially practicable solution to prevent irreparable and unnecessary injury to any of the parties.[26] To satisfy such a duty, the tribunal might also adopt a remedy by agreement of the parties, without recourse to the making of reasoned procedural orders or interim awards provided for in Article 23. In this situation, the tribunal, generally through the chairman, after consultation between the co-arbitrators, will make the tribunal's provisional view of measures to be taken during the pendency of the arbitration known to the parties and allow for possible modification after comments from the parties.[27]

While it is accepted that the making of an order for security for costs is possible under Article 23(1), it is less clear in what circumstances an ICC arbitral tribunal would make such an order.[28] A security for costs order conditions the right of a claimant (or occasionally a counterclaimant) to bring its claim (or counterclaim) on payment of an amount to guarantee, in the case of lack of success, payment of such of the arbitration and opposing party's legal costs as the arbitral tribunal may order the unsuccessful claimant or counterclaimant to pay in the final award. Security for costs is not expressed as a form of interim measure in the ICC Rules, as the draughtsmen did not wish to encourage the view that such orders were routine: it was intended as a measure to be adopted in exceptional circumstances, and there was therefore a concern not to encourage the proliferation of applications for security for costs.[29] That is especially so in ICC arbitrations, since, as often argued in this context, the Rules provide for the payment of advances on costs. However, those advances contain no element to reflect likely party legal costs attendant upon the prosecution of the arbitration. Recourse to Article 23, it was felt, would create an additional overlay that was unnecessary and contrary to the parties' agreement to agree to arbitration under the ICC Rules.

Craig, Park and Paulsson summarize the view as follows:

> *"This expression of the contractual intent of the parties should be given effect and it may be said arguably to exclude additional measures to secure a party from the possibility that its adversary would not be able to pay a costs order made against it in a final award. In order for a claimant to pursue its claim in arbitration it will have already had to advance a substantial amount fixed by the Secretariat or the ICC Court. It is not as if the claimant will not have been willing or required to make a substantial arbitration costs investment in the prosecution of its claim. The ICC practice of advances on costs offers a certain guarantee against abusive and extravagant claims."[30]*

However, as noted above, the counterargument is that the advance on costs is only a contract for the payment of the arbitral expenses, not the legal costs, which in the vast majority of cases constitute the lion's share of the costs of conducting an international arbitration.

The number of applications for security for costs in international arbitrations is increasing, but there remains a reticence on the part of ICC arbitral tribunals to award security for costs.[31] The advance on costs remains a relevant factor in the thinking of many ICC tribunals. It is suggested that two reasons that might be fundamental to the thinking of many ICC arbitrators are that (a) security for costs was long seen as a peculiarly English remedy; and (b) that peculiarity derived from the fact that the English courts (and those which accepted its procedures) routinely made orders for costs in favour of the prevailing party. That is not part of the court tradition in the United States or in civil law courts. More to the point, an arbitral tribunal is likely to take a dim view of a respondent's application for security for costs if the respondent is itself in default of its contractual obligation to pay any or all of its share of the advance on costs.

It is now well established that the arbitral tribunal may act as soon as the file is transmitted to it, i.e. prior to the finalization of the terms of reference. There was some conjecture prior to the 1998 revision of the ICC Rules that this was not the case. The grant of interim remedies may also be conditioned on the posting of security by the requesting party to remedy any damage if it is ultimately determined that the applicant is not entitled to relief.[32]

As to the form in which the remedy is granted, the ICC Rules provide that it may be an order or an award. However, in practice, it is much more likely to be an order. This is both a reflection of the nature of the remedy generally sought and also of the institutional framework of the ICC. Any award rendered under the ICC Rules is first subject to scrutiny by the ICC International Court of Arbitration. This requirement inevitably entails some delay. An application for an interim remedy is made to avoid harm or prejudice to the applicant's interests in a situation of urgency. That object may be frustrated if the relief is contained in an award subject to the completion of the scrutiny process.

## 2. German International Arbitration Rules

*"Section 20 – Interim measures of protection*

*20.1 Unless otherwise agreed by the parties, the arbitral tribunal may, at the request of a party, order any interim measure of protection as the arbitral tribunal may consider necessary in respect of the subject-matter of the dispute. The arbitral tribunal may require any party to provide appropriate security in connection with such measure.*

*20.2 It is not incompatible with an arbitration agreement for a party to request an interim measure of protection in respect of the subject-matter of the dispute from a court before or during arbitral proceedings."*

The German International Arbitration (DIS) Rules were amended in 1998, at the same time as the German Arbitration Law. The amendments to the arbitration law drew heavily on the UNCITRAL Model Law and introduced provisions on interim measures for the first time. Section 20 of the DIS Rules is identical to the arbitration law provisions and also introduced provisions on interim measures for the first time. The DIS Rules contain a potentially restrictive reference to the "subject matter of the dispute", which is discussed below in the context of the UNCITRAL Rules. The dual jurisdiction of the courts is also explicitly recognized.

## 3. International Centre for Dispute Resolution Rules (ICDR/AAA)

*"Article 21 – Interim measures of protection*
1. *At the request of any party, the tribunal may take whatever interim measures it deems necessary, including injunctive relief and measures for the protection or conservation of property.*
2. *Such interim measures may take the form of an interim award, and the tribunal may require security for the costs of such measures.*
3. *A request for interim measures addressed by a party to a judicial authority shall not be deemed incompatible with the agreement to arbitrate or a waiver of the right to arbitrate.*
4. *A tribunal may in its discretion apportion costs associated with applications for interim relief in any interim award or in the final award."*

The ICDR/AAA International Rules draw heavily upon the UNCITRAL Rules, but they have a wider scope, since there is no reference to the "subject matter of the dispute".[37] Tribunals constituted under the ICDR International Rules have the option to make an order in the form of an award and to make the grant of the remedy conditional on the posting of security by the requesting party. Article 21(4) also contains a statement dealing with the apportioning of the costs of such applications.

## 4. London Court of International Arbitration Rules (LCIA Rules)

*"Article 25 – Interim and conservatory measures*
*25.1 The Arbitral Tribunal shall have the power, unless otherwise agreed by the parties in writing, on the application of any party:*
  *(a) to order any respondent party to a claim or counterclaim to provide security for all or part of the amount in dispute, by way of deposit or bank guarantee or in any other manner and upon such terms as the Arbitral Tribunal considers appropriate. Such terms may include the provision by the claiming or counterclaiming party of a cross-indemnity, itself secured in such manner as the Arbitral Tribunal considers appropriate, for any costs or losses incurred by such respondent in providing security. The amount of any costs and losses payable under such cross-indemnity may be determined by the Arbitral Tribunal in one or more awards;*

(b) *to order the preservation, storage, sale or other disposal of any property or thing under the control of any party and relating to the subject matter of the arbitration; and*

(c) *to order on a provisional basis, subject to final determination in an award, any relief which the Arbitral Tribunal would have power to grant in an award, including a provisional order for the payment of money or the disposition of property as between any parties.*

25.2 *The Arbitral Tribunal shall have the power, upon the application of a party, to order any claiming or counterclaiming party to provide security for the legal or other costs of any other party by way of deposit or bank guarantee or in any other manner and upon such terms as the Arbitral Tribunal considers appropriate. Such terms may include the provision by that other party of a cross-indemnity, itself secured in such manner as the Arbitral Tribunal considers appropriate, for any costs and losses incurred by such claimant or counterclaimant in providing security. The amount of any costs and losses payable under such cross-indemnity may be determined by the Arbitral Tribunal in one or more awards. In the event that a claiming or counterclaiming party does not comply with any order to provide security, the Arbitral Tribunal may stay that party's claims or counterclaims or dismiss them in an award.*

25.3 *The power of the Arbitral Tribunal under Article 25.1 shall not prejudice howsoever any party's right to apply to any state court or other judicial authority for interim or conservatory measures before the formation of the Arbitral Tribunal and, in exceptional cases, thereafter. Any application and any order for such measures after the formation of the Arbitral Tribunal shall be promptly communicated by the applicant to the Arbitral Tribunal and all other parties. However, by agreeing to arbitration under these Rules, the parties shall be taken to have agreed not to apply to any state court or other judicial authority for any order for security for its legal or other costs available from the Arbitral Tribunal under Article 25.2."*

The LCIA Rules contain a list of specific interim measures which it is within an arbitral tribunal's power to order. These measures fall into three categories: security for the amount claimed or counterclaimed; measures dealing with property that forms the subject matter of the dispute; and any relief that the tribunal would have power to grant in an award. Article 25(1)(c) specifically provides the power to order interim financial relief – important where reliability of a regular cash flow is a significant factor in carrying on business in the industry in which the parties are involved. Any such relief granted will be subject to later review and readjustment in a later award.[38]

Article 25(2) makes a specific provision relating to applications for security for costs. In the same way as the English Arbitration Act 1996 made clear that the power to order security for costs in arbitration proceedings had been removed from the English courts, the inclusion of this provision arose as a reaction to the *Ken-Ren* case with the objective of spelling out in unequivocal terms the tribunal's powers in this regard.

## 5. Singapore International Arbitration Centre Rules

*"Rule 24 – Additional powers of the Tribunal*
*In addition and not in derogation of the powers conferred by any applicable law of the arbitration, the Tribunal shall have the power to:*

g. *order the preservation, storage, sale or disposal of any property or item which is or forms part of the subject-matter of the dispute;*

   ...

j. *order an interim injunction or any other interim measure;*

   ...

l. *direct any party to ensure that any award which may be made in the arbitral proceedings is not rendered ineffectual by the dissipation of assets by a party;*

m. *order any party to provide security for legal or other costs in any manner the Tribunal thinks fit;*

n. *order any party to provide security for all or part of any amount in dispute in the arbitration. ..."*

The SIAC Rules (third edition) were updated with effect from July 1, 2007. The intention of the revision was firmly to establish SIAC as a world-class arbitration institution in Asia. There is no specific provision in the new Rules that deals exclusively with interim remedies. Instead, the power to grant various forms of interim remedy is included among other powers of the tribunal adumbrated in Rule 24. Rule 24 (m) and (n) are new. They make clear that an arbitral tribunal has the power to order security for legal or other costs and to order any party to provide security for all or part of any amount in dispute in the arbitration.

Although presented in a different manner than in other rules examined here, the SIAC Rules confer a broad discretion on the arbitral tribunal to grant various forms of interim remedy. The broad ambit of Rule 24 (j) is a "catch-all". It ensures that a party cannot mount an argument that the measure sought did not fall within one of the specific powers set out in Rule 24. In contrast to the UNCITRAL Rules and to the other institutional rules considered in this paper, the SIAC Rules do not make it a prerequisite to a tribunal's exercise of these powers that it should first have received an application from one of the parties.

## 6. Rules of the Arbitration Institute of the Stockholm Chamber of Commerce (SCC)

*"Article 32 – Interim measures*

1. *The Arbitral Tribunal may, at the request of a party, grant any interim measures it deems appropriate.*

2. *The Arbitral Tribunal may order the party requesting an interim measure to provide appropriate security in connection with the measure.*

3. *An interim measure may take the form of an order or an award.*

4. *A request for interim measures made by a party to a judicial authority is not incompatible with the arbitration agreement or with these Rules."*

The Arbitration Institute of the SCC revised its arbitration rules in 2006. The new rules came into effect on January 7, 2007. Consideration was given to the extent to which the provisions on interim measures should be amended to take account of the revised UNCITRAL Model Law provisions. With the aim of enhancing the enforceability of an interim measure, it was decided to provide that interim measures may be granted in the form of an award. The new rules eschew setting out in detail the types of interim measure available to a tribunal, preferring to leave the arbitral tribunal's discretion unfettered.[33]

## 7. Swiss Rules of International Arbitration (Swiss Rules)

*"Article 26 – Interim measures of protection*

1. *At the request of either party, the arbitral tribunal may take any interim measures it deems necessary or appropriate.*

2. *Such interim measures may be established in the form of an interim award. The arbitral tribunal shall be entitled to order the provision of appropriate security.*

3. *A request for interim measures addressed by any party to a judicial authority shall not be deemed incompatible with the agreement to arbitrate, or as a waiver of that agreement.*

4. *The arbitral tribunal shall have discretion to apportion the costs relating to a request for interim measures in the interim award or in the final award."*

The Swiss Rules came into force in January 2006 and replaced the separate rules on international arbitration of the six Chambers of Commerce in Switzerland.[34] The Swiss Rules are based on the UNCITRAL Arbitration Rules with two main additions and changes, which were made to take account of modern practice and comparative law in the field of international arbitration and to reflect the application of these Rules to institutional arbitration. Consistent with a general trend in international arbitration to afford the arbitral tribunal a broad discretion to grant interim remedies tailored to the circumstances of the case, the listing of examples has been removed. In order to avoid the potential for tribunals to view language such as "subject matter of the dispute" as restricting their jurisdiction, these arbitration rules have, like others, deliberately adopted broad language.[35]

The Swiss Rules also provide that a request for interim measures filed with a judicial authority is not deemed incompatible with, or a waiver of, the agreement to arbitrate. In a sense, this provision, which can be found in some other institutional rules, is less restrictive than the ICC Rules, which contain a presumption that, once constituted, the arbitral tribunal should be in charge of the determination of applications for interim remedies, absent "appropriate circumstances".[36]

## 8.  UNCITRAL Rules

*"Article 26*

1.  *At the request of either party, the arbitral tribunal may order any interim measure it deems necessary in respect of the subject matter of the dispute, including measures for the conservation of the goods forming the subject-matter in dispute, such as ordering their deposit with a third person or the sale of perishable goods.*

2.  *Such interim measures may be established in the form of an interim award. The arbitral tribunal shall be entitled to require security for the costs of such measures.*

3.  *A request for interim measures addressed by any party to a judicial authority shall not be deemed incompatible with the agreement to arbitrate, or as a waiver of that agreement."*

The UNCITRAL Rules stipulate that the interim measures must be "necessary" and "in respect of the subject matter of the dispute." The question of necessity is to be considered against the basic function of interim measures, which is to preserve the rights of the arbitrating parties.[39]

The language "in respect of the subject matter of the dispute" has led some commentators to question whether or not it places a limitation on the types of interim remedies that may be granted.[40] However, the words that follow that phrase in the text have been accepted as illustrative only, as opposed to prescriptive limits on the arbitral tribunal's power to order any other measures "it deems necessary".[41] Interim remedies granted to avoid prejudicing the status quo have included an order that parallel proceedings initiated in another forum in breach of the agreement to arbitrate be terminated or stayed until further notice.[42] The rules also provide that a tribunal may "require security for the costs" caused by the interim remedy.

Following the completion of its work on the Model Law, the UNCITRAL Working Group has turned its attention to the UNCITRAL Rules. It has been suggested that the provisions dealing with interim remedies should be amended so as to make them consistent with the provisions of the Model Law. If that was done, it would also have the effect of removing the apparent limitation upon the scope of a tribunal's ability to act inherent in the words "the subject matter of the dispute", which have been a source of confusion. The consensus within the Working Group is that these words should be deleted. Insofar as the suggestion of making the rules consistent with the revised Model Law provisions is concerned, the Working Group has agreed that a number of the provisions contained in Chapter IV A of the Model Law should not be replicated, such as the provisions on enforcement. The view was also expressed that provisions that were contentious and had given rise to divergent views such as preliminary orders should not be included, in order not to prejudice the chances of the rules gaining wide acceptability.[43] This topic remains open for discussion.[44] Otherwise, the Working Group is currently considering a revised Article, which closely follows the revisions in the UNCITRAL Model Law, Chapter IV A.[45]

## VI. CONSIDERATION OF THE GRANT OF INTERIM MEASURES: WHAT FACTORS SHOULD BE TAKEN INTO ACCOUNT?

Perhaps so as not to inhibit the discretion of arbitrators, little or no guidance is offered as to the various factors that an arbitral tribunal should take into account when determining whether or not it is appropriate to order an interim measure.[46] The inclination of some arbitral tribunals may be to apply the law of the place of the arbitration to the determination of an application for interim remedies or the applicable substantive law. The place where the interim remedy is to be enforced may also be relevant. Since the arbitration laws at the place of arbitration often offer little guidance, there may also be a tendency on the part of arbitral tribunals to import into their reasoning criteria used to determine applications for interlocutory relief before their own national courts. Inevitably that may of itself give rise to further difficulty, if the arbitrators themselves come from different jurisdictions.

Certainly, an internationally constituted tribunal is likely to have regard to criteria and circumstances that, from the standpoint of a domestic state court judge, might seem irrelevant or simply not susceptible to an order for such relief under a particular domestic law. Nevertheless, it is possible to discern a number of criteria and principles to which international arbitral tribunals typically have regard.[47]

They include:

*Prima facie jurisdiction* – It is generally accepted that the applicant for interim measures must establish that the tribunal has *prima facie* jurisdiction[48] to rule on the merits of the case.[49] In some Iran-US claims tribunal cases,[50] tribunals have stated that the applicant should be given the benefit of the doubt. In finding that it does have *prima facie* jurisdiction, a tribunal does not purport finally to determine the issue of its jurisdiction. A finding of *prima facie* jurisdiction is a prerequisite for the grant of an interim remedy, rather than a jurisdictional finding. The tribunal must ascertain that it is not manifestly lacking in jurisdiction. Were that the case, it should decline jurisdiction rather than consider the application for an interim remedy.

*Assessment of the merits* – If, on its provisional assessment of the strength of the applicant's case and the likelihood of success on the merits, it seems to the tribunal that there may be no arguable case, then it may conclude that the grant of an interim remedy will serve no useful objective. Since the tribunal has not had an opportunity to consider all of the evidence at so early a stage, this assessment is sometimes referred to as a *prima facie* assessment only.[51] There are obvious difficulties with such an approach. Unlike the situation that often obtains in court proceedings, where the judge determining the application for interim relief will in most cases not be the judge who ultimately hears the case on the merits, an arbitrator faced with an application for interim relief will also be determining the substance of the case. Any suggestion that a tribunal has prejudged the outcome of the case is antithetical to the need to ensure that both parties have been given a fair opportunity to present their case. For that reason, this criterion, which requires an element of analysis of the strength of the case at a very early stage in the proceedings, has received a mixed reception.[52]

*No pre-judgment of the merits* – There is an interrelation between the arbitral tribunal's assessment of the strength of the case and this negative requirement, namely that a tribunal should not pre-judge the merits of the dispute. Arbitral tribunals may be asked to consider an application for interim measures at an early stage of the proceedings when little of the evidence has been presented.

The tribunal must be careful not to jeopardize due process and remain astute to ensure that both parties have a fair opportunity to present their case. It is a balancing act for the tribunal. An arbitral tribunal (or a court for that matter) should also refrain from considering an application for interim relief if, in effect, what it is being asked to do is to determine the substance of the arbitration.[53]

In a procedural order on "interim measures" made in an ICC arbitration, the tribunal stated as follows:

> "*The Arbitral Tribunal emphasises that, at this stage of the proceedings, it may and can only conduct a* prima facie *examination of the Parties' respective claims. It may not rule on the substance of the dispute. In particular, the Arbitral Tribunal is not in a position to rule on the issue of the validity of the termination of the [(Contract)] or on the claim of nullity of the Contract or of the validity or the effectiveness of the orders rendered by the Court of the State of X.*"

The dispute concerned the lease of offshore drilling units. The principal question for determination was whether the lessee had failed to make payments due and whether the lessor was entitled to terminate the lease. The issue was compounded by the fact that some of the platforms were situated in the waters of a state (allegedly) favourable to one party, while other platforms had been moved (allegedly unlawfully) to the waters of a state (allegedly) friendlier to the other party. The lessee had obtained, before the municipal courts of the country (allegedly) favourable to it, an order by way of interim relief that the lessor should not move the rig in question.

The lessee was requesting that the platforms resume work. Otherwise, the lessee stood to lose a considerable amount of money (non-performance of its drilling obligations towards third parties). Conversely, the owner of the rigs was requesting a provisional payment of the outstanding invoices and access to the platforms to perform repairs or even to move them to a more neutral place to perform such repairs.

The tribunal ruled that both parties had shown some likelihood of success on the merits, but it did not undertake a factual investigation. It heard the parties and decided that the applications had failed on two other grounds mentioned below, namely the threat of irreparable harm and urgency.

*The threat of irreparable or substantial harm that cannot be compensated by damages* – The absence of any such demonstrable risk is most likely going to militate against the grant of the measure sought, since the claiming party's claims will be compensable in damages or otherwise susceptible to effective remedy in the final award.

The preservation of the rights of the arbitrating parties "may be threatened by actions 'capable of prejudicing the execution of any decision, which may be given by the tribunal'",[54] or, in other words, the purpose of interim remedies is "to prevent irreparable prejudice or harm to the rights of a party".[55] It is worth noting, however, that Iran-US Tribunals have determined that an "injury that can be made whole by monetary relief does not constitute irreparable harm".[56] A reflection of that conclusion is to be found in Article 17A(1)(a) of the revised UNCITRAL Model Law. The tribunal in the offshore platform case referred to above adopted the same reasoning.

Interim relief may be ordered so as to avoid an aggravation of the dispute, but it is not available to protect against an increase of the amount in dispute. It is necessary to keep in mind this distinction between the aggravation of the dispute and any impact upon the amount in dispute such as to increase it. Other factors that are taken into account and perhaps subsumed within the question of irreparable and substantial harm are urgency[57] and proportionality.[58]

*Security/cross-undertaking in damages* – Many rules also provide for the posting of security against the possibility that it should later be found that the measure was unwarranted or that the decision on the merits is in favour of the party against whom the interim measure was granted. A tribunal is in a position to safeguard the interests of the party against which a measure is granted in the event that it is later found to be unjustified by dint of the provision of some form of satisfactory security at the same time as the interim order is made.

The form of the security will be fashioned to the circumstances of the case. It may take the form of an undertaking backed by a guarantee or some form of payment into a specified account.

## VII. *EX PARTE* INTERIM MEASURES

In order for an interim measure to be effective, it may be necessary on some occasions to maintain an element of surprise in order to avoid a real risk of potential harm and to ensure that the remedy is effective. This will be the case where the requesting party has a valid basis for concern that the other party will take steps to dissipate its assets and so render any eventual award in the requesting party's favour nugatory. The topic of *ex parte* interim measures in international arbitration is a controversial one. It has been the subject of much debate during the UNCITRAL Working Group sessions dealing with the revisions of the Model Law provisions.

Redfern and Hunter summarize the current position as follows:

> *"The laws of the most popular arbitration seats and the rules of the leading institutions do not currently expressly envisage such a power for arbitrators and some commentators have suggested that it is incompatible with the consensual nature of arbitration and the respect for due process."*[59]

One commentator has concluded that it is most unlikely that an arbitral tribunal operating under the ICC Rules would grant interim measures on an *ex parte* basis, suggesting that, in the view of most ICC arbitration practitioners, such an action would be inconsistent with the Rules, not least because granting an interim remedy on an *ex parte* basis could undermine the confidence of the other party in the neutrality of the arbitral tribunal.[60]

Part of the difficulty seems to stem from a difference in appreciation as to what *ex parte* means in the context of an application to a court or arbitral tribunal. If proper notice of an application may be shown to have been given and the respondent party fails to attend the hearing, a tribunal, faced with an urgent application that appears, *prima facie*, to be meritorious, might (and, the authors submit, should) pause before declining to make an order simply because the respondent party is not present, despite all reasonable efforts to contact it.

There may be scope for making an order with a very tight return date of, say, 48 hours for further review and argument. Such a situation of an application, which is, in effect, *ex parte* on notice, is very different from a truly *ex parte* application, which is made without any prior notice whatever to the opposing party. It was applications of this latter kind that gave rise to such controversy within the UNCITRAL Working Group.

As mentioned above, some commentators considered that allowing *ex parte* measures would be contrary to the underlying principles of international arbitration, including: (i) the duty to treat all parties with equality; (ii) the duty to afford each a fair hearing including the opportunity of putting its case and answering that of the other party; (iii) the principle that neither party is to have unilateral contact with the arbitrator; (iv) the requirement of impartiality and the arbitrators not having prejudged the issues; and (v) the consensual nature of the arbitral process.[61] For the reasons outlined above, that is not always the appropriate conclusion to draw.

The contrary view is that true *ex parte* interim remedies (that is to say, applications made without any prior notice) are also necessary in international arbitration for precisely the reason that the element of surprise is sometimes essential to make them effective. They do not violate due process *per se*, and in exceptional circumstances *ex parte* measures are necessary to achieve a fair resolution of the dispute. Provided that there are sufficient safeguards and that the parties are aware that either the institutional rules or the law of the place of arbitration allow them, *ex parte* interim remedies should be allowed.[62]

The outcome of the debates within the UNCITRAL Working Group was a compromise. Articles 17 B. and 17 C. of the revised Model Law provide for a preliminary orders regime. It is made clear that the preliminary orders stand apart from other interim measures due to their temporary and extraordinary nature. An order may be granted if the tribunal considers that prior disclosure of the request for the interim measure to the party against which it is directed would risk frustrating the purpose of the interim measure. There are safeguards to protect the interests of the party against which the preliminary order is granted.

The order expires within 20 days from the date on which it was issued, and the tribunal must immediately notify all parties of the determination of an application for a preliminary order and afford the party against which the order is made the opportunity to present its case. It remains to be seen how many countries will amend their arbitration legislation to include this provision.[63]

## VIII. FORM OF THE GRANT OF AN INTERIM REMEDY

Many arbitral institutions leave it to the arbitral tribunal to decide whether to grant the interim measure in the form of an order or a partial award.[64] In most instances, interim measures will be granted in the form of an order, thereby allowing for ready amendment or variation of its terms should circumstances change. Unless there are compelling reasons that cause a tribunal to determine that its decision should be published in the form of an award, such as a perception that it will aid compliance with its terms, most ICC tribunals will avoid doing so.

Attention has already been drawn to the real prospect of delay attendant upon the formality of submitting an award in draft form for scrutiny by the ICC Court. A possible way around this problem is to grant the interim remedy as an order with the reasons to follow in a detailed award. An award is also subject to setting-aside procedures and enforcement procedures, which may result in side litigation with the further consequence that the arbitration will become more complex.

An interim remedy, by definition, is not intended finally to resolve any point in dispute. It is to the substance of the relief furnished, rather than the form of its presentation, that a court called upon to enforce an "award" granting an interim measure is likely to have regard. The absence of finality is inconsistent with the requirements of the New York Convention, which stipulate that an award must be "binding on the parties".[65] When it comes to the enforcement of such interim awards, that point has been taken up, for example, by the Australian courts.[66] In an attempt to overcome these difficulties in respect of enforcement, some states have sought to "label" interim remedies ordered by tribunals as awards, at least so far as their own legislation is concerned.[67]

The recent revisions to the UNCITRAL Model Law contain extensive provisions on enforcement, which are beyond of the scope of this paper. Although the UNCITRAL Rules provide that orders granting interim remedies may be in the form of an interim award, some urgent matters may require that action be taken before the "final" interim remedy may be issued in the form of an interim award. The availability of tribunal members to deliberate and sign an award, or the time required for the award to be circulated between the tribunal members for signing, can result in a delay. The practice has developed of allowing the chairman to direct the party against which the interim measure is requested to refrain temporarily from any actions that might aggravate the situation, pending formal notification of the tribunal's decision.[68]

## IX. A NOTE OF CAUTION

If the remedy sought is unusual or particularly sweeping, an arbitral tribunal will doubtless wish to proceed with particular care. Mindful of its concern to ensure, insofar as it is reasonably able to do so, that its award will be enforceable, an arbitral tribunal will have regard to the location where the remedy may be enforced, since the relevant national court, if called upon to enforce an order, may refuse to do so on the grounds that such a remedy is unknown (or unlawful) in its jurisdiction. Alternatively, a national court requested to enforce an unfamiliar interim remedy imposed by an arbitral tribunal seated outside its jurisdiction may recast it into a form acceptable in the enforcing jurisdiction, even to the extent of undermining the effectiveness of the order originally made.

## X.   COMPLEMENTARY REMEDIES

## 1.   The role of national courts

In certain circumstances, most notably that an arbitral tribunal is not yet in place or there is some doubt that it would have the necessary powers (and powers of coercion in any event), the option of making an application of the kind envisaged in the rules considered above simply does not arise, and a party may be well advised (or simply have no choice but) to go to a national court to seek interim measures.

Courts in a considerable number of jurisdictions would regard themselves, many with some justification, as being astute to exercise their powers in support of the arbitral process. That role is very significant, since courts have coercive powers to ensure compliance with interlocutory orders. Furthermore, those powers may be exercised against parties whose compliance may be required by an interim measure but who are not themselves parties to the arbitration. An arbitral tribunal may order that a party take an action with respect to property that is held by a third party, but the tribunal has no jurisdiction to order the third party itself to take an action or refrain from doing something. For example, a third-party order addressed to a bank holding deposits of a party would not be enforceable against the bank.[69]

The extent and effectiveness of this interaction between state judges and arbitrators will depend on the relevant national arbitration law(s) and the scope of the agreement to arbitrate from which the tribunal derives its powers.

It will be a matter for national courts to determine the circumstances in which they will entertain an application for interim remedies once an arbitral tribunal has been formed. In those jurisdictions where there is a well-developed appreciation on the part of the judiciary of the role of international arbitration and arbitral tribunals and of the relationship between the courts and arbitration, the courts will uphold the parties' agreement to resolve their dispute by arbitration and will only intervene insofar as it is necessary to aid the arbitral process.

Certain arbitral rules contain a statement that applications for interim measures before a state court will not be deemed to be incompatible with the agreement to arbitrate. For example, Article 23(2) of the ICC Rules provides:

> *"Before the file is transmitted to the Arbitral Tribunal, and in appropriate circumstances even thereafter, the parties may apply to any competent judicial authority for interim or conservatory measures. The application of a party to a judicial authority for such measures or for the implementation of any such measures ordered by an Arbitral Tribunal shall not be deemed to be an infringement or a waiver of the arbitration agreement and shall not affect the relevant powers reserved to the Arbitral Tribunal. Any such application and any measures taken by the judicial authority must be notified without delay to the Secretariat. The Secretariat shall inform the Arbitral Tribunal thereof."*

The AAA/IDRC Rules (Article 21(3)) and UNCITRAL Rules (Article 26(3)) state that a request to a judicial authority for interim measures shall not be deemed incompatible with the agreement to arbitrate or a waiver of the right to arbitrate. The LCIA Rules (Article 25(3)) contain a similar provision. The ICC Rules, in common with the LCIA Rules, curtail the parties' ability to seek interim remedies from a judicial authority once the arbitral tribunal is constituted. In the case of the ICC Rules, it is restricted to "appropriate" circumstances and, in that of the LCIA Rules, to "exceptional circumstances".

Even if the arbitral tribunal has jurisdiction to grant interim measures under the applicable institutional rules or the agreement to arbitrate, a further consideration to be taken into account (not least for the tribunal in the exercise of its discretion) is the attitude of the courts at the place of arbitration to the granting of interim measures by an arbitral tribunal. The powers vested in an arbitral tribunal under the various arbitral rules are subject to any mandatory rules of law at the place of arbitration.

In Italy, for example, public policy requires that interim measures may only be granted by the courts. The Italian Code of Civil Procedure provides as follows:

> *"The arbitrator may not grant attachment or other interim measures of protection."* [70]

The number of such jurisdictions in which such restrictions obtain is dwindling, as more and more countries, seeking to attract international arbitrations and to foster a reputation as an investor-friendly environment, enact modernized arbitration laws.

Most often, a neutral venue with an arbitration-friendly environment will be chosen as the place of arbitration. If that is the case, it is unlikely to be the jurisdiction where the assets of the parties are located or where the subject matter of the dispute arose. It is important, therefore, that the parties have the opportunity to access the courts in other jurisdictions, particularly insofar as enforcement is concerned.

In practical terms, parties faced with the prospect of arbitral proceedings will most likely need to consider their options, to the extent that it may be possible to obtain interim relief from a court, prior to the constitution of the tribunal. If measures backed by a threat of financial or penal sanction may be required and/or a third party is involved, the courts will again have an important role to play.

## 2.  Within the arbitral process

In the absence of a validly constituted arbitral tribunal, there may be reason to question whether the courts from which a party might otherwise seek assistance in the form of measures of interim relief will be in a position (or willing) to provide it. Such relief may not be available at all or be of such limited scope as to be inadequate. In certain jurisdictions, interlocutory relief, which might be available in support of an arbitration pending in that jurisdiction is not available in the case of an arbitration pending in a foreign jurisdiction. One such jurisdiction, based on the current state of the law, is Singapore.[71] There may be little or no experience of such applications in the context of international arbitration among the judiciary in a particular country. There may be legitimate cause for concern that, in a dispute between a "foreign" entity and their "home" state, the courts in question will be reluctant to intervene at the expense of the "host" government.

A number of arbitral institutions have developed procedures intended to address the problem posed by the delay between the filing of a request for arbitration and the constitution of a tribunal seized of the substantive dispute(s) between the parties. By way of illustration, attention is drawn to ICC's own Rules for a Pre-Arbitral Referee Procedure (which date from January 1990), the ICDR's (AAA's) Emergency Relief procedures under Article 37 of the ICDR International Arbitration Rules (effective 1 May 2006) and the NAI's Article 42 Summary Arbitral Procedure, available since January 1988.

They have in common a recognition of the need to provide prompt access to a neutral third party competent to order provisional measures of relief of limited duration in circumstances in which interim relief is not available from a court or arbitral tribunal.

However, they differ in that the ICDR procedure is only available as an adjunct to pending ICDR arbitration proceedings: a party may not seek emergency relief before it has filed its Notice of Arbitration. In contrast, it is not a precondition to an application to a referee under the ICC procedure that arbitration – or court – proceedings be on foot or even imminent. The referee may, however, make the carrying out of his order subject to the condition that: "… a party shall commence proceedings before the Competent Authority [defined in Art. 1.1 as: "the arbitral tribunal or national court competent to deal with the case"] on the substance of the case within a specific period."[72] The NAI Summary Arbitral Procedure is a 'stand-alone' arbitral procedure in its own right, independent of the interlocutory relief that the parties may request from an arbitral tribunal seized of the substantive dispute. As Professor Albert Jan van den Berg has observed to the authors: "the Netherlands Arbitration Act is, to my knowledge, the only arbitration law to date [to contain] provisions for arbitral interim relief proceedings independent from the arbitration proceedings on the merits (Article 1051 of the Dutch Code of Civil Procedure)."

It must be remembered that when the ICC introduced its Pre-Arbitral Referee Procedure in 1990, it was breaking new ground: the concept of seeking emergency or temporary relief from an entity other than a court was then a novel one. To that extent, ICC procedure may seem rather formal by comparison with the more recent US and Dutch procedures, which have had the benefit of following the ICC's lead.

Recourse to the Pre-Arbitral Procedure must be the subject of an agreement in writing between the parties, who alone may bring their dispute to the referee. The referee may be designated in advance by the parties or else appointed by the Chairman of the ICC Court:

> *"... in the shortest time possible, taking account of his technical or professional qualifications, nationality, residence, other relationships with the countries in which the parties are established or with which they are otherwise connected, and any submissions of any party concerning the choice of a Referee."*[73]

There is, however, no specific requirement that the referee be and remain independent of the parties. Once appointed, the referee is required to make and send his order within 30 days of transmission of the file to the referee.[74]

The rules for the NAI Summary Arbitral Procedure contemplate the appointment of a sole arbitrator "as soon as possible" after the receipt of the request (in practice, the authors understand that appointments are generally made within 24 hours).[75] Once again, the parties may conclude a specific agreement on a method of appointment of a summary proceedings tribunal, but they may not simply carry over by implicit reference any agreement made between them insofar as the constitution of an arbitral tribunal seized of the merits of the dispute is concerned. Failing such an agreement, the appointment is made by the NAI administrator. An arbitrator appointed under these rules is required to be independent and impartial, but nationality alone is not a reason to preclude a person from appointment. Experience of these procedures in operation suggests that a decision will generally be forthcoming within one to three weeks of the appointment of the arbitrator.

Turning now to the ICDR procedure, it is incumbent upon the administrator to appoint within one business day of receipt of a notice a single emergency arbitrator from a special panel of emergency arbitrators designated to rule on emergency applications.[76] It is incumbent upon anyone approached to accept such an appointment that he or she disclose to the administrator any circumstances likely to give rise to justifiable doubts as to the arbitrator's impartiality or independence. Should any matter be raised, a challenge must be made within one business day of notice to the parties of the circumstances that have been disclosed.[77]

Once appointed, the emergency arbitrator is required, within two business days of appointment, to establish a schedule for consideration of the application for emergency relief.[78] No time limit is fixed for the conclusion of the procedure, but it is generally expected that it will be completed within 7-14 days.

### Competence to order provisional measures of relief of limited duration

The powers of the Pre-Arbitral Referee, which may be altered by express written agreement between the parties, are defined in Article 2 of the ICC Pre-Arbitral Referee Procedure Rules. They include a power to order any conservatory measures urgently necessary to prevent either immediate damage or irreparable loss; a power to order payments to be made; orders necessary to preserve or establish evidence; and orders requiring a party to take any step that ought to be taken according to the contract between the parties. Notwithstanding that remit, no order may be made by the referee other than an order requested by any party in accordance with the provisions of Article 3 of the Rules. Any order made by the referee must be reasoned. While it does not prejudge the substance of the case, nor bind any competent authority, the order is intended to remain in force unless and until the referee or the competent authority has decided otherwise.[79] Uniquely among the rules under consideration, the ICC procedure contemplates that a referee may retain the power to make an order within the time provided under the Rules, even if a competent authority has become seized of the case during the currency of the referee's tenure of office, unless the parties otherwise agree or the competent authority orders otherwise.[80]

While a decision of a summary arbitral tribunal appointed under the NAI Rules is deemed a "provisional decision [which] shall in no way prejudice the final decision of the arbitral tribunal that decides on the merits of the case",[81] the decision in the summary arbitral proceedings is deemed to be an arbitral award for the purposes of Article 1051(3) of the Dutch Code of Civil Procedure.[82] As the authors understand it, it is often the case that, once the Summary Arbitral Tribunal's decision has been handed down, that ruling provides a sound basis for eventual settlement of the dispute between the parties, a point echoed in the introduction to the ICC Pre-Arbitral Referee Procedure Rules, which states:

> *"The order should therefore provide a temporary resolution of the dispute and may lay the foundations for its final settlement either by agreement or otherwise."*

Against this background, Professor Pierre Tercier's description of measures ordered by pre-arbitral referees as being "definitively provisional" seems particularly apt.

In some respects, the powers of an ICDR emergency arbitrator are more circumscribed. The emergency arbitrator's decision, which may be in the form of an interim award or of an order, may include:

> "*Any interim or conservancy measure ... [deemed] necessary, including injunctive relief and measures for the protection or conservation of property.*"

The rules expressly provide that the emergency arbitrator has no further power at all to act once the tribunal that is to be seized of the merits of the dispute has been constituted. Pending the constitution of that tribunal, the emergency arbitrator himself may modify or vacate the interim award or order for good cause shown, but thereafter the tribunal dealing with the merits alone may reconsider, modify or vacate the interim award or order.[83]

While these measures are intended to fill what is rightly perceived to be a gap in the arbitral process, it must be acknowledged that the number of applications made under these various rules to date is very small. Insofar as the authors can ascertain, a mere handful of cases have been the subject of referrals to a pre-arbitral referee under the ICC Rules;[84] the ICDR, in the 18 months during which its emergency rules have been available, has received three notices of request, while the NAI now receives some 10-20 cases a year out of an overall annual case load of some 120-150 cases. It would seem, therefore, that pending the constitution of an arbitral tribunal, most parties will still look first and foremost to the courts in the relevant jurisdiction(s) for such interim relief as might be available to them.

A compromise utilized under the LCIA Rules is to allow for the possibility of the expedited formation of the tribunal. Article 9 of the LCIA Rules allows any party to apply to the LCIA "in exceptional urgency" for the expedited formation of the arbitral tribunal. A party must make an application to the LCIA setting out the specific grounds for the exceptional urgency in the formation of the arbitral tribunal. The LCIA Court then has the discretion to abridge or curtail any time limit under the Rules for the formation of the arbitral tribunal.

Even after an arbitral tribunal has been constituted, it may take time for an application for interim measures to be heard. It may be difficult to convene a meeting between the parties and the members of the arbitral tribunal within a sufficiently short timeframe. The likely fallback, contemplated in many institutional rules – and certainly those of ICC[85] – is that the parties will apply to a court for measures intended to "hold the ring" until the tribunal itself is in a position to deal with the application.

## XI. CONCLUSION

Interim remedies provide a very important mechanism intended to enhance the prospect that the outcome of the resolution of a dispute by arbitration will be effective. Important evidence may be preserved and made available to the tribunal; the subject matter of the dispute may be preserved; the status quo between the parties may be maintained; and assets out of which to satisfy the eventual award or pay the costs of the arbitration may be secured.

Most institutional rules and national arbitration legislation make provision for interim remedies. The absence of uniformity between these provisions (and the need to have regard to the effect of any particular agreement entered into by the parties insofar as interim measures are concerned) requires arbitral tribunals and practitioners to be alert to the potential limits on the grant of interim remedies.

While in many instances the courts remain a "first port of call" for a party seeking interim relief, particularly in the period prior to the constitution of an arbitral tribunal, there is ample evidence to support the proposition that arbitrators are increasingly called upon to exercise their jurisdiction to grant interim measures. To the extent that it is indicative of a willingness on the part of those involved in an international dispute to bring the dispute entirely within the arbitral process, that is encouraging. However, arbitrators (and the arbitral institutions) should be astute to ensure that resort to applications for interim relief as a tactical ploy intended to derail the arbitration through delaying tactics that increase the costs and apply pressure on the other party to settle the dispute is discouraged. It is submitted that, if such a development were to be allowed to go unchecked, it would be inimical to the arbitral process.

It would give rise to a potential source of real dissatisfaction with a means of dispute resolution that has demonstrated a remarkable degree of adaptability to all manner of international disputes and prejudice the prospects of reducing still further the extent of court intervention in the arbitral process.

## END NOTES

[1] *Electricity Company of Sofia and Bulgaria (Belgium v. Bulgaria)*, PCIJ, Series A/B, No. 79, 1939, at 199 (December 5, 1939).

[2] It should be noted that a number of different terms, such as "interim measures of protection", "conservatory measures", "precautionary measures" and "recommendations", are used in the mass of relevant rules and legislation. While these variations of nomenclature may be of some significance in their respective immediate contexts, the term "interim remedies" is used in this paper to encompass all of these different terms.

[3] See J. Lew, L. Mistelis and S. Kroll, *Comparative International Commercial Arbitration* (2003) p. 586.

[4] D.F. Donovan, 'The Scope and Enforceability of Provisional Measures in International Commercial Arbitration: A Survey of Jurisdictions, the Work of UNCITRAL and Proposals for Moving Forward', ICCA Congress Series No. 11 (2003) p. 82. See also D.A. Redfern and J.M.H. Hunter, *Law and Practice of International Commercial Arbitration*, 4th edn. (2004) p. 332, where the purpose of interim remedies is described as "the preservation of evidence, the protection of assets, or in some other way the preserving of the status quo pending the outcome of the dispute." In a similar vein, see A. Yesilirmak, 'Interim and Conservatory Measures in ICC Arbitral Practice', 11(1) *ICC International Court of Arbitration Bulletin* (2000) at p. 31: "Interim and conservatory measures are designed to prevent or minimize any disadvantage which may be due to the duration of the arbitral proceedings until the final settlement of the dispute and the implementation of its result. Their purpose is therefore to uphold justice by protecting parties' interests until the award is recognized or enforced."

[5] L. Craig, W. Park and J. Paulsson, *International Chamber of Commerce Arbitration*, 3rd edn. (2001) p. 460.

[6] Ibid.

[7] Those interim remedies aimed at procedural matters such as the production of documents are not pertinent to the topic of this paper and so are not discussed. The aim of such measures is to afford the parties an equal opportunity to present their case. Examples of measures that would fall within this category are inspection of goods, merchandise or equipment within the other party's control.

[8] Redfern and Hunter, *supra* note 4, at p. 339.

[9] Ibid., at p. 338, note that the orders of an arbitral tribunal are not "writ in water". Reference is made to Schwartz, *Conservatory and Provisional Measures in International Arbitration*, ICC Publication No. 519 (1993), which states:
" *Ultimately, of course, the arbitrators' greatest source of coercive power lies in their position as arbiters of the merits of the dispute between the parties. Parties seeking to appear before arbitrators as good citizens who have been wronged by their adversary would generally not wish to defy instructions given to them by those whom they wished to convince of the justice of their claims.*"

[10] See D. Williams QC, 'Chapter 8 – Interim Measures', *Asian Leading Arbitrators' Guide* (2007) pp. 242-243. Some arbitrators may also use the threat of monetary penalties (*astreintes*). Whether they may order them is a matter of jurisdiction rather than procedure. Therefore, a tribunal requires either the legal entitlement or the parties' (implied at least) consent.

[11] Craig, Park and Paulsson, *supra* note 5, at p. 462. Art. 17 of the recently revised UNCITRAL Model Law describes four categories of interim measures. They are: (a) maintain or restore the status quo pending determination of the dispute; (b) take action that would prevent, or refrain from taking action that is likely to cause, current or imminent harm to the arbitral process itself; (c) provide a means of preserving assets out of which a subsequent award may be satisfied; or (d) preserve evidence that may be relevant and material to the resolution of the dispute.

[12] G. Marchac, 'Interim Measures in International Commercial Arbitration Under the ICC, AAA, LCIA and UNCITRAL Rules', 10 *The American Review of International Arbitration* (1999) p. 123.

[13] Y. Derains and E. Schwartz, *A Guide to the ICC Rules of Arbitration*, 2nd edn., ICC Publication No. 961 (2005) pp. 296-297, opine that remedies granted in ICC arbitrations go beyond mere conservation or disposal of goods to injunctions of all kinds, the preservation of evidence, the protection of trade secrets, orders for provisional payment, the appointment of experts to report upon factual matters and the posting of guarantees.

[14] See Craig, Park and Paulsson, *supra* note 5, at p. 463.

[15] Williams, *supra* note 10, at p. 229.

[16] R. Merkin, *Arbitration Act 1996* (2005) p. 102. It has been suggested recently that there is as yet no clear precedent confirming the arbitrator's power to grant freezing orders as such. See P. Runeland and G. Blanke, 'On Provisional Measures in English Arbitrations: A Brief Overview', 73(2) *Arbitration* (2007) p. 189. See also Yesilirmak, *supra* note 4, at p. 33, pointing out that tribunals acting under the ICC Rules have rejected applications for a Mareva injunction or a post-award attachment as being beyond the competence of the tribunal by reason of its contractual nature.

[17] Section 18(3) of the English Arbitration Act 1996 provides: "The tribunal may order a claimant to provide security for the costs of the arbitration", and Art. 25.2 of the LCIA Rules contains a provision vesting the arbitral tribunal with power to order any claiming or counterclaiming party to provide security for the legal or other costs of any other party. The United Kingdom is, however, something of a special case, since these very specific provisions arose as a reaction to the controversial English case of *Coppee-Lavalin N.V.* v. *Ken-Ren Chemicals and Fertilizers Limited* [1995] 1 A.C. 38, [1994] 2 All E.R. 499.

[18] Derains and Schwartz, *supra* note 13, at pp. 109-110, note 169.

[19] For a comprehensive discussion of anti-suit injunctions, see E. Gaillard (ed.), *Anti-Suit Injunctions in International Arbitration* (2005).

[20] L. Lévy, 'Summary of Laurent Lévy's presentation on interim relief in oil and gas matters', ICC Paris, 29 October 2007, p. 8.

[21] Note by the Secretariat, 30 January 2002, UN Doc. A/CN.9/WG.II/WP.119, p. 6.

[22] Ibid., at p. 7.

[23] Alternatively, the capacity to order interim remedies may be derived from the *lex arbitri*. For example, Art. 183 of the Swiss Private International Law Act provides: "Unless the Parties have agreed otherwise, the Arbitral Tribunal may, at the request of a Party, order provisional or protective measures." See also Art. 17(1) of the UNCITRAL Model Law.

[24] There are exceptions to this general rule. For example, Rule 24 of the new SIAC Rules would appear to empower an arbitral tribunal to order interim relief of its own accord.

[25] Derains and Schwartz, *supra* note 13, at p. 296.

[26] Craig, Park and Paulsson, *supra* note 5, at p. 462.

[27] Ibid., at pp. 463-464.

[28] Ibid., at p. 468.

[29] Derains and Schwartz, *supra* note 13, at p. 297.

[30] Craig, Park and Paulsson, *supra* note 5, at p. 469.

[31] Ibid., at pp. 467-469.

[32] Ibid., at p. 461.

[33] K. Hober and W. McKechnie, 'New rules of the Arbitration Institute of the Stockholm Chamber of Commerce', 23 *Arbitration International* (2007) pp. 261-291.

[34] These rules constitute a unified set of rules for the Swiss Chambers of Commerce.

[35] W. Peter, 'Some Observations on the New Swiss Rules of International Arbitration', in A.J. van den Berg (ed.), *YB Com. Arb.*, Vol. XXIX (2004) pp. 440-447:

> " *By departing from the formulation of the UNCITRAL Arbitration Rules which appeared too restrictive and indeed outdated in view of prevailing international arbitration practice, the drafters of the Swiss Rules wanted to stress the considerable freedom and discretion given to Arbitral Tribunals in respect of the object as well as the nature of interim measures that may be ordered.*"

[36] See L. Burger, 'The New Swiss Rules of International Arbitration: A Comparative Analysis', 19(6) *Mealey's International Arbitration Report* (2004) p. 21.

[37] G. Marchac, *supra* note 12, at p. 128. However, Redfern and Hunter, *supra* note 4, at p. 341 consider that they show a similar narrow concern for goods and property.

[38] Runeland and Blanke, *supra* note 16, at pp. 197-198.

[39] Ibid., at p. 536.

[40] See Redfern and Hunter, *supra* note 4, at p. 341:

> " *The references to 'subject-matter' of the dispute and to 'measures for the conservation of goods forming the subject-matter of the dispute' suggest that the measures contemplated relate to preserving or selling of goods rather than, for instance, preventing the flight of assets. In this sense, they fall short of the interim measures that are needed in the modern world of international commerce.*"

[41] D. Caron, L. Caplan and M. Pellonpää, *The UNCITRAL Arbitration Rules, A Commentary* (OUP, 2006) p. 539; and Donovan, *supra* note 4, at p. 102.

[42] Caron, Caplan and Pellonpää, *supra* note 41, at p. 539.

[43] Report of the Working Group I (Arbitration and Conciliation) on the work of its forty-fifth session, Vienna, September 11-15, 2006, UN Doc. A/CN.9/614.

[44] Report of the Working Group II (Arbitration and Conciliation) on the work of its forty-seventh session, Vienna, September 10-14, 2007, UN Doc. A/CN.9/641.

[45] See UN Doc. A/CN.9/WG.II/WP.145/Add.1.

[46] The recent revisions to the Model Law do provide a set of conditions for granting interim measures in Art. 17 A. The party requesting an interim measure must satisfy the arbitral tribunal that:

> "*(a) Harm not adequately reparable by an award of damages is likely to result if the measure is not ordered, and such harm substantially outweighs the harm that is likely to result to the party against whom the measure is directed if the measure is granted.*
>
> *(b) There is a reasonable possibility that the requesting party will succeed on the merits of the claim, provided that any determination on this possibility shall not affect the discretion of the arbitral tribunal in making any subsequent determination.*"

[47] See, for example, Redfern and Hunter, *supra* note 4, at p. 343.

[48] See Lévy, *supra* note 20, at p. 4, concerning the necessity to characterize this as a *prima facie* assessment only.

[49] Several institutional rules provide that an arbitral tribunal may grant an interim remedy as soon as it has been constituted (e.g. Art. 23(1) ICC Rules). At such an early stage of the proceedings, an arbitral tribunal will not yet have determined its jurisdiction, which may be disputed.

[50] *Military and Paramilitary Activities in and against Nicaragua* (*Nicaragua* v. *United States of America*), Provisional Measures, Order of 10 May 1984, *ICJ Reports* 1984, cited in Caron, Caplan and Pellonpää, *supra* note 41, at p. 536.

[51] See *Occidental Petroleum Corporation and Occidental Exploration and Production Company* v. *Republic of Ecuador*, ICSID Case No. ARB/06/11, Decision on Provisional Measures, August 17, 2007, p. 29, paras. 63-64, where it is stated that the claimants:

*"need only to show that they alleged to the claims that – if ultimately proven – would entitle Claimants to substantial relief...*

*At this stage, the Tribunal reiterates that the right to be preserved only has to be asserted as a theoretically existing right, as opposed to proven to exist in fact."*

[52] Lew, Mistelis and Kroll, *supra* note 3, at p. 604.

[53] See *Channel Tunnel Group Ltd* v. *Balfour Beatty Construction Ltd* [1993] A.C. 334, 367-368. A further example is the Iran-US Claims Tribunal case of *Behring International, Inc.* v. *Iranian Air Force*, 8 *Iran-US CTR* 44, in which the Tribunal refused the relief sought as it would have achieved the result sought by the respondent in its counterclaim.

[54] Caron, Caplan and Pellonpää, *supra* note 41, at p. 536.

[55] Ibid. Caron, Caplan and Pellonpää express the view that "grave" or "substantive" would be a more appropriate characterization of the required harm than "irreparable". This is part of a discussion on Art. 26 of the UNCITRAL Rules under which an arbitral tribunal may take any interim measures it deems "necessary".

[56] Ibid, at p. 538, citing Iran and the United States of America (A/15 and A/24), Award No. ITL 33-A-4/A-15(III)-2, February 1, 1984, 21, 5 *Iran-US CTR* 131 (1984-I).

[57] See Lévy, *supra* note 20, at p. 6.

[58] The requirement of proportionality is encompassed in the revised Model Law provisions, where Art. 17 A.(1)(a) provides as a condition for granting interim measures that the arbitral tribunal shall be satisfied that "harm not adequately reparable by an award of damages is likely to result if the measure is not ordered, and such harm substantially outweighs the harm that is likely to result to the party against whom the measure is directed if the measure is granted."

[59] Redfern and Hunter, *supra* note 4, at p. 335.

[60] Derains and Schwartz, *supra* note 13, at p. 299.

[61] H. van Houtte, 'Ten Reasons Against a Proposal for *Ex Parte* Interim Measures of Protection in Arbitration', 20 *Arbitration* (2004).

[62] K. Hober, 'The Trailblazers v. the Conservative Crusaders, Or Why Arbitrators Should Have the Power to Order *Ex Parte* Interim Relief', ICCA Congress Series No. 12 (2005) pp. 272-277.

[63] Redfern and Hunter, *supra* note 4, at p. 336, consider that any change to national arbitration laws may take some time, since most leading arbitral venues have recently renewed their laws without including such a power. One jurisdiction that has already taken steps to amend its laws – in part, due to fortuitous timing – is New Zealand. The New Zealand Parliament at the same time as approving some other minor amendments to the Arbitration Act 1996 has recently approved the adoption of all of the revised Model Law provisions on interim measures.

[64] In court proceedings, state courts have shown a willingness to look beyond the title of a decision of an arbitral tribunal. For instance, in *True North* v. *Publicis*, a US Federal Court granted the enforcement of interim relief, finding that, rather than a provisional order, the arbitrators had actually handed down an award. Conversely, the *Cour d'Appel de Paris* quashed a provisional order on the basis that the arbitrators had actually made an award and had not abided by the ICC Rules (scrutiny of the ICC Court): *Brasoil* v. *Libya*, *Rev. Arb.* 1999, 834.

[65] Art. V(1)(e) of the New York Convention. As Redfern and Hunter, *supra* note 4, have observed at p. 335, "the interim measures ordered by an arbitral tribunal do not, by definition, finally resolve any point in dispute. Such an order is therefore unlikely to satisfy the requirement of finality imposed by the New York Convention for an award."

[66] See the case of *Re Resort Condominiums International Inc.* [1995] 1 Q.D.R. 406.

[67] Redfern and Hunter, *supra* note 4, at p. 335.

[68] Caron, Caplan and Pellonpää, *supra* note 41, at pp. 541-542.

[69] Redfern and Hunter, *supra* note 4, at pp. 334-335.

[70] See also Arts. 28 and 45 of the Arbitration Law of the People's Republic of China. Italian law does now provide an exception in the field of company law whereby the arbitral tribunal is granted the power to grant an interim remedy staying the effect of the resolutions of a company meeting where the dispute concerns such resolutions.

[71] See *Swift-Fortune Ltd* v. *Magnifica Marine S.A.* [2006] S.G.C.A. 42. For a more detailed commentary, see also Chang Leng Sun, 'Injunctions in Aid of Foreign Arbitration: the Singapore Experience', 3(2) *Asia International Arbitration Journal* (2007).

[72] Art. 6.4 of the Rules for a Pre-Arbitral Referee Procedure.

[73] Ibid., Art. 4.2.

[74] Ibid., Art. 6.2. It is important to note that any extension of that time limit lies within the sole discretion of the Chairman of the ICC Court.

[75] Art. 42(f) of the Rules for Summary Arbitral Proceedings.

[76] Art. 37(3) of the ICDR Emergency Measures of Protection.

[77] Ibid.

[78] Ibid., Art. 37(4).

[79] Art. 6.3 of the ICC Rules for a Pre-Arbitral Referee Procedure.

[80] Ibid., Art. 2.4.

[81] Art. 42(m) of the NAI Rules.

[82] Ibid., Art. 42(l).

[83] Arts. 37(e) and 37(f).

[84] The Statistical Reports of the ICC for 2000-2006 published in the *Bulletin of the International Court of Arbitration* reveal that for this period there were five applications for a pre-arbitral referee procedure.

[85] Art. 23(2) of the ICC Rules of Arbitration.

# 5

# Issues of applicable law and uniform law on interest: basic distinctions in national and international practice

## By **Andrea Giardina**

## I.    INTRODUCTORY REMARKS

The question of awarding interest in international disputes is crucial. Court and arbitral proceedings are often initiated for the settlement of disputes involving significant amounts of money. Once a party has succeeded in its damages claim, interest is usually added in order to fully compensate that party for the damage it has suffered, also with regard to the length of the period between the beginning of the procedure, the issuance of the award and, finally, the actual payment.

Although the legal approaches and solutions differ, even radically in the various legal systems, it is generally recognized that interest is due for delayed payments. There are also a few countries that forbid interest in principle, because they consider it inconsistent with their religious beliefs, but they provide alternative mechanisms in order to compensate the damaged party.[1] Moreover, in some countries, interest is qualified as a procedural matter, while in others it is considered a substantive issue. There is still no uniformity as to the determination of interest rates, the period of time over which interest is due or the applicable rate.[2] It may be added that the determination of the interest rate and period is generally fact-specific.[3]

Obviously, judges and arbitral tribunals generally consider the contractual provisions applicable to the case as the primary source for their power to award interest. The parties might have provided in the contract that interest is due in the case of late payment, specifying the rate and date for the calculation of interest. If the contract does not contain any provision concerning the payment of interest or designate the law applicable in this regard, the court or tribunal usually applies domestic law to solve the problem.

As national statutory law and case law vary considerably on the issue of interest, the choice of the applicable law or rules is of extreme importance in the process of deciding a case. The choice of law on interest can turn an outstanding success on the issue of responsibility and damages into an unsatisfying compensation, due to the application of simple interest at a low rate. In contrast, a limited outcome in terms of responsibility and damages can be transformed into an outstanding success in terms of effective compensation, due to the awarding of compound interest at a high rate.

Obviously, international conventions and other international instruments – when applicable – make a significant contribution in favour of the uniformity of solutions, which is traditionally desirable in international trade. In the present chapter, the issue of interest in international commercial cases will be examined, taking into particular consideration the 1980 Vienna Convention on Contracts for the International Sale of Goods (CISG) and its related case law. Article 78 CISG provides: "If a party fails to pay the price or any other sum that is in arrears, the other party is entitled to interest on it, without prejudice to any claim for damages recoverable under article 74." According to this rule, interest is due, but the Convention does not specify the accrual period, the rate of interest to be applied or how the rate should be determined. For these reasons, the analysis of national case law and international arbitration practice becomes of great importance.[4]

Particular attention will also be given to the UNIDROIT Principles. Articles 7.4.9 and 7.4.10 of the UNIDROIT Principles contain provisions that are clearly and substantially in line with international trade require-ments. In consideration of these characteristics, recent practice shows that the Principles are often applied or referred to by courts and arbitration tribunals.[5]

Moreover, various authors have dealt extensively with the issue of interest, carefully examining national and international practices[6] and often suggesting solutions that have been derived from or inspired by the practice and trends of international trade.

Nevertheless, they sometimes seem to pay insufficient consideration to the particular frameworks (national jurisdictions or different kinds of international arbitration) in which the problems arise and to the content of the applicable national or international rules. In a general context characterized by different approaches and solutions, it is understandable that authors, national courts and arbitral tribunals have tried to free themselves from the constraints of traditional conflict of laws methods and the strict application of national statutory laws or international rules, in order to freely promote the uniformity of solutions that is necessary for the protection and development of international trade.

However, it should be pointed out that uniformity of solutions cannot be sought by applying abstract and subjective criteria, as this would be detrimental to certainty and foreseeability, which are also fundamental values for international trade.

The necessity of assuring certainty and stability of solutions is particularly important nowadays, when international litigation is growing significantly and participants in international trade are located all over the world. Thus, the lack of certainty and variability of the decisions adopted by the competent judicial and/or arbitral bodies severely endanger the development of international economic cooperation.

The present chapter intends to indicate some points that could contribute to promoting clearer and more coherent solutions in the decisions of national courts and arbitral tribunals on the issue of interest. In doing so, it distinguishes carefully between the various fields of international trade in which the problem arises, while at the same time applying a comparative approach and taking into account recent positions suggested by commentators and international case law.

It therefore seems necessary to maintain the traditional approach as a starting point and then to distinguish different models, such as the CISG, the UNIDROIT Principles and other uniform principles, as well as the rules of some arbitration institutions. Next, the practice of the Iran-US Claim Tribunal and other arbitral institutions (mainly ICSID and other mechanisms for the solution of investment disputes) will be analyzed. Finally, some concluding observations are presented.

## II. THE TRADITIONAL APPROACH: INTEREST DETERMINED ACCORDING TO THE LAW GOVERNING THE CONTRACT

The issue of awarding interest is primarily dealt with by judges and arbitrators by having regard to the parties' agreement. In fact, the parties to the dispute may have inserted provisions expressly addressing this issue and also determining the date from which interest is expected to be paid. There may also be contractual provisions designating the law governing the matter of interest. In such cases, the interest claim is therefore resolved, at least in principle,[7] by courts and arbitral tribunals by awarding interest in the amount and at the rate agreed directly by the parties or stipulated by the law designated by them.

Frequently, however, the contract or the agreement from which the dispute originates does not contain any reference to the possibility of awarding moratory and/or compensatory interest in case of default by one of the parties with respect to its contractual obligations. In these circumstances, national courts usually apply the conflict rules of the *forum* to select the law applicable to solve the issue. In contrast, international arbitrators enjoy greater freedom of approach and have recourse to different methods for determining the interest to be applied. The issue can actually be resolved by the arbitrators through a traditional conflict of law method by selecting an applicable national law for the contract and then applying it to the determination of interest. As will be seen later, however, a number of decisions of international tribunals show that it is also possible for arbitrators to disregard national statutory law and apply general principles of law.

When arbitrators opt for the choice of law approach, their analysis will face the difficult process of initially selecting the applicable conflict of laws rules. In this context, it is worth mentioning that some national laws on arbitration provide specific rules concerning the way in which tribunals that have their seat in the country concerned have to determine the substantive law applicable to the disputed issues.

In Switzerland, Article 187 of the Federal Code on Private International Law provides:

"*(1) Le tribunal arbitral statue selon les règles de droit choisies par les parties ou, à défaut de choix, selon les règles de droit avec lesquelles la cause présente les liens les plus étroits.*

*(2) Les parties peuvent autoriser le tribunal arbitral à statuer en équité.*"

Article 834 of the Italian Code of Civil Procedure, as introduced by Law No. 25 of 1994 (and abrogated in 2006[8]), provided:

"*Le parti hanno facoltà di stabilire d'accordo tra loro le norme che gli arbitri debbono applicare al merito della controversia oppure di disporre che gli arbitri pronuncino secondo equità. Se le parti non provvedono, si applica la legge con la quale il rapporto è più strettamente collegato. In entrambi i casi gli arbitri tengono conto delle indicazioni del contratto e degli usi del commercio.*"

Broader powers are conferred on arbitrators by French law. For instance, Article 1496 of the *Nouveau Code de Procédure Civile*[9] provides:

"*L'arbitre tranche le litige conformément aux règles de droit que les parties ont choisies; à défaut d'un tel choix, conformément à celles qu'il estime appropriées. Il tient compte dans tous les cas des usages du commerce.*"

Depending on the powers conferred on the arbitrators, the issue of interest may be decided according to: (i) the substantive law applicable to the contract as designated by the parties; (ii) the substantive law applicable to the contract as chosen or deemed appropriate by the arbitrators; (iii) the law of the place of the arbitration; (iv) the applicable international conventions; or (v) the rules of international arbitration institutions.

## III.  THE TRADITIONAL APPROACH IN NATIONAL CASE LAW

The traditional approach to the question of awarding interest in the process of solving international disputes can be detected in the national case law of most countries. Examples are numerous, especially in less recent case law, and do not require specific references here.[10]

However, a US case of 2004 deserves to be mentioned, because the issue of interest was examined in some detail. In this case, the Northern District Court of Illinois observed that, on the matter of interest, there is no single approach used by courts and that, when the parties to the contract fail to address the interest issue and fail to provide information necessary to "customize" a rate, the court has to award interest "according to the principles used by the federal courts in determining choice of law issues".[11] In particular, making reference to the Vienna Convention, the Court determined that the substantive law applicable to the dispute was the law of Illinois, given that this state was the place of performance of the contractual obligations.[12] The determination reached in that case also indicated that, despite the CISG's evident purpose to promote uniformity, the result of applying the *forum*'s interest rate is quite common in comparative CISG case law, thus generating significant variability in terms of solutions.

The traditional conflict of law method for determining the accrual period and rate of interest is also confirmed in the Swiss and Italian case law, where the problem is often solved by making reference to the conflict of laws system of the *forum*.

As to Swiss law, a decision of the *Tribunal Cantonal du Valais* of 2005[13] is worth mentioning. The Court decided that the respondent owed the plaintiff the delayed payment together with interest. In the absence of any reference to the Vienna Convention, the Court stated that, in order to determine interest,

> "*celui-ci doit dès lors être déterminé selon le droit désigné par les règles de conflit du for. Conformément aux articles 118 LDIP et 3 al. 1 de la convention de La Haye de 1955 … il s'agit, à nouveau, de la loi interne du pays où le vendeur a sa résidence habituelle au moment où il reçoit la commande, soit le droit italien.*"

In the framework of the CISG,[14] the Tribunal of Padua, despite affirming that, in principle, "an approach different from the international private approach must nevertheless be preferred", favoured "the direct application of the norms of substantive law" and subsequently decided that the interest rate should be determined by reference to the substantive law applicable by virtue of the rules of conflict of the forum.[15] The Court observed that the Vienna Convention, which was applicable to the merit of the dispute, recognized the right of the party to be awarded interest in addition to compensation, but that it was silent as to the method of determining the interest. Therefore, in order to determine the law applicable to this issue, the Court made reference to the Italian private international law rules, incorporating the Hague Convention of 1955 on the law applicable to international sale contracts. Article 3(1) of the Hague Convention provides:

> "*In default of a law declared applicable by the parties under the conditions provided in the preceding Article, a sale shall be governed by the domestic law of the country in which the vendor has his habitual residence at the time when he receives the order.*"

As a result, in compliance with the Hague rule, the Court awarded interest according to Italian substantive law, this being the "law of the seller".[16]

A more recent example of this trend is the case decided in 2006 by the *Cour de Justice* of Geneva concerning a dispute initiated by a French seller and a Swiss buyer. The Swiss Court recognized that Article 78 CISG provides for the awarding of interest but that it does not mention the applicable rate or the *dies a quo* and concluded that

> "*En cas de contestation, la question est régie par le droit désigné par les règles de conflit de lois de l'État du for ... En l'espèce, l'intimée s'est référée au droit suisse (art. 104 al. 1 CO) et a réclamé un intérêt moratoire 5% à compter du 1er juin 1999. Ce point n'a pas fait l'objet d'une controverse, et le Tribunal était dès fondé d'y donner suite.*"

IV.  THE METHOD OF CONFLICT OF LAWS AND THE DIRECT DETERMINATION
OF INTEREST IN INTERNATIONAL COMMERCIAL ARBITRATION

In recent years, the practice of international arbitration has shown significant variability in decisions concerning the awarding of interest, which have focused mainly on the awarding of compensatory interest rather than moratory interest. There are three major approaches in international arbitration practice concerning the awarding of interest to the party that has to be compensated. The first is represented by the application of the traditional method of conflict of laws. As already noted above with regard to national case law, the arbitrators decide whether interest should be awarded and determine the rate and the accrual period according to the law governing the contract.

Under the second approach, the arbitrators resolve the claim for interest pursuant to general principles of law and the relevant practice of international arbitration.

Under the third approach, the arbitrators freely decide the issue of interest on the basis of the principles they deem applicable and in relation to the circumstances of the case under dispute.[17]

## 1.  Interest determined by the law applicable to the contract as indicated by the parties

International arbitral tribunals sometimes resolve the issue of interest simply by applying the law that has been chosen by the parties for the interpretation and application of their contract. In this case, the *lex causae* governing the merits of the dispute also applies to interest, which could be awarded against the party that is condemned to pay compensation. An example of this solution is offered by ICC Award No. 9448 of 1999.[18] In this arbitration case, the parties had provided that "the laws of Switzerland shall apply to all matters respecting the making, interpretation and performance of this contract". As the parties had chosen Swiss law, and Switzerland is a contracting state of the CISG, the Arbitral Tribunal thus considered that the 1980 Vienna Convention on Contracts for the International Sale of Goods formed part of Swiss substantive law and was applicable to the contract, as all the necessary preconditions had been fulfilled.

The Tribunal noted that,

> *"according to Article 78 CISG, if a party fails to pay the price or any other sum that is in arrears, the other party is entitled to interest. The rate to be applied is, however, a matter, in the first place, for the domestic law".*

The Tribunal thus decided that the Swiss Code of Obligations was applicable.[19]

## 2. Interest determined by the law designated by the conflict rules of the place of arbitration

A different approach is followed when arbitrators, having decided to award interest on the sums to be paid to the injured party, determine the interest rate on the basis of the conflict of law rules of the *lex fori*.

## 3. Interest determined according to the conflict of laws rules deemed applicable or appropriate by arbitrators

Article VII(1) of the 1961 Geneva Convention on International Commercial Arbitration can be taken as the best example. It provides:

> *"The parties shall be free to determine, by agreement, the law to be applied by the arbitrators to the substance of the dispute. Failing any indication by the parties as to the applicable law, the arbitrators shall apply the proper law under the rule of conflict that the arbitrators deem applicable. In both cases the arbitrators shall take account of the terms of the contract and trade usages."*

It is also worth mentioning the ICC Rules of Arbitration as in force from 1975 to 1998. Article 13(3) of those Rules provided:

> *"The parties shall be free to determine the law to be applied by the arbitrator to the merit of the dispute. In the absence of any indication by the parties as to the applicable law, the arbitrator shall apply the law designated as the proper law by the rule of conflict which he deems appropriate."*

Another example of interest determined by arbitrators on the basis of the applicable or appropriate conflict of laws rules are the UNCITRAL Arbitration Rules. Article 33(1) of these Rules provides:

> *"The arbitral tribunal shall apply the law designated by the parties as applicable to the substance of the dispute. Failing such designation by the parties, the arbitral tribunal shall apply the law determined by the conflict of laws rules which it considers applicable."*

## 4. Interest determined according to the direct choice by the arbitrators of the rules governing the contract

French law provides an important example in this regard. Article 1496 of the *Nouveau Code de Procédure Civile* provides:

> *"L'arbitre tranche le litige conformément aux règles de droit que les parties ont choisies; à défaut d'un tel choix, conformément à celles qu'il estime appropriées. Il tient compte dans tous les cas des usages du commerce."*

It is also worth mentioning Article 17 of the ICC Rules as introduced in 1998, which provides:

> *"The parties shall be free to agree upon the rules of law to be applied by the Arbitral Tribunal to the merits of the dispute. In the absence of any such agreement, the Arbitral Tribunal shall apply the rules of law which it determines to be appropriate."*

In ICC Case No. 11849 of 2003, the interest issue was decided according to the substantive law deemed appropriate by the arbitral tribunal. First, the sole arbitrator determined that the Vienna Convention was applicable to the contract, as agreed by the parties, although the claimant argued that it was governed by Italian substantive law, because the CISG could not be applied to a long-term distributorship agreement.

Having quantified the sums due by one party to the other, the arbitrator came to the award of interest on these sums and noted that

> *"The Agreement does not contain any indication as to the interest rate applicable to the sums due by respondent to claimant. Claimant has submitted that the legal rate applicable in the State of Washington should apply because this is the place where it is registered. The Arbitrator does not believe such solution to be appropriate. As a matter of fact, by submitting the Agreement to the CISG, the parties have clearly indicated their intention to avoid their respective internal law rules, and to resort to neutral solutions. This will should be respected also regarding interest."*

In this respect, the arbitrator added that

> *"In international arbitration, arbitrators have the broadest powers to determine interest on the basis of the most appropriate rate, without resorting to any rule of conflict. As indicated above, the interest rate to be applied should correspond to a generally accepted rate, applied on the international financial markets to the currency in which the damages shall be paid."*

An interesting position was expressed by the sole arbitrator in ICC Case No. 9771 of 2001 when determining first the applicable conflict of law rules to govern the contract and then the issue of interest. The arbitrator noted that the contract did not contain any explicit designation on the choice of law and that neither party had made precise reference to any applicable law. Instead, he observed:

> *"it seems likely that the parties in this case would not have been inclined to accept the case being treated with the application of the substantive law ... of the other party's country [Italy and Cyprus]. ... The indication of Stockholm as the place of arbitration could be interpreted as an indication of the will of the parties to let the law of the place of arbitration govern their contract."*

Then, the sole arbitrator, also referring to Article VII (erroneously indicated as Article III) of the 1961 Geneva Convention regarding the conflict of law system "deemed applicable" by the arbitrators, concluded that the contract was governed by Russian law, designated by the Swedish conflict of law rules.

As to the issue of interest, the arbitrator considered that

> *"[t]he general view in Sweden (as elsewhere) is that the matter of interest is an issue of substance and thus is governed by the applicable substantive law. The latter is thus to be determined under the appropriate provisions of the internal Russian legislation",*

being the law governing the contract as determined by the Swedish conflict of law rules. It followed that

> *"[t]he proper construction of Russian law with regard to interest ... shall therefore in the opinion of the sole arbitrator lead to the application of the official discount rate as applicable from time to time in the claimant's domicile, i.e., Italy."*

The *dies a quo* was left to the discretion of the arbitrator, who found it reasonable to award interest from the time the request for arbitration was filed.

## 5.  Interest freely determined on the basis of arbitration rules

Arbitrators can also freely determine interest without any reference to the law governing the contract in cases where the arbitration rules applicable to the procedure allow them to do so. In this regard, Article 60 of the WIPO Rules, which regulates currency and interest with respect to the sums to be awarded, provides that

> *"the Tribunal may award simple or compound interest to be paid by a party on any sum awarded against that party. It shall be free to determine the interest at such rates as it considers to be appropriate, without being bound by legal rates of interest, and shall be free to determine the period for which the interest shall be paid."*

Similarly, Article 26.6 of the LCIA Arbitration Rules provides that

> *"the Arbitral Tribunal may order that simple or compound interest shall be paid by any party on any sum awarded at such rates as the Arbitral Tribunal determines to be appropriate, without being bound by legal rates of interest imposed by any state court, in respect of any period which the Arbitral Tribunal determines to be appropriate ending not later than the date upon which the award is complied with."*

The freedom of the arbitral tribunal in the determination of interest is perhaps more limited under the AAA Arbitration Rules, which in Article 28.4 provide that

> *"the tribunal may award such pre-award and post-award interest, simple or compound, as it considers appropriate, taking into consideration the contract and applicable law."*

## V. SPECIAL CONFLICT RULES ON INTEREST

As evidenced by the arbitral award in ICC Case No. 9771 of 2001, another problem in the process of determining interest is the fact that the rules on interest may be qualified differently in different countries. In particular, these rules are considered as procedural in some countries and substantive in others. In this respect, it has been stated that

> *"similar differences exist as to the classification of the rules governing interest. Most national laws consider interest as part of damages and therefore part of the substantive law. ... In some countries, such as England, the issue of interest is considered at least partly as procedural. The natural consequence of this is that the law that governs the arbitration, the* lex arbitri, *has to deal at least with the question of which items are classified as procedural and which are substantive."*[20]

Under English law, only the question whether interest should be awarded is classified as a matter of substantive law and is therefore governed by the *lex causae* applicable to the contract, while the issues of the *dies a quo* and the rate of interest are regarded as procedural matters and have to be governed by the *lex fori*. As clearly evidenced by Lew, "in arbitration, however, no such *lex fori* exists", and arbitrators are generally free to apply the conflict of law rules they deem appropriate.

The search for a specific rule of conflict on the matter of interest can be detected both in national case law and in international arbitration. Therefore, the examples of the various solutions presented here come from both domestic and international case law.

## 1. Interest determined by the law of the place of payment

In a recent case concerning an international sales contract,[21] the judges of the Court of Appeal of Antwerp had to determine the interest rate to be applied to the sums claimed by the plaintiff. In particular, the seller claimed compound interest and a rate of 9% from the date of payment until the date of full payment. The court held that *"according to Belgian law [which was the law applicable to the contract], the conventional interest claimed by the [seller] on the basis of Article 5 of [seller]'s general conditions – which are deliberately reduced to 9% – are certainly not exaggerated"* and applied the 9% rate.

## 2. Interest determined by the law of the country of the currency of payment

This solution is well evidenced in a case decided by a Belgian District Court in 2001[22] concerning a sales contract between a Belgian plaintiff and Czech defendant. As to the substantive law governing the contract, the Court found that the CISG was applicable to the dispute, as both countries were contracting states and the obligation concerned the sale of movable goods. According to the Court's ruling, the seller-plaintiff was entitled to interest under Article 78 CISG because of the late payment, but, *"whereas the CISG does not itself determine the interest rate in the case of late payment, this interest rate is determined according to the law of the currency of payment"*, which was Belgian law.

Similarly, in ICC Case No. 11849 of 2003, the sole arbitrator, having applied the CISG rules to a sale contract, observed that, as a matter of fact, the parties had clearly indicated their intention to avoid their respective internal law rules and to resort to the neutral solution of the Vienna Convention and that their will should also be respected regarding interest. Hence, the arbitrator ruled differently on the issue of interest, making a distinction between interest to be awarded on the sums due from the claimant and interest to be awarded on the sums due from the respondent, applying two different interest rates. The reasoning was that, in international arbitration, arbitrators have the broadest powers to determine interest on the basis of the most appropriate rate without resorting to any rule of conflict. In this case, the arbitrator decided that "the interest rate to be applied should correspond to a generally accepted rate, applied on the international financial markets to the currency in which the damages shall be paid".

## VI.  THE VIENNA CONVENTION ON CONTRACTS FOR THE INTERNATIONAL SALE OF GOODS (CISG) AND ITS ARTICLES 74 AND 78

As already noted, the Article 78 CISG specifically provides that a party is entitled to interest if the other party fails to pay the price or any other sum that is in arrears *"without prejudice to any claim for damages recoverable under article 74"*.[23] However, the CISG does not contain any specific indications regarding the interest rate or the date from which interest is due. Farnsworth notes that the reason why Article 78 was conceived without an express definition of the interest rate and the time for calculation is that the problem proved to be "too intractable" within the Working Group to adopt more than a limited solution.[24] It is clear that the major source of difficulty was that some countries forbid interest in principle, because it is considered inconsistent with their religion, and that others impose a limit on the applicable rate. It was therefore unconceivable to fix a standard rate in the Convention that would be valid for all member states. On the other hand, however, it was still necessary to provide at least a general rule, in order to avoid that the matter would be regulated exclusively by national statutory law.

As a consequence, whenever the CISG has been considered applicable to a case, the issue of interest according to Article 78 has received different interpretations in both national courts and international arbitrations.

In particular, there is one general view according to which the issue of interest is outside the scope of Article 78 and should therefore be decided according to the domestic substantive law designated by the applicable conflict rules. In this case, interest could be awarded according to (i) the applicable law chosen by the parties; or (ii) the applicable law determined by the court or the arbitral tribunal.

In some cases, however, judges and arbitrators have considered that Article 78 affirmed the right of a party to be awarded interest, despite being silent on how it should be determined and that the issue therefore had to be solved according to the general principles of the CISG.

There are many examples of the first approach. In ICC Case No. 7565 of 1994, the arbitrators stated:

> *"As the general principles do not settle the matter ... and the parties have referred to the laws of Switzerland, it seems justified to refer to Article 73 of the Swiss Code of Obligations whereby, in the absence of a determination of the rate of interest by agreement or law or usages, that rate shall be 5% per annum".*

Similarly, in ICC Case No. 9187 of 1999, the arbitral tribunal determined that the law governing the contract was Swiss law, given the explicit reference to that statutory law contained in the contract, and, therefore, that any of the conventions applicable in Switzerland, including the CISG, were applicable to the case. As to the rate of interest, the tribunal noted that *"Article 78 CISG is silent. Therefore, national law is supplementarily applicable."*

In a case decided by an arbitral tribunal of the International Commercial Arbitration Court of the Russian Federation in 2000,[25] the parties had expressly agreed in their contract to apply the law of the Russian Federation and, as a consequence, the Vienna Convention. The tribunal issued the final award, granting the claim for interest and noted that "considering that the CISG does not provide the rate of interest, the amount of interest should be calculated in accordance with the rules of subsidiary applicable Russian law", thus deciding that

> *"under Article 395(1) of the Russian Federation Civil Code, the amount of interest for failure to perform a monetary obligation is calculated according to the actual credit rate of interest offered by banking institutions at the place of location of the creditor."*

More recently, in a judgment of the Court of Appeal of Antwerp in 2006, it was decided that the CISG was applicable, and the issue of interest was then determined according to the law applicable to the contract. The Court stated that

> *"According to article 78 CISG, interest is due in case of late payment and interest commences to run without the need for an order. Since the interest rate is not determined by the CISG, it is determined by the* lex contractus, *in casu Belgian law."*[26]

Given the general principle contained in Article 78 CISG, and in the absence of a choice of law expressed by the parties in the contract, the law governing interest is determined by judges or arbitrators having regard to the appropriate conflict of law rules. There are many cases in which the issue of interest has been solved by turning to the conflict of law rules of the *lex fori*.

In 1999, the Tribunal of Pavia decided that

> *"Per quanto riguarda gli interessi sulle somme non pagate, va rilevato che la Convenzione delle Nazioni Unite prevede solo un generale diritto agli interessi, senza specificare quale sia il tasso da applicare. Alla luce del fatto che i redattori della Convenzione hanno intenzionalmente lasciato irrisolto il problema del tasso applicabile, come si evince dai lavori preparatori, non si può ritenere che si tratti una delle materie che, in virtù dell'art. 7, comma II della Convenzione, dovrebbero essere regolate dai principi generali cui la Convenzione stessa si ispira. Si tratta invece di una questione per niente disciplinata dalla Convenzione e che quindi va risolta alla luce del diritto applicabile (da determinarsi in virtù delle norme di diritto internazionale privato italiano) ossia alla luce del diritto italiano (quale diritto del venditore, al quale rinvia l'art. 3, comma I della Convenzione dell'Aja del 1955). Conseguentemente gli interessi vengono determinati nella misura del tasso legale vigente in Italia."*[27]

In a more recent case decided in 2006 by the *Oberlandesgericht Köln*,[28] the Court noted that *"hinsichtlich der Zinshöhe ist auf das niederländische Recht als Recht der charakteristischen Leistung abzustellen, da das CISG keine Regelung enthalt"*.

A different position has also been expressed by judges and arbitrators who considered that, in the absence of any specific determination in Article 78, the issue of interest had to be solved according to the general principles of the CISG as affirmed in Article 7(2).

This approach is reflected in a case decided by the *Internationales Schiedsgericht der Bundeskammer der gewerblichen Wirtschaft Österreich* in 1994.[29] The arbitrators considered, first of all, that Article 78 CISG, while granting the right to interest, says nothing about the level of the interest rate payable. They also recalled that, in various international legal writings and case law, it is disputed whether the question is outside the scope of the Convention or whether there is a true gap in the Convention within the meaning of Article 7(2), meaning that the applicable interest rate should possibly be determined autonomously in conformity with the general principles underlying the Convention. In relation to this, the arbitral tribunal decided that

> *"this second view is to be preferred, not least because the immediate recourse to a particular domestic law may lead to results which are incompatible with the principle embodied in Art. 78 of the CISG, at least in the cases where the law in question expressly prohibits the payment of interest."*

## VII. INTEREST ACCORDING TO UNIFORM PRINCIPLES AND DIRECTIVE 2000/35/EC ON COMBATING LATE PAYMENT IN COMMERCIAL TRANSACTIONS

Uniform laws applicable to international commercial transactions also provide for the awarding of compensatory interest in favour of the party to which the payment is due. In this regard, the UNIDROIT Principles 2004 deserve special attention.[30] The right to interest is clearly affirmed in Article 7.4.9, which determines the accrual period and gives a general indication as to the rate to be applied. According to this rule, in case of late payment of the sum due, *"[t]he aggrieved party is entitled to interest upon that sum from the time when payment is due to the time of payment whether or not the non-payment is excused"*, and the rate to be applied is *"the average bank short-term lending rate to prime borrowers prevailing for the currency of payment at the place for payment, or where no such rate exists at that place, then the same rate in the State of the currency of payment"*. Article 7.4.9 also provides that, in cases where such a rate cannot be determined at either place, the rate of interest shall be that fixed by the law of the state of the currency of payment. It is worth noting that according to the preamble, the Principles may be used to interpret or supplement international uniform law instruments or to interpret or supplement domestic law.

Moreover, the Principles provide an additional rule on interest that is applicable when judges or arbitrators have to determine the *dies a quo* of interest on damages for non-performance. Article 7.4.10 provides that *"unless otherwise agreed, interest on damages for non-performance of non-monetary obligations accrues as from the time of non-performance"*.

It is not superfluous to underline the importance of the UNIDROIT Principles for international trade and arbitration,[31] as national courts and international arbitral tribunals have made useful references to the Principles in numerous cases.[32]

With particular regard to the application of the UNIDROIT Principles by arbitrators in determining interest to be awarded to one of the parties, the Arbitral Tribunal of the Stockholm Chamber of Commerce considered, in a case decided in 2005,[33] that

> *"this claim is based on the Treaty and is therefore a claim under international law. In accordance herewith, the interest should, in the Arbitral Tribunal's opinion, be based on international rather than national rules. The Arbitral Tribunal considers the UNIDROIT Principles of International Commercial Contracts, relied on by X, to be an appropriate basis for determining the interest"*.[34]

The Principles of European Contract Law 1998 contain a rule providing for the payment of compensatory interest when the payment of a sum of money is delayed. Under Article 9:508,

> *"the aggrieved party is entitled to interest on that sum from the time when payment is due to the time of payment at the average commercial bank short-term lending rate to prime borrowers prevailing for the contractual currency of payment at the place where payment is due."*[35]

The 1992 UNCITRAL Model Law on International Credit Transfers also allows interest for the benefit of a party that has been damaged in a payment order. The Model Law affirms the principle that a receiving bank that does not comply with its obligations under the Model Law when the credit transfer is completed is liable to the beneficiary.

In this respect, under Article 17, the receiving bank has

> *"to pay interest on the amount of the payment order for the period of delay caused by the receiving bank's non-compliance. If the delay concerns only part of the amount of the payment order, the liability shall be to pay interest on the amount that has been delayed."*[36]

EC Directive 2000/35/EC of June 29, 2000[37] provides a uniform standard aimed at discouraging delays in payments in commercial transactions. The Directive applies to all commercial relations involving the delivery of goods or the provision of services for remuneration between undertakings or between undertakings and public authorities whenever the payment due has exceeded the contractual or statutory period.[38] In particular, according to the Directive, the debtor's liability is automatically established, and, unless the debtor can demonstrate that he is not responsible for the delay, a fixed rate of interest will be applied with the special purpose of discouraging late payments and protecting the creditors established in the Community.

With regard to interest rates, Article 3 provides that the member states have to ensure that the level of interest for the delayed payment imposed to the debtor shall be the sum of the interest rate applied by the European Central Bank to its most recent refinancing operations, plus at least seven percentage points, unless otherwise specified in the contract.[39]

The interest rate determined by Directive 2000/35/EC was taken into consideration in a case submitted to the Commercial Court of Hasselt in 2006. The dispute concerned an international sale of goods between a Dutch seller and a Belgian buyer, in which the creditor-seller claimed compensation for delayed payment as provided under the 2002 Belgian Act. At first, the Court considered the problem of the applicable law, noting that

> *"if internal law were to be applied to determine the interest, then this would have to be the law of the* lex contractus, *in this case Dutch law. Dutch law has transposed Directive No. 2000/35 of 29 June 2000 concerning compensation for delay in payment in commercial transactions."*

However, the court also stated that

> *"the interest rate, determined by the Directive, does not only have the intention to reimburse the creditor for the loss of funds, but is also intended as a sanction for late payment and an incentive to pay in a timely manner. The latter seems contradictory to the international context in which the CISG must be considered. In these matters, article 78 of the CISG is applicable."*[40]

In conclusion, the court agreed that the interest rate should be viewed in an international context, without recourse to the national law applicable to the contract.

However, it is worth mentioning that, in an award of the *Internationales Schiedsgericht der Wirtschaftskammer Österreich* issued in 2006,[41] the arbitral tribunal applied an interest rate of 9.47% as provided for by Article 1333(2) the Austrian Civil Code, as modified by Directive 2000/35/EC, without making reference to the CISG. The arbitrators argued that, although many authors share the opinion, which is confirmed by the relevant case law, that Article 78 CISG has to be interpreted independently from national statutory law, in the case at issue the national rule on interest could be applied in the absence of any objection by the debtor.

## VIII. INTEREST IN THE CASE LAW OF THE IRAN-UNITED STATES CLAIMS TRIBUNAL

The Iran-US Claims Tribunal was established in 1981. Since the beginning, the practice of awarding interest to the prevailing party was limited and not uniform. In particular, the decisions rendered by the Tribunal have generally been positive as to whether interest should be awarded, but the practice remains divided as to the rate to be applied, with a clear trend towards the allocation of simple interest instead of compound interest.[42]

In the *Sylvania* award of 1985,[43] the Tribunal[44] considered the claimant's request for interest on the awarded amounts and noted that, in order to have uniformity of treatment of the parties, a rate of interest based on return of investment during the relevant period would be more appropriate.

The Tribunal found that

*"So far the Tribunal's practice in awarding interest does not show a great degree of uniformity. While the Chambers are consistent in generally awarding interest, when claimed, on the basis of compensation for damages suffered due to delay in payment, and while the Tribunal has never awarded compound interest, the rates applied by the Tribunal show little uniformity. In the absence of a contractually stipulated rate, however, the Tribunal has exercised its discretion, applying rates varying from 8.5 percent to 12 percent, which it determined to be 'fair rates'."*

Consequently, in the absence of a contractually determined interest rate, the Tribunal applied a rate of interest based approximately on the amount that a successful claimant would have earned if it had been paid in time and thus would have had *"the funds available to invest in a form of commercial investment in common use in its own country"*.

In the *McCollough* award of 1986,[45] the Tribunal[46] noted that *"a large variety of rates of interest have been awarded"* and concluded that

*"no uniform rule of law relating to interest has emerged from the practice in transnational arbitration, in contrast to the well developed rules regarding the determination of the standard of compensation for damages resulting from a breach of contract, where the rule of full compensation usually is applied."*

However, the Tribunal also noted that *"the absence of a uniform rule does not, however, imply the absence of general principles"*. Two principles are therefore indicated by the Tribunal. The first is that *"under normal circumstances, and especially in commercial cases, interest is allocated in the amounts awarded as damages in order to compensate for the delay with which the payment to the successful party is made"*. The second principle is that *"the rate of interest must be reasonable, taking into account all pertinent circumstances, which the Tribunal is entitled to consider by virtue of the discretion it is empowered to exercise in this field"*. The Tribunal, which awarded the successful party a flat interest rate of 10%, also considered that the difficulty in the application of a fixed rate is due to the diversity of the cases submitted and that, for the same reason, the accrual period has to be determined on a case-by-case approach, taking into account all relevant factors.[47]

It may be noted that the solutions adopted in the various decisions of the Iran-US Claims Tribunal are certainly influenced by the significant impact of the interstate origin of the Tribunal and the solutions in the matter of interest traditionally adopted in interstate relations. As will be seen below, this also applies to investment arbitration practice, at least in its initial stage.

## IX. INTEREST IN INVESTMENT ARBITRATION

In recent years, disputes concerning international investments and the amount of related case law have increased dramatically, especially when the applicable national or international rules allow investors to present their claims against host states directly before international arbitral tribunals. As is well known, these developments are essentially due to the creative decisions of some arbitral tribunals operating under the aegis of ICSID, which has rapidly consolidated and expanded. According to this case law, the consent of the host state to ICSID arbitration can be found not only in a compromissory clause contained in an investment contract but also in a national piece of legislation (mainly a law for the promotion of investments) in which the state generally undertakes to submit possible disputes with foreign investors to ICSID or other kinds of international arbitration.[48] Subsequently, the consent of the state was regarded as being explicitly expressed in the clauses contained in bilateral investment treaties (BITs) concluded by the host state with the home states of the investors indicating ICSID arbitration as one of the means for investors to solve their disputes with the host state.[49]

On the matter of interest, ICSID case law also seems to show an interesting evolution. This phenomenon appears in those cases where reference to the ICSID mechanism is not contained in BITs but in treaties with a much broader participation, such as the North American Free Trade Agreement (NAFTA)[50] and the Energy Charter Treaty.[51] It also appears in other kinds of investment arbitration that take place in different frameworks and apply different arbitration rules, such as the UNCITRAL Rules, those of the Stockholm Arbitration Institute and those of the International Chamber of Commerce.

The rather prudent attitude to matters of interest initially followed by the tribunals dealing with investment disputes was probably influenced by the public international law character of the ICSID Convention and its mechanism of arbitration, as well as by the same interstate nature of the applicable bilateral investment treaties.[52] Traditionally, interest – particularly compound interest – was restrictively and rarely awarded in interstate litigation, even in cases where states sought to provide diplomatic protection to their citizens who suffered damage abroad.[53]

The prudent approach in matters of interest traditionally followed in interstate arbitration had a strong influence on the arbitration between states and foreign enterprises in matters of protection of property and investments prior to the recent increase in and development of ICSID disputes. Actually, the doctrine according to which *"state contracts"* are submitted to public international law resulted in the expansion to those contracts of the principles on interest usually applied in interstate commerce. In cases where a national law was considered applicable, the relevant national rules on interest were faithfully respected. Famous cases do not need to be recalled, particularly the three Libyan arbitrations of the 1970s involving British Petroleum, Texaco-Calasiatic and LIAMCO.[54] The only case that appears of special interest in the framework of this presentation is the *Aminoil* v. *Kuwait* case of 1982.[55] In that case, the Tribunal awarded Aminoil damages of USD 83 million, adding interest and inflation rates for a global annual rate of 17.5 %, which was compounded and produced an additional sum of USD 96 million. The case, which obviously forms a famous example of compound interest in international arbitration, has recently been subject to new analysis indicating that the high compounded rates of interest and inflation were a sort of disguised compensation of Aminoil for an expropriation that, notwithstanding the fact that it was officially considered lawful, the Tribunal intended to compensate with a global amount corresponding to the higher level due for an unlawful expropriation.[56]

In order to properly evaluate ICSID case law concerning interest, it seems useful to take into consideration the basic discipline provided for in Article 42 of the Washington Convention as to the law to be applied by ICSID tribunals.

According to Article 42.1:

> *"The Tribunal shall decide a dispute in accordance with such rules of law as may be agreed by the parties. In the absence of such agreement, the Tribunal shall apply the law of the Contracting State party to the dispute (including its rules on the conflict of laws) and such rules of international law as may be applicable."*

Thus, in order to solve an issue related to interest, ICSID tribunals have first to respect the agreement of the parties on the direct determination of the interest and then their possible agreement as to the "rules of law"[57] governing the particular issue of interest, or the investment contract in its entirety. In the absence of choice by the parties, the solution to the entire dispute, or some aspects of it such as interest, will be adopted by applying the relevant rules of the host state of the investment.

At first, the attitude of ICSID tribunals on the issue of interest showed a general reference to the law of the host state and appeared founded on strict compliance with Article 42 of the Washington Convention. In that earliest period, the case law of the *ad hoc* committees ruling on annulment claims[58] somehow encouraged strict compliance with the law of the host state, because the committees regarded as a manifest excess of power, justifying the annulment, the failure by tribunals to apply to the case concerned the law that should be applicable according Article 42 of the Washington Convention. An example of this attitude can be found in one of the first ICSID awards in the case *Agip SpA* v. *République du Congo* of 1979,[59] in which the tribunal awarded the claimant what the claimant itself had requested in terms of interest, presenting its claims in compliance with the applicable law of the Republic of Congo (at the time Article 1153 of the French Civil Code for moratory interest and Article 2028 for additional compensatory interest). Consequently, the tribunal awarded only simple interest at 5% for debts in CFA and interest at the lowest rate in effect in the markets concerned for debts in other currencies[60]

The ICSID arbitral tribunal in the *Aucoven* v. *Venezuela* case of 2003 made a reference to the law of the host state to solve the issue of interest.[61]

The tribunal held that

> *"Aucoven's submission that international law requires an award of compound interest must thus be rejected. Having concluded that the applicable Venezuelan law combined with the pertinent contract provision does not allow compound interest and that international law does not require it, the Tribunal can dispense with making a determination whether the specific circumstances of the case prevent an award of compound interest in the present arbitration."*

Accordingly, the decision applied Venezuelan simple interest, adding the relevant finding that international law does not require the application of compound interest, so that the solution of the national applicable law cannot be superseded because that would be contrary to international law.

The *CME v. Czech Republic* case of 2003[62] provides an example of a similar ruling on interest adopted by an *ad hoc* international tribunal deciding on an investment dispute according to the UNCITRAL Rules. The tribunal concluded in favour of the application of the Czech rate of interest, as established in Article 517 of the Civil Code and the ensuing Government Decree, after having found that "[n]either the Treaty [the applicable BIT] nor international law provide for an interest rate to be applied". The tribunal added that no particular circumstances in the case justified the award of compound interest.[63]

An important development took place in the *Compania de Desarollo de Santa Elena v. Costa Rica* case of 2000,[64] in which an ICSID tribunal for the first time awarded compound interest to a foreign investor who had suffered damage. This was done in order to assure compensation to the investor in a case where the "taking" of the property had taken place several years before the award and was initially creeping (or indirect), becoming direct afterwards. The case is also worth mentioning because the tribunal attached no apparent relevance to the environmental reasons on which the public authorities had based the taking.

In particular, the tribunal considered that, on the one hand, simple interest would not be justified, given the long period of time that had elapsed between the measure of taking and the arbitral award, and, on the other hand, that full compound interest would not do justice to the parties in the case at issue, in which the investor maintained its property for a long period but with a reduced capacity to exploit it.[65]

More recent practice seems to confirm, with limited exceptions, a trend in favour of awarding compound interest to investors who have suffered damage. To start with the exceptions, reference can be made to the ICSID arbitration award of 2007 in the *Siemens AG* v. *Argentine Republic* case.[66] The tribunal decided the issue of interest on the basis of the guiding principle of the *"full reparation for the injury suffered as a result of the internationally wrongful act"*. The tribunal then considered it inappropriate to take into account the rate of interest paid by the company for its borrowings and preferred to adopt the *"interest rate the amount of the compensation would have earned had it been paid after the expropriation"*.[67]

A recent trend in favour of compound interest thus seems to be consolidating. For example, compound interest has been adopted as a means to assure full compensation to the investor in some recent ICSID awards, such as in the *ADC Affiliate Ltd and ADC & ADMC Management Ltd* v. *Republic of Hungary* case[68] in 2006 and in the *LG&E* v. *Argentine Republic* case[69] and the *Sempra Energy International* v. *Argentine Republic* case[70] in 2007. The tribunal in the first case decided for post-award compound interest on a monthly basis, affirming that compound interest constituted *"the current trend in investor-State arbitration"* and going against the traditional findings in public international law contrary to compound interest still *"echoed"* by the Iran-US Claims Tribunal.[71] In the *LG&E* case, the tribunal also considered compound interest an appropriate means to assure *"full reparation"* and added the general explanation that such interest *"would better compensate the Claimants for the actual damages suffered since it better reflects contemporary financial practice"*.[72]

Having examined the decisions of various arbitral tribunals in relation to investments, and especially the recent trend in favour of awarding compound interest to compensate investors for the damages suffered, a note of some interest can be added.

In some decisions awarding compound interest, such as in the *Aminoil* and *Santa Elena* cases, it appears that the basic reason for such an award is represented by the will of the tribunal to reach a certain global amount of compensation that it considers justified in the circumstances of the case. In the first case, it was stated that the awarding of compound interest was due to the fact that, although the tribunal formally considered the expropriation suffered by the investor legitimate, it intended to fully compensate the investor as if the expropriation was unlawful. In the second case, the awarding of compound (but adjusted) interest was apparently due to the difficulty of assessing the initial value of the taken property and the extremely long period of time elapsed from the taking until the arbitral award.[73]

This observation invites us to attribute the real and proper value to the findings of the tribunals on the issue of interest. The tribunals sometimes do not intend to solve the issue according to rules or principles of law but rather take into consideration the particular characteristics of the case and the practical results that the tribunals deem justified and intend to reach.

## X.   SOME CONCLUDING OBSERVATIONS

Concluding the analysis of the practices of state courts and international arbitration tribunals, which solve different kinds of disputes, namely in the commercial and investment sectors, it clearly appears that it is difficult or even impossible to find at a uniform solution to the problems relating to interest. Various factors encourage scepticism as to the possibility of reaching conclusions that can be generally valid and applicable worldwide.

The first factor inducing careful consideration of distinctions in relation to interest-related issues relates to the various laws that may be applicable, the litigation contract in its entirety or the specific issue of interest. This basic difficulty is strictly connected to the traditional functioning of a conflict of laws method, which is still widely employed by state courts, also in cases where international conventions on uniform law are applicable (such as Article 78 CISG) but which leaves the issue subject to the choice made by the competent court.

Obviously, the difficulty can be overcome to the extent that the classic conflict method does not need to be applied to the specific issue. As has been shown above, this happens more frequently in international arbitration than before state courts. Actually, arbitrators frequently have the possibility of making a direct choice on the rules governing the contract or the specific issue of interest on the basis of national laws governing the arbitration (e.g. Article 1496 of the French NCCP) or the arbitration rules applicable in the case (e.g. Article 17 of the ICC Arbitration Rules, Article 22.3 of the LCIA Rules, Article 28.4 of the AAA Rules or Articles 59(a) and 60(b) of the WIPO Rules).

Another important distinction relates to the subject matter or field to which the interest-related dispute refers. In principle, different solutions on interest are conceivable and appear justified if one compares commercial arbitration to investment arbitration. The commercial character of a dispute appears to justify the payment of a high rate of interest, at least *in abstracto* and in due compliance with the applicable law or rules of law. This is due to the personal characteristics of the disputing parties, who are normally involved in commercial and financial transactions and accustomed to earning and paying interest, in their capacity as creditors or debtors in those transactions. The practice of state courts and international arbitration tribunals basically appear to follow the same approach, with inevitable differences due to the different applicable rules and powers attributed to the deciding bodies.

In contrast, in the investment sector, the parties involved in a dispute where an issue of interest arises have different personal characteristics, one being a state often exercising its public or regulatory powers and the other being an investor often acting on the basis of a legal instrument, a piece of legislation of the host state or an investment treaty in force between the host state and the home state of the investor, which was not directly negotiated and concluded by the parties to the dispute. In such cases, the legitimate interest of the investor regarding the preservation and protection of its investment is not usually faced with the non-performance of a contractual obligation by the host state but with measures that the latter has adopted in its capacity as a public or regulatory authority. As a result, at least in principle, the conditions are basically different from those underlying the awarding of interest in commercial or financial disputes.

It thus appears doubtful whether, for the purpose of determining interest in investment disputes, reference should be made to solutions adopted by state courts or international arbitration tribunals acting in different frameworks and in the presence of parties having the same commercial or financial nature. Actually, it seems that the peculiar position of host states should be taken into account, namely when they act in the legitimate use of their public and regulatory powers in order to protect, for instance, welfare objectives such as public health, safety and the environment.[74] In those cases where the measures affecting investors do not constitute direct or indirect expropriation, if any compensation should be provided to the investor, this will be done through a different method for the assessment of damages, and especially the calculation of possible interest, so that the adoption by the state of such legitimate measures will not be jeopardized.

One final point of distinction can be made on the issue of compensation and related interest in the case of measures of taking adopted by states that can be considered legitimate in view of their specific welfare objectives. The point is suggested by the case law of the European Court of Human Rights concerning the protection of the right of property according to Article 1 of Protocol 1 to the 1950 Rome Convention.[75] The Court constantly differentiates between legitimate expropriations that violate Article 1 of Protocol 1 only because of the inadequate level of compensation provided and expropriations considered unlawful because they were adopted in violation of the rule of law. In the first case, according to the Court, reasons of *utilité publique* allow the state to pay compensation that is lower than the value of the property taken. This important case law seems to confirm the opportunity to differentiate, also in the case of the taking of investors' rights, between the compensation and interest due in consideration of the proper character and objectives of the public measures adopted by the host state and the compensation and interest due in the case of unlawful takings.

## END NOTES

[1]  Tarek Fouad A. Riad, 'The Issue of Interest in Middle East Laws and Islamic Law', Report to the ICC Annual Meeting (2007) (in this volume).

[2]  J.Y. Gotanda, 'Awarding Interest in International Arbitration', 90 *Am. J. Int'l L.* (1996) p. 40; ibid., 'A Study of Interest', Report to the ICC Annual Meeting (2007) (in this volume).

[3]  C. McLachlan, L. Shore, and M. Weiniger, *International Investment Arbitration* (Oxford, 2007) p. 343 ff.

[4]  An important collection of cases concerning the awarding and determination of interest is available at: <http://www.unilex.info/dynasite.cfm?dssid=2376&dsmid=13356&x=1>.

[5]  See the collection of case law made available at: <http://www.unilex.info/dynasite.cfm?dssid=2377&dsmid=13617>. See also the case law on the UNIDROIT Principles reproduced in Italian in M.J. Bonell and E. Finazzi-Agrò, *Diritto del Commercio Internazionale, Rassegna giurisprudenziale sui Principi UNIDROIT dei contratti commerciali internazionali* (2002, 2004 and 2007).

[6]  Many authors have dealt with the issue: F.A. Mann, 'Compound Interest as an Item of Damages in International Law', in F.A. Mann (ed.), *Further Studies in International Law* (Oxford, 1990) p. 377 ff.; Y. Derains, 'Intérêts moratoires, dommages-intérêts compensatoires et dommages punitifs devant l'arbitre international', in *Etudes offertes à Pierre Bellet* (Paris, 1991) p. 101 ff.; P. Karrer, 'Transnational Law of Interest in International Arbitration', in E. Gaillard (ed.), *Transnational Rules in International Commercial Arbitration*, ICC Pub. No. 480 (Paris, 1993) p. 223 ff.; H. Schönle, 'Intérêts moratoires, intérêts compensatoires et dommages-intérêts de retard en arbitrage international', in *Etudes de droit international en l'honneur de Pierre Lalive* (Basle, 1993) p. 649 ff.; P. Cerina, 'Interest as Damages in International Commercial Arbitration', *Am. Rev. Int'l Arb.* (1993) p. 255 ff.; M.S. Schwebel, 'Compound Interest in International Law', in *Scritti in onore di Arangio Ruiz* (Naples, 2004) p. 881 ff.; N. Comair-Obeid, 'Recovery of Damages for Breach of an Obligation of Payment', in *Evaluation of Damages in International Arbitration*, ICC Institute of World Business Law Dossiers (Paris, 2006); J.Y. Gotanda, 'Awarding Interest', *supra* note 2; ibid., 'Compound Interest in International Disputes', (2004) Oxford U Comparative L Forum 1, at: <http.ouclf.iuscomp.org> ; ibid., 'A Study of Interest', *supra* note 2; C. Brower, 'Awarding Interest – Ex Officio or Only If Requested, at What Rate, as of When, Compound or Not?', in *Resolution of the Dispute – from the Hearing to the Award*, ASA Special Series No. 29 (2007) p. 70 ff.

[7]  This conclusion applies only "in principle", because it depends on the characterization of the national rules on interest. If they are considered as simple national *ordre public*, they cannot be derogated from by the parties after they have selected that national law as applicable or, in the case of absence of choice, once the court has found that such national law governs the contract. However, they can be derogated from by a party's choice of a foreign law governing the entire contract or the special issue of interest. On the other hand, if the rules of the forum on interest are considered "international mandatory rules" or rules of "*ordre public vraiment international*", then their application cannot be avoided by any other party's choice concerning both the substantive and the conflict regulation of the issue.

[8]  Art. 834 of the Code of Civil Procedure was abrogated along with the entire chapter devoted to international arbitration by the *Decreto Legislativo* Legal Decree No. 40 of February 2, 2006, which entered into force on March 1, 2006.

[9]  Art. 1496 was introduced by *Décret* n° 81-500 of May 12, 1981, published in *Journal Officiel* of May 14-21, 1981.

[10] See *supra* note 4. A selection of cases is also reproduced in Italian in A. Veneziano, and V.M. Donini, *Diritto del Commercio Internazionale, Rassegna giurisprudenziale sulla compravendita internazionale di beni mobili* (2002, 2004 and 2007).

[11] U.S. District Court Illinois, *Chicago Prime Packers Inc.* v. *Northam Food Trading Co.*, May 21, 2004, available at: <http://www.unilex.info/case.cfm?pid=1&id=974&do=case>.

[12] The court observed that, "in determining the conflict of laws in contract disputes, Illinois follows the Restatement (Second) of Conflict of Laws, which refers either to a choice of law provision in the contract at issue, or to the place of performance".

[13] Tribunal Cantonal Valais, Case No. C1 04 33, September 19, 2005, available at: <http://www.unilex.info/case.cfm?pid=1&id=1083&do=case>.

[14] Cf. *infra* section VI for other relevant case law on the issue of interest in the framework of the Vienna Convention.

[15] See Tribunal of Padua, March 31, 2004, available at: <http://www.unilex.info/case.cfm?pid=1&id=966&do=case>.

[16] A similar decision was taken by the Tribunal of Pavia on December 29, 1999, in Case No. 468 concerning a textile sale contract between an Italian seller and a Greek buyer, available at: <http://www.unilex.info/case.cfm?pid=1&id=734&do=case>.

[17] J.D.M. Lew, 'Interest on Money Awards in International Arbitration', in *Making Commercial Law. Essays in Honour of Roy Goode* (Oxford, 1997) p. 543 ff., notes that a fourth approach is sometimes suggested, based on the reference to usages of international trade in the particular sector concerned. These usages "will expect or provide for interest to be charged to outstanding amounts".

[18] ICC Case No. 9448 of July 1999, Final Award, available at: <http://www.unilex.info/case.cfm?pid=1&id=467&do=case>.

[19] See also the ICC Case No. 6527 of 1991, Final Award, in *YB Com. Arb.*, Vol. XVIII (1993) p. 44 ff., in which the arbitral tribunal extended the application of the law governing the contract to the issue of interest.

[20] Lew, *supra* note 17.

[21] Hof van Beroep Antwerpen, *Gmbh Lothringer* v. *NV Fepco Int.*, Case No. 20002/AR/2087, April 24, 2006, available at: <http://www.unilex.info/case.cfm?pid=1&id=1152&do=case>.

[22] Rechtbank van Koophandel Veurne, *BV BA G-2* v. *A.S. C.B.*, Case No. A/00/00665, April 25, 2001, available at: <http://www.unilex.info/case.cfm?pid=1&id=953&do=case>.

[23] Art. 74 provides that: "Damages for breach of contract by one party consist of a sum equal to the loss, including loss of profit, suffered by the other party as a consequence of the breach. Such damages may not exceed the loss which the party in breach foresaw or ought to have foreseen at the time of the conclusion of the contract, in the light of the facts and matters of which he then knew or ought to have known, as a possible consequence of the breach of contract."

[24] E.A. Farnsworth, 'Art. 78', in Bianca and Bonell, *Commentary on the International Sales Law. The Vienna 1980 Sales Convention* (Milan, 1987) p. 568 ff. See also V. Behr, 'The Sales Convention in Europe: From Problems in Drafting to Problems in Practice', *Journal Law and Comm.* (1998) p. 263 ff.

[25] Russian Federation Chamber of Commerce and Industry, Case No. 340/1999, February 10, 2000, available at: <http://www.unilex.info/case.cfm?pid=1&id=876&do=case>.

[26] Hof van Beroep Antwerpen, *supra* note 21. This judgment is also of particular relevance. After briefly discussing the issue of simple and compound interest, it affirms that "the CISG is silent on the question whether compound interests is possible. Article 78 CISG mentions 'interest on the price or any other sum' from which some authors conclude that no interest on interest is due. Other authors state that interest on interest can be framed in the practices between parties in the sense of article 9 CISG."

[27] Tribunal of Pavia, *supra* note 16. See also Cour d'appel Grenoble, November 28, 2002, available at: <http://www.unilex.info/case.cfm?pid=1&id=923&do=case>; Tribunal of Padua, *supra* note 15; *Tribunal Cantonal Valais*, *supra* note 13.

[28] Oberlandesgericht Köln, Case No. 16U17/05, April 3, 2006, available at: <http://www.unilex.info/case.cfm?pid =1&id=1133&do=case>.

[29] Internationales Schiedsgericht der Bundeskammer Wien, Case No. SCH-4366, June 15, 1994, available at: <http://www.unilex.info/case.cfm?pid=1&id=55&do=case>.

[30] Institute of International Business Law and Practice, *UNIDROIT Principles for International Commercial Contracts: A New Lex Mercatoria?*, ICC Pub. No. 490/1 (1995); A. Giardina, *Les Principes UNIDROIT sur les contrats internationaux* (Clunet, 1995) p. 547 ff.; M.J. Bonell, *An International Restatement of Contract Law. The UNIDROIT Principles of International Commercial Contracts*, 2nd edn. (Ardsley, NY, 1997); ibid. (ed.), *A New Approach to International Commercial Contracts. The UNIDROIT Principles of International Commercial Contracts* (The Hague, 1999); *UNIDROIT Principles of International Commercial Contracts. Reflections on their Use in International Arbitration*, ICC Pub. No. 642 (2002).

[31] A collection of case law on the UNIDROIT Principles is also available in M.J. Bonell, *The UNIDROIT Principles in Practice. Case Law and Bibliography on the Principles of Commercial Contracts* (New York, 2002). See also *supra* note 4.

[32] F. Marrella, *La nuova lex mercatoria. Principi UNIDROIT ed usi dei contratti del commercio internazionale* (Padua, 2003) especially pp. 390-489.

[33] *Petrobart Ltd* v. *Kyrgyzstan*, SCC Case No. 126/2003, IIC 184, March 29, 2005, available at: <http://www.investmentclaims.com>.

[34] Similarly, the arbitral tribunal of the Russian Federation Chamber of Commerce and Industry in Case No. 100/2002, available at: <http://cisgw3.law.pace.edu/cases/040519r1.html>, stated that "the CISG does not does provide for interest rate nor for the method of its calculation (art. 78 CISG). Art. 395 of the Russian Civil Code provides that the interest rate is to be determined with respect to the bank rate in the country of the creditor's place of business on the day on which the payment was performed. When making a ruling on the recovery of the debt, the Tribunal can grant a creditor's claim taking into account either the bank rate on the day of the bringing of the action or on the day of making an award. [The buyer's] representatives insisted on the application of the bank rate fixed on the day of the bringing of the action, that is, July 5, 2002. The Tribunal granted [the buyer's] request. As in Russia, the creditor's ([buyer's]) place of business, there is no interest rate in Indian rupees, the Tribunal had recourse to an international practice established in such situations and which is reflected in the UNIDROIT Principles (art. 7.4.9(2)). In accordance with this practice, 'the rate of interest shall be the average bank short-term lending rate to prime borrowers prevailing for the currency of payment at the place for payment, or where no such rate exists at that place, then the same rate in the State of the currency of payment'." See also Supreme Economic Court of the Republic of Belarus, Case No. 7-5/2003, May 20, 2003, available at: <http://cisgw3.law.pace.edu/cases/030520b5.html>.

[35] Art. 9:508 (ex Art. 4.507) provides as follows: "(1) If a payment of a sum of money is delayed, the aggrieved party is entitled to interest on that sum from the time when payment is due to the time of payment at the average commercial bank short-term lending rate to prime borrowers prevailing for the contractual currency of payment at the place where payment is due. (2) The aggrieved party may in addition recover damages for any further loss so far as these are recoverable under this Section."

[36] Art. 17 provides as follows: "(1) A receiving bank that does not comply with its obligations under article 8(2) is liable to the beneficiary if the credit transfer is completed. The liability of the receiving bank is to pay interest on the amount of the payment order for the period of delay caused by the receiving bank's non-compliance. If the delay concerns only part of the amount of the payment order, the liability shall be to pay interest on the amount that has been delayed."

[37] The Directive was published in *OJ* L 200 of August 8, 2000.

[38] It is worth noting that the Directive is not applicable to payments made as remuneration for commercial transactions or to transactions involving consumers.

[39] On the impact of the EC Directive on late payments on the CISG rule on interest, see M. del Pilar Perales Viscasillas, 'La Ley 3/2004 y la Directiva 2000/35: pasado, presente y futuro e impacto en el Derecho Mercantil', *REDUR* (2007) p. 5 ff. According to the opinion of this author, the Directive "funcionara integrando las lagunas del regimen vienés".

[40] Rechtbank van Koophandel Hasselt, *Scanlift Nederland BV* v. *Belgium Coach Service BVBA*, Case No. A.R.06/1436, May 10, 2006, available at: <http://cisgw3.law.pace.edu/cases/060510b1.html>.

[41] Internationales Schiedsgericht der Wirtschaftskammer Österreich, Case No. SCH-4921, May 11, 2006, unpublished but available in *Diritto del Commercio Internazionale* (2007) p. 456 ff.

[42] See C. Brower and J. Brueschke, The *Iran-United States Claims Tribunal* (The Hague, 1998), for the cases decided by the Tribunal; C. Brower and J.K. Sharpe, 'Awards of Compound Interest in International Arbitration: The Aminoil Non-Precedent', in *Liber Amicorum in Honour of Robert Briner* (Paris, ICC, 2005) p. 155 ff. One clear position in favour of awarding compound interest in a case decided by the Iran-US Claims Tribunal is that expressed by Holtzmann, in his Concurring Opinion in *Starret Housing Corporation, Starret Systems, Inc., et al.* v. *The Government of the Islamic Republic of Iran*, Award No. 314-24-1, August 14, 1987, in Iran-US CTR (1987) 112 ff., arguing that "only an award of interest on a compound basis can adequately compensate Starret [claimant] for the damages it suffered due to the Respondent's wrongful taking" (at 252).

[43] Iran-US Claims Tribunal, *Sylvania Technical Systems, Inc.* v. *The Government of the Islamic Republic of Iran*, Award No. 180-64-1, June 27, 1985, in Iran-US CTR (1985) 298 ff.

[44] The Tribunal was composed of Bockstiegel (Chairman) and Mostafavi and Holtzmann (members).

[45] Iran-US Claims Tribunal, *McCollough & Company, Inc.* v. *Ministry of Post, Telegraph and Telephone*, Award No. 225-89-3, April 22, 1986, in Iran-US CTR (1986) 35.

[46] The Tribunal was composed of Virally (Chairman) and Brower and Ansari (members).

[47] See the Concurring and Dissenting Opinion of Judge Brower on the issue of interest, *supra* note 45, at 42 ff.

[48] The first case in which the above-mentioned construction was adopted in order to found the ICSID jurisdiction and the competence of the Tribunal was the decision on jurisdiction in the *S.P.P.* v. *Egypt* case of 1985, *ICCA Yearbook* (1991) p. 19 ff. The comments on this decision have been numerous and generally favourable. Cf., also for further references, I Shihata and A. Parra, 'The Experience of the International Center for Settlement of Investment Disputes', *Foreign Investment Law Journal* (1999) p. 304 ff.; E. Gaillard, 'L'arbitrage sur le fondement des traités de protection des investissements', *Revue de l'arbitrage* (2003) p. 883 ff; G. Sacerdoti, 'Investment Arbitration Under ICSID and UNCITRAL Rules: Prerequisites, Applicable Law, Review of Awards', *ICSID Review* (2004) p. 1 ff; A. Giardina, 'International Investment Arbitration: Recent Developments as to the Applicable Law and Unilateral Recourse', in A. Del Vecchio, (ed.), *New International Tribunals and New International Proceedings* (Milan, 2006) p. 42 ff.

[49] BIT clauses relating to the settlement of disputes (with reference to the ICSID mechanism) were first considered a sufficient legal basis for ICSID arbitration in the *A.A.P.P.* v. *Sri Lanka* case of 1990, and then rapidly consolidated. Cf. S. Alexandrov, 'The "Baby Boom" of Treaty-Based Arbitrations and the Jurisdiction of ICSID Tribunals. Shareholders as Investors under Investment Treaties', *Journal of World Investments and Trade* (2005) p. 387 ff.; M.R. Mauro, 'Nuove questioni in tema di arbitrato fra Stato ed investitore straniero nella recente giurisprudenza dei tribunali ICSID', in *Riv. Dir. Int. Priv. Proc.* (2006) p. 67 ff.

[50] Chapter XI of NAFTA, at Art. 1115 ff., provides the mechanisms of disputes resolution. Art. 1120 contains the reference to ICSID arbitration for disputes of investors and host states. Cf. G. Marceau, 'NAFTA and WTO Settlement Rules. A Thematic Comparison', *Journal of World Trade Law* (1997) p. 25 ff; A. De Mestral, 'The North American Free Trade Agreement: A Comparative Analysis', *Recueil des Cours*, Vol. 275 (The Hague, 1998) p. 255 ff.

[51] On the mechanisms for the settlement of disputes between investors and host states provided for by the Energy Charter Treaty, and particularly its Art. 26, see J. Touscoz, 'Le Traité de la Charte de l'énergie. Aspects juridiques', *Revue de l'énergie* (1996) p. 494 ff; R. Babadji, 'Le traité sur la charte européenne de l'énergie', *Annuaire Français de Droit International* (1996) p. 872 ff; T.W. Waelde (ed.), *The Energy Charter Treaty: An East-West Gateway for Investment and Trade* (The Hague, 1996); A. Giardina, 'Energy Charter Treaty', *Enciclopedia degli Idrocarburi*, Vol. IV (Rome, 2007) p. 551 ff.

[52] It seems worth recalling that for decades BITs were considered mere interstate instruments, incapable of constituting the basis for direct claims of foreign investors against host states before international arbitral tribunals. Only in 1990 (cf. *supra* note 50), the case law was initiated, permitting investors to file direct international claims against states responsible for the violation of the treatment obligations assumed with the BITs.

[53] Reference was and is frequently made to a statement by M. Whiteman, *Damages in International Law*, Vol. III, (Washington, 1943) p. 1997, according to which "few rules within the scope of the subject of damages in international law ... are better settled than the one that compound interest is not allowed". Cf. Brower and Sharpe, *supra* note 42.

[54] On these famous cases and the question of the legal regime of state contracts as directly governed by public international law, see J. Verhoven, 'Droit international des contrats et droit des gens', *Revue belge de droit international public* (1978-1979) p. 209 ff; B. Stern, 'Trois arbitrages, un meme problème, trois solutions', *Revue de l'Arbitrage* (1980) p. 5 ff; A. Giardina, 'State Contracts: National versus International Law?', *The Italian Yearbook of International Law* (1980-1981) p. 147 ff. For a new examination of the issue in the light of the recent developments in the law of international investments, see C. Leben, 'La théorie du contrat d'Etat et l'évolution du droit international des investissements', *Recueil des Cours*, Vol. 302 (The Hague, 2003) p. 207 ff.

[55] *International Legal Materials* (1982) p. 976 ff. On the interest issue as decided in the case, see Brower and Sharpe, *supra* note 42.

[56] For a convincing explanation of the case along the lines indicated in the text, see Brower and Sharpe, *supra* note 42, at pp. 159 and 160 ff.

[57] It is well known that doctrine and case law substantially share the view that this expression allows the parties to also select non-national rules of law, such as the UNIDROIT Principles and the Principles of European Contract Law (PECL). For references in this respect, see A. Giardina, 'La legge regolatrice dei contratti di investimento nel sistema ICSID', *Riv. Dir. Int. Priv. Proc.* (1992) p. 677 ff; C. Schreuer, *The ICSID Convention. A Commentary* (Cambridge, 2001) p. 549 ff.

[58] Reference is made here to the well-known annulment decisions in the *Kloeckner* v. *Cameroon* case of 1985 and the *Amco* v. *Indonesia* case of 1986. Cf. M. Reisman, 'The Breakdown of the Control Mechanism in ICSID Arbitration', *Duke Law Journal* (1989) p. 739 ff.

[59] *YB Com. Arb.* (1983) p. 133 ff.

[60] On the *Agip SpA* case, see the commentary by Derains, *supra* note 6, at 114 ff. The author submits that the rather moderate decision of the Tribunal on the issue of interest, especially on the issue of compensatory interest for debts in foreign currencies, was the result of the request made by the claimant, which could not be overcome by the Tribunal without pronouncing *ultra petita*.

[61] Available at: <http://icsid.worldbank.org/ICSID/FrontServlet>.

[62] Available at: <http://www.investmentclaims.com/IIC_62_(2003).pdf>.

[63] The reason for this conclusion was the following: "The calculation of the compensation itself already fully compensates Claimant for the damage suffered. Awarding simple interest compensates the loss of use of the principal amount of the award in the period of delay."

[64] Available at: <http://icsid.worldbank.org/ICSID/FrontServlet>; also reproduced in *Rivista dell'Arbitrato* (2001) p. 111 ff., with commentary by A. Giardina, 'Diritto internazionale e diritto interno in tema di espropriazione: il momento della valutazione del bene espropriato e l'interesse da applicare'. Cf. C.N. Brower and J. Wong, 'General Valuation Principles. The Case of Santa Elena', T. Weiler (ed.), *International Investment Law and Arbitration* (London, 2005) p. 747 ff., in particular p. 768 ff.

[65] The Tribunal held that "[i]t is not the purpose of compound interest to attribute blame to, or to punish, anybody for the delay in the payment made to the expropriated owner; it is a mechanism to ensure that the compensation awarded the Claimant is appropriate in the circumstances. In the instant case, an award of simple interest would not be justified, given that ... for almost twenty-two years, CDSE has been unable either to use the Property for the tourism development it had in mind when it bought Santa Elena or to sell the Property. On the other hand, full compound interest would not do justice to the facts of the case, since CDSE, while bearing the burden of maintaining the property, has remained in possession of it and has been able to use and exploit it to a limited extent. Consequently, Claimant is entitled to an award of compound interest adjusted to take account of all the relevant factors." In this case, the Tribunal granted the claimant USD 16 million in compensation for a property valued at USD 4.15 million at the time of the "taking" 22 years earlier. This global result was reached by the Tribunal based on a semi-annual compound interest of about 6.40% that was added to the assessed original value of the property taken.

[66] Available at: <http://icsid.worldbank.org/ICSID/FrontServlet>.

[67] The Tribunal held that "[t]hus, in determining the applicable interest rate, the guiding principle is to ensure 'full reparation for the injury suffered as a result of the internationally wrongful act'. The Tribunal considers that the rate of interest to be taken into account is not the rate associated with corporate borrowing but the interest rate the amount of compensation would have earned had it been paid after the expropriation. Since the awarded compensation is in dollars, the Tribunal considers that the average rate of interest applicable to US six-month certificates of deposit is an appropriate rate of interest."

[68] Available at: <http://icsid.worldbank.org/ICSID/FrontServlet>.

[69] Available at: <http://icsid.worldbank.org/ICSID/FrontServlet>.

[70] ICSID case No ARB/02/16, IIC 304, 2007. The Tribunal held "that interest ... will be computed at the successive 6-month LIBOR rates, plus a 2% annualized premium or portion thereof. Interest shall be compounded semi-annually." The Award is available at: <http://www.investmentclaims.com/IIC_304_(2007).pdf>.

[71] The Tribunal also considered that "[a]s to post-Award interest, contrary to Respondent's submission, the current trend in investor-State arbitration is to award compound interest. Respondent relies on the statement 'there are few rules within the scope of the subject of damages in international law that are better settled than the one that compound interest is not allowable' ... While the Iran-U.S. Claims Tribunal echoed Ms. Whiteman's statement, tribunals in investor-State arbitrations in recent times have recognized economic reality by awarding compound interest ... Accordingly, the Tribunal determines that interest is to be compounded on a monthly basis in the present case."

[72] The Tribunal noted that "[i]n the Tribunal's view, interest is part of the 'full' reparation to which the Claimants are entitled to assure that they are made whole. In fact, interest recognizes the fact that, between the date of the illegal act and the date of actual payment, the injured party cannot use or invest the amounts of money due. ... The Tribunal is of the opinion that compound interest would better compensate the Claimants for the actual damages suffered since it better reflects contemporary financial practice."

[73] It is worth nothing that the Tribunal, having awarded compound pre-award interest, did not apply the same interest for the post-award period, but simple interest at a rate of 6%.

[74] The expression is adopted in at para. 4.b of Annex B (Expropriation) to the US Model BIT of 2004, as well as in Annex B 13 (1) to the Canadian Model BIT, also of 2004. The purpose of the annexes is to define expropriation, including indirect or creeping expropriations but excludes those measures "designed and applied to protect public welfare objectives such as public health, safety, and environment [which] do not constitute indirect expropriations".

[75] This case law has recently been confirmed by the decision of the European Court of Human Rights of March 6, 2007 in the *Scordino* v. *Italy (No. 3)* case, available at: <http://cmiskp.echr.coe.int/tkp197/portal.asp?sessionSimilar=5257002&skin=hudoc-en&action=similar&portal=hbkm&Item=3&similar=frenchjudgement>. Cf. also the references to previous and consolidated case law in the decision.

# A study of interest

### *By* **John Y. Gotanda**
*Associate Dean for Faculty Research, Professor of Law
and Director, J.D./M.B.A. Program,
Villanova University School of Law*

## INTRODUCTION

In recent years, the subject of interest has garnered significant attention from the international community, in the contexts of both international commercial disputes and international investment disputes. This is in sharp contrast to the not too distant past, when such claims were often decided without much attention from the parties and tribunals. Today, parties discuss the question of interest extensively, and it is not uncommon in an arbitration involving significant amounts of money for both sides to submit opinions of experts on its calculation and for tribunals to hold hearings on issues relating to interest and to devote pages in the final award addressing the award of interest.[1]

Perhaps the change in attitudes towards interest arises because claims today, particularly in investment disputes, involve millions of dollars and because there may be a lengthy period of time between the origin of the dispute and the final award. In cases where a tribunal awards interest, the rate may be as significant from a monetary standpoint as the principal claim itself.[2]

This new interest in interest has caused a number of tribunals, mainly those deciding investment disputes, to re-examine traditional practices concerning the award of interest, particularly whether interest should be awarded at market rates and on a compounded basis.[3] However, many tribunals deciding transnational contracts disputes continue to follow the traditional practice of applying national laws on interest, which often results in the application of domestic statutory interest rates calling for a fixed rate of interest to accrue on a simple as opposed to compound basis.[4]

These statutory rates often do not change to reflect economic conditions and thus may undercompensate or overcompensate a claimant.[5]

In this paper, I argue that, when tribunals award interest in both international investment disputes and transnational contract disputes, they should strive to fully compensate the aggrieved party for the loss of the use of its money. In many cases, then, they should award interest at a market rate and on a compound basis. I begin by providing an overview of interest and a brief comparative study of laws providing for its payment, the period during which interest should accrue and the rate of interest. I then compare the practice of awarding interest in international commercial disputes and international investment disputes. I conclude by offering a proposal that essentially provides a framework for awarding interest as damages and achieves the goal of awarding interest to make a party whole after being deprived of the opportunity to earn a return on the use of its money.

## I. OVERVIEW OF PRACTICE OF AWARDING INTEREST

Interest is a sum of money paid or payable as compensation for the temporary withholding of money.[6] Today, interest is often awarded without proof of actual loss.[7] Courts and tribunals presume that the delayed payment of money deprives the injured party of the ability to invest the sum owed. Thus, a party is entitled to compensation for this loss.[8]

There are several reasons for requiring a respondent to pay interest to a claimant that has succeeded on its damages claims. First, the payment of interest furthers the principle of full compensation, because it helps restore the claimant to the position it would have enjoyed if the breach had not occurred.[9] Second, an award of interest prevents unjust enrichment of the respondent by requiring it to pay compensation to the claimant for the benefit that the respondent received by using the money it wrongfully withheld. In other words, since the respondent has received the earning capacity of the borrowed money without compensating the claimant for the loss of its use, the respondent should pay the opportunity cost of the money that it withheld from the claimant.[10]

Third, the payment of interest promotes efficiency. Without interest, respondents may be insufficiently deterred, may not try to avoid future litigation and, indeed, may even take steps to delay the resolution of the dispute because respondents profit from the use of claimants' money while the dispute is being resolved. Likewise, the failure to require the payment of interest as a general rule may cause claimants to be overdeterred and to take excessive precautions to avoid future litigation.[11]

There are two major types of interest: pre-judgment interest and post-judgment interest. Pre-judgment interest, which is also known as pre-award or compensatory interest, is interest as part of an award. By contrast, post-judgment interest, which is also known as post-award interest, is interest on an award.[12]

Interest is calculated either on a simple or compound basis. In the case of simple interest, the interest is calculated only on the principal owed; the interest owed for a certain period does not merge with the principal and become part of the base upon which future interest is calculated. An award of compound interest means that the interest payment for a certain period is added to the principal sum owed and that sum is treated as a new principal for calculating the interest for the next period. In other words, the claimant receives interest upon interest.[13]

Claims for interest typically raise three issues. The first issue is whether there exists the authority to award interest. If the court or tribunal decides that it has the authority to award interest, the second issue is how to determine the period over which interest accrues. The final issue is the rate at which interest accrues. The resolution of these issues often depends on the parties' agreement and applicable laws or rules.

## 1.  Liability to pay interest

The laws of most countries hold a respondent liable for the payment of interest to ensure that the claimant is fully compensated for the loss of the use of money.[14] This rule applies to interest on the payment of late debts, interest as damages, interest on damages and post-award interest.[15] Most countries will also enforce an agreement to pay interest, unless it violates the public policy of that country.[16]

For example, Article 1153 of the French Civil Code provides "in obligations which are restricted to the payment of a certain sum, the damages resulting from delay in performance shall consist … in awarding interest at the statutory rate… Those damages are due without the creditor having to prove any loss."[17] Similar statutes exist in Italy[18] and Switzerland.[19]

In the United States, the payment of interest in private actions is typically governed by local law, and states have enacted statutes providing for the payment of interest. For example, in New York, a party has a statutory claim for interest when the action is for "breach of performance of a contract, or … depriving or otherwise interfering with title to, or possession or enjoyment of, property."[20]

The payment of interest in England has a colourful history. At common law, England did not allow the recovery of interest on judgment debts.[21] Today, however, the prohibition on the payment of interest has been relaxed by both judicial decisions and statutes.

English courts have held that a claimant may recover interest for delayed payment if the agreement expressly provides for interest to be paid.[22] In addition, courts have sometimes awarded interest where its payment could be inferred from the course of dealing between the parties or through trade usage.[23] Furthermore, courts have allowed interest as special damages if, because of the respondent's action, the claimant had actually incurred interest charges and it "may reasonably be supposed to have been in the contemplation of both parties, at the time they made the contract, as the probable result of the breach of it."[24]

Statutes in England also provide the authority to award interest.[25] Originally, statutory power to award interest was limited by Lord Tenterden's Act. This statute provided that interest was payable on "all debts or sums certain, payable at a certain time or otherwise … by virtue of some written instrument" or otherwise if there was a demand of payment in writing giving notice to the debtor that interest will be claimed.[26]

In 1934, the power to award interest was modified in the Law Reform (Miscellaneous Provisions) Act.[27] The 1934 Act provided that

> *"in any proceedings tried in any court of record for the recovery of any debt or damages, the court may, if it thinks fit, order that there shall be included in the sum for which judgment is given interest at such rate as it thinks fit on the whole or any part of the debt or damages for the whole or any part of the period between the date when the cause of action arose and the date of the judgment."*[28]

However, interest on interest was not authorized.[29] In 1982, the Administration of Justice Act removed any application of the 1934 Act to the Supreme Court and County Courts with respect to the awarding of interest and added a section on interest to the Supreme Court Act 1981.[30] The Supreme Court Act 1981 and the County Courts Act 1984 now provide the authority for those courts to award interest on debts and damages.

In England, arbitrators have even broader authority than judges to award interest.[31] Under section 49 of the Arbitration Act 1996:

> *"The tribunal may award simple or compound interest from such dates, at such rates and with such rests as it considers meets the justice of the case –*
> *(a) on the whole or part of any amount awarded by the tribunal, in respect of any period up to the date of the award;*
> *(b) on the whole or part of any amount claimed in the arbitration and outstanding at the commencement of the arbitral proceedings but paid before the award was made, in respect of any period up to the date of payment."*[32]

It should also be noted that, in 2000, the European Parliament and the Council of the European Union issued a Directive that required member states to introduce measures to protect commercial creditors against late payment by creating, among other things, a right to interest for late payments.[33]

By its terms, this Directive is

*"limited to payments made as remuneration for commercial transactions and does not regulate transactions involving consumers, interest in connection with other payments, e.g., payments under the laws on cheques and bills of exchange, payments made as compensation for damages, including payments from insurance companies."*[34]

International treaties, conventions and uniform law also may provide the authority to award interest. The UN Convention on the International Sale of Goods (CISG) provides for the payment of interest.[35] In addition, the North American Free Trade Agreement (NAFTA) provides that a tribunal deciding a dispute pursuant to NAFTA may award "monetary damages and any applicable interest".[36] And uniform laws, such as the UNIDROIT Principles and the Principles of European Contract Law, also provide for the payment of compensatory interest.[37]

A number of countries prohibit the payment of interest.[38] Most of these countries have legal systems based on Islamic law or *Sharia*, which expressly forbids the taking of interest.[39] However, even some of these countries have allowed it in certain commercial transactions.[40]

Courts and arbitral tribunals deciding transnational contract disputes also typically award compensatory interest.[41] The practice is so widespread that the liability to pay interest as part of an award of damages is now an accepted international legal principle.[42]

There are exceptions to the general rule concerning liability for the loss of the use of money. For example, parties may agree that no interest shall be paid on sums in arrears.[43] Claims for interest may be denied if the payment of interest would result in injustice, be otherwise unconscionable or violate public policy.[44] In addition, interest may not be awarded if the respondent can show proof of laches, bad faith, duress or fraud on the part of the claimant.[45]

## 2. Accrual period

Once a court or tribunal has determined that the respondent is liable for the payment of interest, it must fix the period for which it allows interest.

In general, agreements between the parties providing for interest to be paid from a certain date in the event of a breach are respected and enforced. In the absence of such an agreement, national laws typically provide that interest accrues from the date of default.

For example, in England, interest typically accrues from the time payment was due or should have been made.[46] By contrast, in many civil law countries, such as Italy[47] and Switzerland,[48] a respondent does not default simply by failing to perform its obligations by the date specified in the contract.[49] For a claimant to receive interest, the respondent must be given some notice of default.[50] Otherwise, the respondent is free to assume that either the claimant is suffering no injury as a result of the delay or the claimant has given implied permission for the respondent to delay performance.[51]

The ways of placing the respondent in default vary widely from country to country. The commencement of a legal action is almost always sufficient to place a respondent in default.[52] In addition, a claimant can usually place a respondent in default by making a demand for perform-ance. This demand must state, in quantitative and qualitative terms, exactly what performance is being demanded of the respondent.[53]

In Italy and Switzerland, for example, a claimant may satisfy the notice-of-default requirement by sending a letter simply stating that payment, together with interest, is due.[54] Generally, however, a claimant may not place a respondent in default merely by sending the respondent an invoice.[55]

As noted, in 2000, the European Union issued a Directive requiring member states to insure that creditors are entitled to interest for late payments in commercial transactions. With respect to the date from which interest accrues, the Directive provides that interest shall be "payable from the day following the date or the end of the period for payment fixed in the contract; ... if the date or period for payment is not fixed in the contract, interest shall become payable automatically without the necessity of a reminder:" (1) 30 days after receipt by the debtor of the invoice or an equivalent request for payment; (2) if the date of receipt of the invoice or the request for payment is uncertain, then 30 days after the receipt of the goods or services; (3) if the request for payment precedes the receipt of goods or services, then 30 days after receipt of the goods or services; or (4) if the request for payment precedes the date for procedures to verify performance as determined by contract or statute, then 30 days after the procedural date.[56]

Some Latin American countries, like Brazil and Panama, also do not award interest until the respondent has received some sort of notice of default.[57] In most Asian countries, a default can occur if there is a set date for performance and the respondent fails to perform by that date.[58] Even when no time is fixed for performance, however, a default can occur if the claimant notifies the respondent that the obligation is due and the respondent still does not perform.[59]

Various exceptions attach to the requirement that the claimant place the respondent in default as a prerequisite to receiving interest. The most widely recognized exception enables a claimant to recover interest without taking any action when the contract expresses an agreement between the parties that the respondent will automatically be in default if the obligation is not performed by a certain date.[60] In addition, a demand for payment is generally unnecessary when the respondent's unwillingness to perform has been made clear to the claimant.[61]

Courts and tribunals have differed over the date from which interest accrues. Some have awarded interest from the moment that the claimant has been deprived of its money (e.g. the date that the contract is breached) while others have awarded interest from the date that the respondent receives notification of default or from the date that the suit or request for arbitration is filed.[62]

## 3. Rate of interest

The final and perhaps most contentious issue is the rate at which interest accrues. Here again, agreements on the payment of interest at specified rates are typically enforced unless they violate public policy, such as usury laws.[63] In the absence of such agreement, in most countries, interest on a sum in arrears accrues at the statutory rate applicable through a choice of law analysis.

Interest rate statutes vary widely. Some countries periodically set the rate of interest, typically basing it on market conditions. In France, for example, the legal rate of interest is equal to the discount rate set by the Bank of France on December 15 of the preceding year.[64] In contrast, many other countries have fixed statutory rates. For example, in Germany, the Commercial Code sets the rate for commercial transactions between merchants and the Civil Code sets the rate for non-commercial transactions,[65] while in Japan the interest rate is set by the Civil Code unless the parties have agreed to a different rate.[66] In many cases, these statutes are not regularly amended and, as a result, may not accurately reflect compensation for the loss of the use of money. In the United States alone, statutes that fix interest at specific rates vary from 6% to 12%.[67]

England gives its courts discretion in fixing the rate at which interest accrues. According to one recent study, most courts apply the prevailing "commercial rate".[68] This rate is based on evidence submitted by the parties or, in some cases, on the rate that a claimant of like characteristics would have had to pay to borrow money during the period in question.[69]

The rate of interest may also be prescribed by statute. For example, the Late Payment of Commercial Debts (Interest) Act 1998 provides for simple interest on debts owed "for the supply of goods or services where the purchaser and the supplier are each acting in the course of a business".[70] This Act was originally designed to protect only small business against the late payment of commercial debts, but it has since been broadened to implement the EU Directive on combating late payment in commercial transactions.

The Directive provided that

> *"Member States shall ensure that ... the level of interest for late payment [of commercial transactions] [('the statutory rate')] which the debtor is obliged to pay, shall be the sum of the interest rate applied by the European Central Bank to its most recent main refinancing operation carried out before the first calendar day of the half-year in question ('the reference rate'), plus at least seven percentage points ('the margin'), unless otherwise specified in the contract."*[71]

In light of this Directive, the Late Payment of Commercial Debts (Interest) Act was amended to apply to claims for interest by all commercial creditors who are owed money by commercial organizations.[72] The applicable interest rate is 8% above the Bank of England base rate.[73]

It should also be noted that, in most countries, statutes and rules provide only for the awarding of simple interest. For example, Switzerland forbids interest to be paid upon interest, even if agreed upon in the contract.[74] In general, compound interest may be awarded when the parties have agreed to it in the contract or when it is payable as a matter of right, such as in the case of special damages.[75]

Courts and tribunals deciding transnational disputes have used various approaches to determine the rate of interest. Some have applied a statutory interest rate as determined by a choice of law analysis. Other approaches taken by courts and arbitral tribunals include awarding interest by applying the law of the creditor's place of business, the law of the debtor's place of business, the law of the country of the currency of payment, the law of the country in which payment is to be made, trade usage or general principles of law, such as the UNIDROIT Principles.[76] Also, some courts and tribunals have based all or part of an award of interest on principles of reasonableness and fairness.[77] Not surprisingly, the rates at which interest has been awarded have varied greatly.[78] However, the traditional practice has been to award only simple interest.[79]

In sum, there exists a general consensus that interest should be paid on overdue debts and damages and that it accrues from the date of default. However, the rates at which interest accrues, as well as the approaches for calculating interest, are controversial issues.

## II. AWARDING OF INTEREST IN INTERNATIONAL COMMERCIAL ARBITRATIONS AND IN INTERNATIONAL INVESTMENT DISPUTES: A COMPARISON

Traditionally, tribunals deciding disputes between transnational parties would resolve claims for interest by using one of a number of approaches. First, if the agreement contained a provision on the payment of interest, tribunals would typically enforce it unless the agreement violated public policy.[80]

Second, if the parties' agreement was silent or ambiguous on the payment of interest, tribunals would resolve the interest claim in accordance with applicable law selected through a choice of law analysis.[81] Alternatively, some tribunals have resolved claims for interest on the basis of general principles of law or on the basis of fairness or reasonableness.[82] The method most commonly used has been to resolve claims for interest pursuant to applicable national law; this method often results in applying a statutory interest rate and an award of only simple interest.[83] However, the trend in investment disputes has been for tribunals to award interest at market rates and on a compound basis.

Starting in the early 2000s, there were a number of cases decided under the auspices of the International Centre for Settlement of Investment Disputes (ICSID) – *Santa Elena*, *Maffezini* and *Wena Hotels* – in which the tribunals awarded interest at rates apart from those found in national laws and allowed it to accrue on a compound basis.[84] In *Compania del Desarrollo de Santa Elena* v. *Costa Rica*, the claimants sought compensation for property that Costa Rica expropriated in 1978.[85] The tribunal initially determined that the sum of USD 4.15 million constituted a "fair and reasonable approximation" of the value of the property at the time of its taking.[86]

With respect to interest, the claimant sought compound interest, while Costa Rica claimed that no interest was due or, that if interest was owed, it should accrue at a nominal rate and on a simple as opposed to compound basis. The tribunal noted that an interest serves two goals: (1) to ensure that the claimant receives "the full present value of the compensation that it should have received at the time of the taking"; and (2) to prevent "the State [from being] unjustly … enrich[ed] … by reason of the fact that the payment of compensation has long been delayed".[87] Interestingly, the tribunal did not discuss what would be an appropriate interest rate in the case, nor did it state the rate at which interest should accrue. Instead, it discussed extensively whether it had the authority to award compound interest. In answering this question, the tribunal acknowledged that there existed "a tendency in international jurisprudence to award only simple interest".[88] However, after surveying the cases and commentary on compound interest, the tribunal determined that an award of such interest was not prohibited by international law.[89]

In addition, it noted that international tribunals tended to award only simple interest in cases of injury or simple breach of contract but that they have awarded compound interest in cases relating to the valuation of property or property rights.[90] The tribunal noted that the determination of interest is a product of the exercise of judgment, taking into account all of the circumstances of the case, especially considerations of fairness.[91] Applying this exercise of judgment to the facts of the case, the tribunal noted that when an owner of property has lost the value of its asset but has not received its monetary equivalent, the compensation should reflect, at least in part, the additional sum that the money would have earned, had it and the income generated by it been reinvested each year at generally prevailing rates of interest.[92] Simple interest would not have been appropriate in this case, the tribunal reasoned, because Santa Elena was unable for 22 years either to use the property for the tourism development for which it was intended or to sell the property.[93] Full compound interest, however, would also not be justified, because Santa Elena had remained in possession of the property and had been able to exploit it to a limited extent.[94] In the end, the tribunal awarded the claimants approximately USD 11.85 million in compound interest, adjusted to take account of all relevant factors. It concluded that this award was needed to provide the claimants with the full present value of the property that was taken 22 years ago.[95]

In *Maffezini* v. *Spain*, the claimant sought the return of 30 million Spanish pesetas that he claimed was improperly transferred from his personal account to the account of a corporation affiliated with the Kingdom of Spain.[96] The tribunal ordered the return of the money plus interest.[97] With respect to the rate of interest, the tribunal ruled that it was reasonable under the circumstances to fix as the interest rate the London Inter Bank Offered Rate (LIBOR) for the Spanish peseta for each annual period since the date the claimant was deprived of funds.[98] The tribunal also ruled that interest should accrue on a compound basis. It explained that interest should be compounded annually "since the funds were withdrawn from [the claimant's] time-deposit account", which would have enabled the claimant to earn compound interest.[99] The tribunal's award of interest totalled ESP 27.6 million Spanish pesetas.[100]

In *Wena Hotels Ltd* v. *Arab Republic of Egypt*, the tribunal ruled that the respondent expropriated the claimant's property and failed to protect the claimant's investment and that, as a result, the claimant was entitled to USD 8 061 896.55 in damages.[101] Although the claimant sought interest on this amount, it neither specified the interest rate at which interest should accrue nor addressed whether the interest should be compounded. In resolving the claim for interest, the tribunal stated that the agreement between the United Kingdom and Egypt required that compensation be "prompt, adequate and effective" and that it "amount to the market value of the investment expropriated immediately before the expropriation itself."[102] This provision showed, the tribunal concluded, that compensation must not be eroded by the passage of time or diminution in market value. Based on this principle, the tribunal determined that the claimant should be granted interest at a rate close to but slightly below long-term government bonds in Egypt. The tribunal ultimately settled on a rate of 9%, which was 1% below the bonds.[103] It then decided that interest should be compounded quarterly. The tribunal explained the reasons for the award of compound interest, which totalled USD 11 431 386.88, as follows:

> "*An award of compound (as opposed to simple) interest is generally appropriate in most modern, commercial arbitrations. ... 'Almost all financing and investment vehicles involve compound interest. ... If the claimant could have received compound interest merely by placing its money in a readily available and commonly used investment vehicle, it is neither logical nor equitable to award the claimant only simple interest'.*"[104]

In more recent cases, tribunals have continued to award interest at market rates and on a compound basis. In *PSEG Global Inc.* v. *Republic of Turkey*, the tribunal ruled that Turkey breached its obligation to provide claimants fair and equitable treatment as provided for in the US-Turkey Bilateral Investment Treaty in their efforts to build and operate a coal power plant in Turkey. It awarded claimants compensation for their actual expenses related to the investment, totalling approximately USD 9 million.[105] With respect to the claim for interest, the claimants sought their alleged lost opportunity costs, which they asserted ranged from 10.6% to 12%, or alternatively the Turkish sovereign rate.

Turkey argued that the appropriate interest rate should be that of the US Treasury Bill. The tribunal rejected an interest rate based on claimants' lost opportunity cost on the grounds that it was too subjective. It declined to use the Turkish bond yield rate or the U. T-Bill rate because there was no evidence that the claimants would have placed the money owed in either financial market. In the end, the tribunal determined that the interest rate that would "compensate adequately an international company such as PSEG Global" under the circumstances was the "6-month average LIBOR plus 2 percent per year for each year during which the amounts" were owed and that interest should be compounded semi-annually.[106]

In *Siemens A.G.* v. *Argentine Republic*, the claimant was awarded a concession to create and operate Argentina's personal identification and electoral information system, which was based on the creation of national identity cards.[107] Argentina caused the claimant to suspend production of the cards and subsequently terminated the contract. The claimant filed for arbitration, alleging violations of the Mutual Protection and Promotion of Investments between the Federal Republic of Germany and the Argentine Republic. The tribunal ruled, *inter alia*, that Argentina's actions amounted to an expropriation and that it also breached its treaty obligation to provide fair and equitable treatment.[108]

With respect to interest, the claimant sought an award of interest at a compound rate of 6%, which it claimed was its average corporate borrowing rate. By contrast, Argentina argued that the Treaty provided for interest at the usual bank rate. The tribunal noted that, in determining the applicable interest rate, the "guiding principle is to ensure 'full reparation for the injury suffered as a result of the internationally wrongful act'."[109] It thus rejected the claim for interest at the corporate borrowing rate on the grounds that the appropriate rate is not the rate associated with corporate borrowing but the rate that reflects the amount of compensation the claimant would have earned if it had been paid after the expropriation. The tribunal concluded that "since the awarded compensation is in dollars, ... the average rate of interest applicable to the U.S. six-month certificates of deposit is an appropriate rate of interest".[110]

It also ruled that interest should be compounded annually because if the compensation had been paid following the expropriation, the claimant would have earned interest on interest on that amount. Compound interest, the tribunal noted, "is a closer measure of the actual value lost by an investor" and furthers the "objectives of prompt, adequate and effective compensation that reflects the market value of the investment immediately before the expropriation".[111]

The tribunal in *Azurix Corp.* v. *Argentine Republic* reached a similar result with respect to interest. There, the claimant alleged that Argentina had breached various obligations owed to Azurix under the 1991 Argentina-US BIT with respect to its concession agreement with the Argentine province of Buenos Aires for the provision of water and sewerage services in the province, which the claimant asserted were terminated because of a series of measures taken by the province.[112] The tribunal rejected the expropriation claims but found that Argentina had breached its obligation to provide the claimant with fair and equitable treatment and thus violated the obligation to afford the investor full protection and security. The tribunal awarded the claimant the fair market value of the concession, which it determined to be approximately USD 165 million. With respect to interest, the tribunal fixed the rate at the US six-month certificates of deposit. It also concluded that such interest should be compounded semi-annually. The tribunal reasoned that this interest rate best "reflects the reality of financial transactions, and best approximates the value lost by an investor".[113]

The trend to award interest at a market rate and on a compound basis continued recently in *LG&E Energy Corp.* v. *Argentine Republic*.[114] In that case, the claimant asserted that the value of its investments in Argentina were destroyed as a result of Argentina's breaches of the Bilateral Treaty between Argentina and the United States. The tribunal agreed that Argentina had breached the treaty but found that its conduct was justified during a certain period when it was under a "state of necessity". It thus awarded the claimants USD 50.9 million for the actual losses incurred as a result of the wrongful acts.[115]

With respect to interest, the tribunal noted:

> *"Interest is part of the 'full' reparation to which the Claimants are entitled to assure that they are made whole. In fact, interest recognizes that fact that, between the date of the illegal act and the date of actual payment, the injured party cannot use or invest the amounts of money due."*[116]

Based on this principle, the tribunal set the rate of interest at the rate of the six-month US Treasury Bills for the applicable period. The tribunal also ruled that interest, which totalled USD 6.5 million, should accrue on a compound basis. It explained that "in 'modern economic conditions', funds would be invested to earn compound interest".[117] Thus, "compound interest would better compensate the Claimants for actual damages suffered since it better reflects contemporary financial practice".[118]

There is one other recent ICSID case of note, *Compañía de Aguas del Aconquija S.A. and Vivendi Universal* v. *Argentine Republic*.[119] In that case, the claimants were the owners of water and sewage services concessions in Tucumán, Argentina. They claimed that acts and omissions of the province, which were attributable to the Argentine Republic, constituted an expropriation of their investment and a violation of the fair and equitable treatment standard as expressed in the bilateral investment treaty between the Argentine Republic and the Republic of France for the Promotion and Reciprocal Protection of Investments. The tribunal agreed and awarded the claimants USD 105 million in compensation.[120]

With respect to interest, the claimants had sought compound interest at a rate of 9.7%, which they alleged corresponded to the discount rate applied in claimants' discounted cash-flow analysis and the quoted rate on an Argentine treasury bond in 1997. However, the tribunal was "not persuaded that the claimants would have earned 9.7%, compounded, on their shares of damages awarded, had such sums been paid timely at the date of Argentina's expropriation of the concession".[121]

Instead, the tribunal ruled that a 6% interest rate represented a reasonable proxy for the return that the claimants could otherwise have earned on the amounts invested and lost in the concession,

> *"having regard to the claimants' business of investing in and operating water concessions, to the anticipated 11.7% rate of return on investment reflected in the Concession Agreement (which [privatized the water and sewage services of the province and in which] the parties had agreed to be appropriate having regard to the nature of the business, the term and risk involved) and the generally prevailing rates of interest since September 1977."*[122]

In addition, the tribunal held that interest should be compounded in order to adequately compensate the claimants for the loss of the use of their money. In doing so, the tribunal noted, "to the extent there has been a tendency of international tribunals to award only simple interest, this is changing, and the award of compound interest is no longer the exception to the rule."[123]

In light of these cases, the question thus arises: why the difference between international commercial arbitration and investment disputes when it comes to the interest rate? One reason could be that the sources of authority are different. Several international sources support authorizing investment tribunals to award interest apart from national law. For example, in *Wena Hotels*, the BIT provided that compensation for expropriation must be "prompt, adequate and effective" and "shall amount to the market value of the investment", which the tribunal saw as including a determination of interest compatible with those principles.[124] As noted, NAFTA is more explicit. Article 1135(1) NAFTA provides that a tribunal may award "monetary damages and any applicable interest".[125] In addition, the Draft Articles on Responsibilities of States adopted by the International Law Commission state that "[i]nterest on any principal sum payable … shall be payable when necessary in order to ensure full reparation" and that "the interest rate and the mode of calculation shall be set so as to achieve that result".[126]

Tribunals deciding breach of contract disputes often must or may feel bound to use a national law that often results in a fixed statutory rate. However, the result is often the same when the governing law in a transnational breach of contract action gives the tribunal seemingly broad discretion to award interest. For example, the CISG provides a general rule requiring the payment of interest whenever "a party fails to pay the price or any other sum that is an arrears...".[127] A few tribunals have interpreted this provision as broadly providing the authority to award interest at market rates in order to effectuate the principle of full compensation that is set forth in the main damages provision of the CISG.[128] However, most courts and tribunals have instead relied on national interest rate statutes to determine the rate at which interest accrues.[129]

There is another reason that could explain the different approaches between tribunals deciding international investment cases and those deciding international commercial disputes. The custom among tribunals deciding investment disputes has been to decide issues of interest and costs and fees apart from national law. As the *ad hoc* committee hearing the annulment application in *Wena Hotels* v. *Egypt* noted, the practice in international investment disputes is for issues concerning interest to be "left almost entirely to the discretion of the tribunal".[130]

Perhaps the explanation for the different approaches stems from the nature of the disputes. Investment arbitrations today often involve millions of dollars and can take many years to resolve. Thus, an award of interest at market rates and on a compound basis can be significantly different.[131] In contrast, while the sums at issue in many transnational contract disputes are significant, many do not involve the large amounts that are at issue in international investment disputes, and the duration of the dispute may not be as long.[132] Thus, the difference between interest at a statutory rate or a compounded market rate may not make much difference from a monetary standpoint.[133]

In any event, the approach taken by these investment arbitration tribunals better compensates claimants for the loss of the use of money; interest awarded at market rates and on a compound basis more accurately reflects what the claimant would have been able to earn on the sums owed if they had been paid in a timely manner.[134]

Investment tribunals often enjoy greater authority to award interest at market rates than their counterparts deciding transnational contract disputes; the latter are often constrained by national laws containing statutory interest rates. These rates remain unchanged for years, and they only provide for the payment of simple interest. However, tribunals deciding transnational contract disputes can achieve the same results as their counterparts deciding international investment disputes in four cases.

First, if the parties' agreement calls for the payment of interest at market rates and on a compound basis, tribunals should enforce that agreement.[135] Of course, the tribunal should not do so if it would violate a fundamental public policy rule, be clearly against the parties' true intentions or result in extreme prejudice or injustice to one party.[136]

Second, if the applicable law or rules allow for the awarding of interest at market rates and on a compound basis, the tribunal may do so. For example, English law gives arbitrators wide discretion to award interest.[137] In addition, if arbitral rules give the tribunal broad discretion to award interest, then the tribunal would have the authority to award interest at market rates and on a compound basis, subject to the exceptions set out above. For example, the rules for the arbitration of international disputes of the London Court of International Arbitration, the American Arbitration Association and the World Intellectual Property Organization expressly grant tribunals broad authority to award interest, indeed, compound interest. Thus, a tribunal deciding a case under any of those rules could award interest at market rates and on a compound basis.[138]

Third, if the breach of contract has caused the claimant to incur financing charges at market rates, the claimant should be entitled to interest at the borrowing rate that it paid.[139] In this case, the claim for interest would be one for interest as damages. Awarding interest at the claimant's borrowing rate (including on a compound basis, if that is what the claimant incurred) furthers the principle of fully compensating the claimant for all damages directly resulting from the respondent's wrongful actions. This principle is well recognized both in many national laws and by international tribunals.[140] Of course, the claim is subject to the traditional limitations on damages, including the principle that such damages must be a foreseeable consequence of the breach.[141]

The final circumstances in which the claimant should be entitled to interest at market rates on a compound basis is when the claimant can prove that, if it had been timely paid, it would have invested the money in a vehicle that would have paid it compound interest at a certain rate (typically reflecting the market rate).[142] Again, the claim is essentially only for interest as damages.

## CONCLUSIONS

It is a settled principle that a respondent is liable for all damages that have accrued naturally as a result of the failure to perform its obligations.[143] Liability includes the obligation to pay the claimant interest for its lost opportunity cost, which may be in the form of interest.[144] However, the opportunity cost in a commercial enterprise is a forgone investment opportunity.[145] Thus, awarding compound interest at the claimant's opportunity cost would be the most appropriate way to compensate it for the loss of the use of its money.

The difficulty for the claimant is to prove its lost opportunity cost. For example, if the claimant can show that it regularly placed its cash surpluses in a standard investment vehicle paying market rates, then it should be entitled to interest at such rates.[146] A business may alternatively reinvest its earning in the business itself or pay excess cash out to its shareholders in the form of dividends.[147] The claimant should be entitled to this amount if it can prove its lost opportunity cost.[148] A claimant may be able to do so by producing historical financial records and through expert testimony to show the rate of its return on investment during the relevant time period.[149] In appropriate cases, this evidence could also provide the basis for the compound rate, because it illustrates profit the business could have earned if it been paid the money owed in a timely manner.[150]

I am not arguing for a relaxation of rules of proof for claims for interest at market rates. On the contrary, I argue that if the claimant can show its lost opportunity cost with reasonable certainty and meet the limitations imposed by the proximate cause and foreseeability (or satisfy any other requirements imposed for the recovery of damages generally), it should be entitled to interest at that rate as damages.[151] This approach would make awards of interest more uniform, bring predictability to the area and ultimately further the goal of compensating the aggrieved party for all losses resulting from the wrongful act.

## END NOTES

[1] See, e.g., *PSEG Global Inc.* v. *Republic of Turkey*, Award, ICSID Case No. ARB/02/5, January 17, 2007, available at: <http://www.investmentclaims.com/decisions/ARB0205%20PSEG%20v% 20Turkey%20-%20Award%20and%20Annex.pdf>.

[2] See, e.g., *Compañía del Desarrollo de Santa Elena* v. *Costa Rica*, ICSID Case No. ARB/96/1, 15 *ICSID* (2000) p. 200, available at: <http://www.worldbank.org/icsid/cases/awards.htm> (awarding of USD 4.15 million in damages and USD 11.85 million in interest); *KCA Drilling Ltd.* v. *Sonatrach*, ICC Case No. 5651 (awarding USD 23 million in damages and USD 26 million in interest), summarized in pertinent part in D. Branson and R. Wallace, Jr., 'Awarding Interest in International Commercial Arbitration: Establishing a Uniform Approach', 28 *Va. J. Int'l L.* (1988) p. 920; *Am. Bell Int'l Inc.* v. *Islamic Republic of Iran*, 12 *Iran-U.S. Cl. Trib. Rep.* (1986) p. 170 (awarding approximately USD 28 million in interest on damages of approximately USD 50 million); *Gov't of Kuwait* v. *Am. Indep. Oil Co.*, March 24, 1982, 21 *ILM* (1982) p. 976 (awarding USD 83 million in damages and USD 96 million in interest); see also *Azurix Corp.* v. *Argentine Republic*, ICSID Case No. ARB/01/12, July 14, 2006, available at: <http:// www.worldbank.org/icsid/cases/awards.htm> (awarding approximately USD 165 million in damages and interest at the average rate applicable to the US six-month certificate of deposit, compounded semi-annually, or approximately USD 17.5 million in interest); *Siemens A.G.* v. *Argentine Republic*, ICSID Case No. ARB/02/8, February 6, 2007, available at: <http:// www.worldbank.org/icsid/cases/awards.htm> (awarding approximately USD 218 million in damages and interest at the average rate applicable to the US six-month certificate of deposit, compounded annually, or approximately USD 34 million in interest); *ADC Affiliate Limited* v. *Hungary*, ICSID Case No. ARB/03/16, October 2, 2006, available at: <http:// www.worldbank.org/ icsid/cases/awards.htm> (awarding approximately USD 76 million in damages and post-award interest at a rate of 6%, compounded monthly).

[3] See, e.g., *Santa Elena*, *supra* note 2; *Wena Hotels* v. *Egypt*, 41 *ILM* (2002) pp. 933, 945; *Emilio Agustín Maffezini* v. *Kingdom of Spain*, ICSID Case No. ARB/97/7, 16 *ICSID* (2001) p. 1, available at: <http://www.worldbank.org/icsid/cases/emilio_AwardoftheTribunal.pdf>; *Azurix Corp.*, *supra* note 2; *Siemens A.G.*, *supra* note 2; *PSEG Global Inc.*, *supra* note 1.

[4] See, e.g., Final Award in ICC Case No. 9839 of 1999, reprinted in 29 *Y.B. Com. Arb.* (2004) p. 66 (awarding in a breach of contract case 9% interest on damages pursuant to New York CPLR, § 5001(a)(b)); ICC Arbitration Case No. 10329 of 2000 (*Industrial product* case), reprinted in 29 *Y.B. Com. Arb.* (2004) p. 108 (awarding in a case governed by the CISG interest at a rate of 5% pursuant to the Swiss Code of Obligations); ICC Arbitration Case No. 9333 of October 1998 (*Services* case), available at: <http://cisgw3.law.pace.edu/cisg/wais/db/cases2/ 989333i1.html> (awarding in a dispute governed by the CISG 5% interest pursuant to Art. 104 of the Swiss Code of Obligations); ICC Arbitration Case No. 8611 of January 23, 1997 (*Industrial equipment* case), available at: <http://cisgw3.law.pace.edu/cisg/wais/db/cases2/ 978611i1.html> (awarding in a dispute governed by the CISG 5% interest pursuant to Art. 352 of the German Commercial Code); see also F. Mazzotta, 'CISG Article 78: Endless Disagreement among Commentators, Much Less among the Courts' (2004) (concluding that most courts and tribunals award interest under the CISG pursuant to national interest rate statutes). But see ICC Arbitration Case No. 8790 of 2000 (*Processed food product* case), 29 *Y.B. Com. Arb.* (2004) p. 13 (awarding in a case governed by the CISG interest at the LIBOR rate for the period in which the default occurred).

[5] A fixed interest rate could actually encourage the respondent to delay resolution. If the prevailing market interest rate is higher than the interest rate set by statute, the respondent could essentially earn money by delaying payment, earning a high return on the invested funds. On the other hand, if the prevailing savings rate is much lower than the fixed statutory rate, the result will be that the claimant is overcompensated. Furthermore, determining which statutory rate applies in a given situation can be difficult. See J. Gotanda, 'Awarding Interest in International Arbitration', 90 *Am. J. Int'l L.* (1996) p. 40.

[6] See *McCollough & Co.* v. *Ministry of Post, Tel. & Tel.*, 11 *Iran-U.S. Cl. Trib. Rep.* (1986) pp. 3, 29; G.H. Hackworth, 5 *Digest of International Law* (1943) p. 735 (citing *Illinois Central Railroad Co.* (*United States* v. *Mexico*), Opinions of the Commissioners (1927) 187, 189); D. Dobbs, *Dobbs Law of Remedies*, 2nd edn. (1993) § 3.6(1).

[7] See *Code Civil* (C. civ.) Art. 1153 (Fr.); *Codice Civile* (C.c.) Art. 1224 (Italy), translated in *The Italian Civil Code* (M. Beltramo, et al. (trans.), 1969) p. 323; *Schweizerisches Obligationenrecht* (OR) Art. 313 (Switz.).

[8] See *Spalding* v. *Mason*, 161 U.S. 375, 396 (1896).

[9] See generally J. Keir and R. Keir, 'Opportunity Cost: A Measure of Prejudgment Interest', 39 *Bus. Law.* (1983) p. 129; R. Haig, 3 *Bus. & Com. Litig. Fed. Cts.*, § 39.3; Restatement (Second) of Contracts, § 344(a) (1981).

[10] See R. Sergesketter, 'Interesting Inequities: Bringing Symmetry and Certainty to Prejudgment Interest Law in Texas', 32 *Hous. L. Rev.* (1995) p. 231; 'Prejudgment Interest as Damages: New Application of an Old Theory', 15 *Stan. L. Rev.* (1962) p. 107; S. Freund, et al., 'Prejudgment Interest in Commodity Futures Litigation', 40 *Bus. Law.* (1985) p. 1268.

[11] See M.S. Knoll, 'A Primer on Prejudgment Interest', 75 *Tex. L. Rev.* (1996) pp. 293, 296-297; L. Sohn and R. Baxter, Convention on the International Responsibility of States for Injuries to Aliens, § 83(1), Explanatory Note, 242 (Draft No. 12 with Explanatory Notes, 1961).

[12] J. Gotanda, *Supplemental Damages in International Law: The Awarding of Interest, Attorneys' Fees and Costs, Punitive Damages and Damages in Foreign Currency Examined in the Comparative and International Context* (1998) pp. 11-93. Other types of interest include, *inter alia*, conventional interest, gross interest, nominal interest, ordinary interest and penalty interest. It should be noted that, in some jurisdictions, moratory interest is sometimes synonymous with post-judgment interest. In other jurisdictions, however, moratory interest is defined as interest due on money claims as soon as the creditor notifies that payment is due.

[13] See E. Bringham and J. Houston, *Fundamentals of Financial Management*, 8th edn. (1998) p. 207. Compound interest is calculated through the use of the following formula: $FV = PV (1 + i)^n$, where FV is the future value of the total award, including interest, PV is the present value of the award (i.e. not including interest), i is the interest rate per compounding period and n is the number of compounding periods.

[14] J. Gotanda, 'Damages in Private International Law: Compensatory Interest', *Recueil des Cours* (2007, forthcoming).

[15] The commercial codes of Mexico, Panama and Brazil contain provisions directing that interest should be paid when the debtor is in default on the payment of a money debt. See *Código de Comercio* (Cód. Com.) Art. 362 (Mex.), translated in M. Gordon (ed.), *Commercial, Business and Trade Laws: Mexico* (1985) p. 37; Commercial Code (Pan. Com. Code) Art. 223 (Pan.), translated in *Panama, Commercial Laws of the World* (Foreign Tax Law Ass'n, 1991) p. 30; *Código Civil* (C.C.) Art. 1063 (Braz.), translated in *Brazil, Commercial Laws of the World* (Foreign Tax Law Ass'n, 1976) p. 165. Some Canadian provinces award interest as damages at the rate the claimant would have paid had it borrowed the money owed from a lending institution. This is the general rule for courts in the western provinces, Prince Edward Island and Nova Scotia. One commentator anticipates that New Brunswick courts would also follow this practice. H. Pitch, *Damages for Breach of Contract* (1985) pp. 210, 213. In England, the Supreme Court Act 1981 and the County Courts Act 1984 gave the High Court and the county courts, respectively, the authority to award simple interest on the recovery of a debt or damages. Supreme Court Act 1981, § 35A (Eng.); County Courts Act 1984, § 69 (Eng.).

[16] A number of countries with legal systems based on *Sharia* do not allow the payment of interest, because *Sharia* is based on the teachings of the Koran, Islam's holy book, which expressly prohibits the taking of interest, or *riba*. See M. Kahn, 'Islamic Interest-Free Banking: A Theoretical Analysis', in 33 *Int'l Monetary Fund Staff Papers* (1986) p. 5; T.S. Abdus-Shahid, 'Interest, Usury and the Islamic Development Bank: Alternative, Non-Interest Financing', 16 *L. & Pol'y Int'l Bus.* (1984) pp. 1095, 1100. *Riba* has been defined as an "[u]nlawful gain derived from the quantitative inequality of the counter-values in any transaction purporting to effect the exchange of two or more species which belong to the same genus and are governed by the same efficient cause." N. Saleh, *Unlawful Gain and Legitimate Profit in Islamic Law*, 2nd edn. (1992) p. 16. See W.M. Ballantyne, *Commercial Laws in the Arab Middle East* (1986) p. 122.

[17] C. civ. Art. 1153 (Fr.).

[18] See C.c. Art. 1224 (Italy), translated in *The Italian Civil Code*, *supra* note 7, at p. 323 ("In obligations having as their object a sum of money ... legal interest ... is due from the day of the default even if it was not due previously and even if the creditor does not prove that he has suffered any damage.").

[19] In Switzerland, for loans of money in commercial transactions, interest is payable even if the agreement fails to provide for interest; however, in non-commercial transactions, interest is payable only if the agreement provides for it. See OR Art. 313 (Switz.).

[20] N.Y. Civ. Prac. L. & R., § 5001(a) (McKinney 1992 and Supp. 1995).

[21] See *President of India* v. *La Pintada Compania Navegacion S.A.* [1985] A.C. 104 H.L.; *London, Chatham and Dover Railway Co.* v. *South E. Ry. Co.* [1893] A.C. 429; *Gordon* v. *Swan* [1810] 12 East 419; *Higgins* v. *Sargent*, [1823] 2 B. & C. 348.

[22] See *Cook* v. *Fowler* [1874] L.R. 7 H.L. 27; *In re Roberts* [1880] 14 Ch. D. 49.

[23] See *In re Anglesey* [1901] 2 Ch. 548; *Great Western Ins. Co.* v. *Cunliffe* [1874] 9 Ch. 525; *In re Duncan & Co.* [1905] 1 Ch. 307; *Ikin* v. *Bradley* [1818] 8 Taunt. 250; *Page* v. *Newman* [1829] 9 B. & C. 378.

[24] *Hadley* v. *Baxendale* [1854] 156 Eng. Rep. 145; see *Trans Trust S.P.R.L.* v. *Danubian Trading Co.* [1952] 2 Q.B. 297, 306-307; *Wadsworth* v. *Lydell* [1981] 1 W.L.R. 598; *Bacon* v. *Cooper (Metals) Ltd.* [1982] 1 All E.R. 397.

[25] See, e.g., Bills of Exchange Act 1882, § 57 (Eng.) (providing for interest on dishonoured bills and notes); Supreme Court Act 1981, § 35A (Eng.) (providing the High Court with the authority to award interest on debt or damages); County Courts Act 1984, § 69 (Eng.) (providing the county courts with the authority to award interest on debts and damages); and Arbitration Act 1996, § 49 (Eng.) (providing arbitrators with the authority to award interest).

[26] Civil Procedure Act 1833, 3 & 4 Will. 4, c. 42, § 28 (Eng.).

[27] See Law Reform (Miscellaneous Provisions) Act 1934, 24 & 25 Geo. 5, c. 41, § 3 (Eng.).

[28] Ibid., at § 3(1).

[29] See ibid., at § 3(1)(a).

[30] See Administration of Justice Act 1982, c. 53, §§ 15(1), 15(5)(a) (Eng.).

[31] See Arbitration Act 1996, § 49 (Eng.).

[32] Ibid; see also A. Samuel, 'Pre-Award Interest: England and Scotland', 5 *Arb. Int'l.* (1989) p. 310 (discussing an arbitrator's power to award interest in England and Scotland).

[33] See Directive 2000/35/EC of the European Parliament and of the Council of 29 June 2000 on combating late payment in commercial transactions, available at: <http://europa.eu.int/smartapi/cgi/sga_doc?smartapi!celexapi!prod!CELEXnumdoc&lg=en&numdoc=32000L0035&model=guichett> (providing for interest in case of late payment).

[34] Ibid., preamble, § 13.

[35] The basic rule on interest is set forth in Art. 78. It provides: "[i]f either party fails to pay the price or any other sum that is in arrears, the other party is entitled to interest on it, without prejudice to any claim for damages recoverable under Article 74." UN Convention on Contracts for the International Sale of Goods, Art. 78, U.N. Doc. A/Conf.97/18 Annex I (1980).

[36] North American Free Trade Agreement, December 17, 1992, U.S.-Can.-Mex., Art. 1135(1), 32 *ILM* (1993) pp. 289, 646 (entered into force January 1, 1994).

[37] UNIDROIT Principles of International Commercial Contracts (2004) Art. 7.4.9; Principles of European Contract Law (1998) Art. 9:508.

[38] See Gotanda, *supra* note 12, at p. 34.

[39] See G.G. Letterman, *Letterman's Law of Private International Business* (1990) p. 43; S. Saleh, 'The Recognition and Enforcement of Foreign Arbitral Awards in the States of the Arab Middle East', in J.D.M. Lew (ed.), *Contemporary Problems in International Arbitration* (1987) pp. 348-349. The rationale for this prohibition on interest is threefold:

   (1) Interest or usury reinforces the tendency for wealth to accumulate in the hands of a few, and thereby diminishes man's concern for his fellow man.

   (2) Islam does not allow gain from financial activity unless the beneficiary is also subject to the risk of potential loss; the legal guarantee of at least nominal interest would be viewed as guaranteed gain.

   (3) Islam regards the accumulation of wealth through interest as selfish compared with accumulation through hard work and personal activity.
Abdus-Shahid, *supra* note 16, at pp. 1102-1103 (quoting I. Karsten, 'Islam and Financial Mediation', 29 *Int'l Monetary Fund Staff Papers* (1982) pp. 108, 111).
It should be noted that Jewish law also prohibits the payment of interest among Jews. See G. Horowitz, *The Spirit of Jewish Law* (1953) pp. 488-494. However, other than in areas reserved to religious jurisdiction, Jewish law is not binding *per se*. See A. Bin-Nun, *The Law of the State of Israel* (D. Furman (ed.) and M. Eichelberg (trans.), 1990) p. 11.

[40] See Gotanda, *supra* note 5, at pp. 48-50 (discussing circumstances where interest may be awarded under Iranian law).

[41] See Gotanda, *supra* note 12.

[42] See *Asian Agric. Prod., Ltd.* v. *Sri Lanka*, June 27, 1990, 30 *ILM* (1991) pp. 580, 625; see also *McCollough & Co.*, 11 *Iran-U.S. Cl. Trib. Rep.* (1986) pp. 26-31; R. Lillich, 'Interest in the Law of International Claims', in *Essays in Honor of Voitto Saario and Toivo Sainio* (1983) p. 55.

[43] See Gotanda, *supra* note 14.

[44] See Gotanda, *supra* note 12, at p. 53.

[45] See M. Whiteman, *Damages in International Law* (1953) pp. 1924, 1990-1993 (discussing cases); C. Gray, *Judicial Remedies in International Law* (1987) p. 30 (discussing circumstances where it would not be appropriate to award interest). Cf. *Metal Box Co. Ltd.* v. *Currays Ltd.* [1988] 1 W.L.R. 175, 179 (ruling that "unreasonable delay by a plaintiff in prosecuting a claim may lead a court not to award interest for the full period"); *In re Bankers Trust Co.*, 658 F.2d 103, 108 (3d Cir. 1981) (stating that interest may be denied where the claimant "has (1) unreasonably delayed prosecuting its claim, (2) made a bad faith estimate of its damages that precluded settlement, or (3) not sustained any actual damages"); *National Bank of Canada* v. *Artex Indus. Inc.*, 627 F. Supp. 610, 616 (S.D.N.Y. 1986) (denying prejudgment interest because the plaintiff's error necessitated litigation, and it would be unfair to charge the defendant for the lost interest); *Malkin* v. *Wright*, 64 A.D.2d 569, 407, N.Y.S.2d 36, 38 (1978) (calculating interest only from the judgment awarding damages and not from the date of the verdict assessing liability because the plaintiff's interlocutory appeal delayed the assessment of damages).

[46] See Law Reform (Miscellaneous Provisions) Act 1934, 24 & 25 Geo. 5, c. 41, § 3 (Eng.); *Panchaud* v. *Pagnan* [1974] Lloyd's Rep. 409.

[47] See C.c. Art. 1219 (Italy).

[48] See Final Award in ICC Case No. 6230 of 1990, reprinted in 17 *Y.B. Com. Arb.* (1992) pp. 164, 176.

[49] See M. Planiol, *Traité Élémentaire De Droit Civil* [Treatise on the Civil Law], 11th edn. (Louisiana St. L. Inst. (trans.), 1959) p. 101; M. Amos and F. Walton, *Introduction to French Law*, 3rd edn. (F.H. Lawson, et al. (eds.), 1967) p. 183. In Italy, however, if the sum owed is liquid and not subject to any conditions, interest automatically accrues. See G. Certoma, *The Italian Legal System* (1985) p. 346.

[50] In France, for example, a claimant places a respondent in default by issuing a formal demand for payment or *mise en demeure*. See J. Reitz, 'The Mysteries of the Mise en Demeure', 63 *Tul. L. Rev.* (1988) p. 85. French law states that this should be done by means of a *sommation*, a written demand for payment that is served upon the respondent by a bailiff, or by an equivalent act. See C. Civ. Art. 1139 (Fr.). This rule has been held to require such formal notice only for a claim of moratory damages but not compensatory damages.

[51] See Planiol, *supra* note 49, at p. 101. In the United States, there is no uniform approach for determining the date from which interest accrues. In some jurisdictions, if a party fails "to pay a definite sum in money or to render a performance with fixed or ascertainable monetary value, interest is recoverable from the time for performance on the amount...". Restatement (Second) of Contracts (1981) § 354 (U.S.). In other jurisdictions, interest does not accrue until the respondent is given some notice of default. See *Knights of Columbus* v. *Writz*, 592 F.2d 466 (8th Cir. 1979); *Ledyard* v. *Bull*, 23 N.E. 444 (1890). Still others give the tribunal discretion to determine the period for which interest accrues. See A. Rothschild, 'Comment: Prejudgment Interest: Survey and Suggestion', 77 *Nw. U. L. Rev.* (1982) pp. 192, 204.

[52] See *Bürgerliches Gesetzbuch* (BGB) Art. 286 (Ger.); see also Final Award in ICC Case No. 4629 of 1989, reprinted in 18 *Y.B. Com. Arb.* (1993) p. 33 (awarding interest from the date of the request for arbitration because the claimants did not give the respondents formal notice that the invoices should be paid as required under Art. 102 of the Swiss Code of Obligations).

[53] See BGB Art. 286 (Ger.); OR Art. 102 (Switz); see also E. Bucher, *Schweizerisches Obligationenrecht, Allgemeiner Teil ohne Deliktsrecht* (1988) p. 357; P. Gauch, *Schweizerisches Obligationenrecht, Allgemeiner Teil, Rechtsprechung des Bundesgerichts* (1989) Art. 102; A. von Tuhr and A. Escher, *Allgemeiner Teil des Schweizerischen Obligationenrechts* (1974) p. 137.

[54] See C.c. Art. 1219 (Italy); Final Award in ICC Case No. 6230 of 1990, reprinted in 17 *Y.B. Com. Arb.* (1992) p. 176.

[55] See, e.g., Final Award in ICC Case No. 6531 of 1991, reprinted in 17 *Y.B. Com. Arb.* (1992) p. 224; Final Award in ICC Case No. 4629 of 1989, reprinted in 18 *Y.B. Com. Arb.* (1993) p. 33.

[56] Directive 2000/35/EC *supra* note 33, at Art. 3.1.(a)-(b).

[57] See C.C. Art. 1063 (Braz.); Pan. Com. Code Art. 227.

[58] See Civil Act (Kor. Civ. Act) Art. 387 (S. Korea); *Minpô* (Civil Code) Art. 412 (Japan); Laws of the Republic of China (ROC Civ. C.) Art. 229 (Law Revision Planning Group, et al. (eds.), 1961); PRC Foreign Econ. Law Art. 23; General Principles of Civil Law of the People's Republic of China (PRC Civ. C.) Art. 88, translated in *The Laws of the People's Republic of China 1983-86* (Foreign Languages Press, 1987) p. 240. In China, when there is a stated time for performance, it is implied that the respondent has notice that, if he does not perform, he will be in default. No extension of time is permitted. See W.S.H. Hung, *Outlines of Modern Chinese Law* (1976) p. 60. In Japan, if a time is agreed upon but it is not stated with certainty, then the respondent is in default from the point in time when he becomes aware that performance is due but still does not perform. See *Minpô* Art. 412.

[59] See Kor. Civ. Act Art. 387; *Minpô* Art. 412; ROC Civ. C. Art. 229; PRC Foreign Econ. Law Art. 23; see also V. Riasanovsky, *Chinese Civil Law* (1938) p. 151.

[60] See C. civ. Art. 1139 (Fr.); Amos and Walton, *supra* note 49, at p. 184. In general, the fact that the contract merely specifies a date by which the respondent must perform in and of itself is not sufficient to meet this requirement. See Reitz, *supra* note 50, at p. 89; C. Aubry and C. Rau, *Cours de Droit Civil Français* [Civil Law Translations], 6th edn. (E. Bartin (ed.) and A.N. Yiannopoulos (trans.), 1965) p. 96. But the agreement need not explicitly state that a respondent will be in default without there being any act on the part of the claimant; an agreement to dispense with the *mise en demeure* requirement can be inferred from the circumstances of the contract. See Planiol, *supra* note 49, at p. 102.

[61] See C.c. Art. 1219 (Italy); F. Dessemontet, 'Country Handbook on Switzerland', in A. Kritzer (ed.), *International Contract Manual* (Supp. 1993) p. 10.

[62] Some Canadian jurisdictions provide for interest to run from the date of breach. See R.S.B.C., ch. 76, § 1(1); R.S.N.B., ch. J-2, § 45(1); R.S.N.S., ch. 2, § 38(a), amended by ch. 55, § 1, ch. 54, § 1. See also R.S.O. 1980, § 36(3)(a)(i) (providing that where the claim is liquid, interest begins to accrue from the time the cause of action arises). In other Canadian jurisdictions, interest does not begin to accrue until the respondent has been given some kind of notice of default. See R.S.P.E.I., ch. 33(2); see also R.S.O., ch. 11, § 36(3)(a)(ii) (providing that where the claim is not liquid, notice must be given before interest will begin to accrue).

In civil law countries, interest generally runs from the date of default. See Planiol, *supra* note 49, at p. 102; M. Hunter and V. Triebel, 'Awarding Interest in International Arbitration', 6 *J. Int'l Arb.* (1989) pp. 7, 17. In some Latin American countries, if there is no date in the agreement, then interest runs from the filing of the suit or service of the claim. See C.W. Urquidi, *A Statement of the Laws of Bolivia in Matters Affecting Business*, 4th edn. (1975) p. 42; T.C. Brea, 'Argentina', in A. Coleman (ed.), *Encyclopedia of International Commercial Litigation* (1991) p. 25; see also H. Zürcher, et al., *A Statement of the Laws of Costa Rica in Matters Affecting Business*, 5th edn. (1975) p. 88 ("If the obligation is the payment of a sum of money, damages always consist solely in the payment of interest on the amount due, counted from the time it fell due."); *A Statement of the Laws of Mexico in Matters Affecting Business*, 4th edn. (1970) p. 75. In Argentina, in non-contact cases where damages are awarded, interest accrues from the date the cause of action arose. Coleman, ibid., at p. 25.

[63] See, e.g., *Anaconda-Iran Inc.* v. *Iran*, 18 *Iran-U.S. Cl. Trib. Rep.* (1988) pp. 199, 233, 238-239 (awarding interest at the prime rate charged by Chase Manhattan National Bank plus 2% as indicated in the contract); *R.J. Reynolds Tobacco Co.* v. *Iran*, 7 *Iran-U.S. Cl. Trib. Rep.* (1984) pp. 181, 191-192 (awarding interest at the rate stipulated in the contract, which was LIBOR plus 2%). Some countries have statutory maximums that cannot be exceeded, even by agreement of the parties. In these cases, the statutory maximum is awarded. Courts in New Zealand have discretion to determine the interest rate, but, if interest is awarded on damages under the Judicature Act, the rate cannot exceed the maximum rate set by the Act. See the Judicature Act 1908 (N.Z.), § 87; *Day* v. *Mead* [1987] 2 N.Z.L.R. 443, 463; S.M.D. Todd, et al. (eds.), *The Law of Torts in New Zealand* (1991) p. 887; R. Howarth (ed.), *Abridgement of New Zealand Case Law* (1992) pp. 398-399. A rate agreed to by the parties in Japan is not enforceable if it exceeds a statutory ceiling set by the Interest Rate Restriction Act. See ROC Civ. C. Art. 205; Z. Kitagawa (ed.), *Doing Business in Japan* (1992) p. 118. Parties in Korea may agree to a rate other than the legal rate as long as it does not exceed the statutory ceiling. See Kor. Civ. Act Art. 397(1) (S. Korea). In Taiwan, the rate is 5% if there is no agreed upon rate, but in any event the rate may not exceed 20%. See Civil Code (ROC Civ. C.) Art. 203 (Taiwan), translated in C.V. Chen and A.P.K. Keesee (eds.), *Commercial, Business and Trade Laws, Taiwan* (1983); ROC Civ. C. Art. 205 (Taiwan) ("If the rate of interest agreed upon exceeds twenty percent per annum, the creditor is not entitled to claim any interest over and above twenty percent.").

[64] See Law No. 75-619 of July 11, 1975, Art. 1, translated in G. Bermann and V.G. Curran, *French Law: Constitution and Selective Legislation* (1998) pp. 4-162. Art. 2 of Law No. 75-619 states: "If the discount rate set by the Bank of France on June 15th differs by three points or more from the discount rate set on the preceding December 15th, the legal interest rate is equal to the new discount rate for the six final months of the year." Two months after a judgment, the legal interest rate is increased by five points. See ibid., Art. 3.

[65] See *Handelsgesetzbuch* Art. 352 (Ger.); BGB Art. 288 (Ger.).

[66] See *Minpô* Art. 404 (Japan). The legal rate of interest for commercial agreements is 6% per annum. *Shôhô* (Commercial Code) Art. 514 (Japan), translated in *Doing Business in Japan* (Statute Volume) (2003) App. 5A.

[67] See, e.g., Alaska Stat., § 45.45.010 (1994) (10.5% interest); D.C. Code Ann., § 28.3302 (1991) (6% interest); Ind. Code Ann., § 24-4.6-1-101 (West 1995) (8% interest); Mass. Gen. Laws Ann., ch. 231, § 6B (West 1995) (12% interest); N.Y. Civ. Prac. L. & R., § 5004 (McKinney 1992 and Supp. 1995) (9% interest).

[68] H. McGregor, *McGregor on Damages*, 14th edn. (1980) § 476, p. 347; Hunter and Triebel, *supra* note 62, at p. 11.

[69] See Hunter and Triebel, *supra* note 62, at pp. 11-12. For example, a large corporation typically will be able to borrow money at a lower rate than a small, independent business owner. See ibid. The rationale for this practice is that the rates at which banks loan money are based upon a number of factors, including the amount and duration of the loan and the degree of risk that they associate with the respondent. An established business may have an extensive credit history and a large amount of collateral, which might entitle it to a low interest rate. On the other hand, a new small business may have neither an established credit history nor much collateral to offer. Because it presents a greater lending risk, that business may be charged a higher interest rate.

[70] Late Payment of Commercial Debts (Interest) Act 1998, c. 20, § 2(1) (Eng.).

[71] Directive 2000/35/EC, *supra* note 33, at Art. 3.1.(d). The Directive further provides that, "[f]or a Member State which is not participating in the third stage of economic and monetary union, the reference rate … shall be the equivalent rate set by its national bank." Ibid.

[72] Late Payments of Commercial Debts Regulations 2002, Statutory Instrument No. 1674 (Eng.), available at: <http://www.legislation.hmso.gov.uk/si/si2002/20021674.htm>. The new regulations apply only to contracts made on or after August 7, 2002. Ibid.

[73] Late Payment of Commercial Debts (Rate of Interest) (No. 3) Order 2002, Statutory Instrument No. 1675 (Eng.), available at: <http://www.legislation.hmso.gov.uk/si/si2002/20021675.htm>.

[74] OR Arts. 105, 314 (Switz.).

[75] See C.c. Art. 1283 (Italy) (allowing compound interest when there has been prior usage or a prior agreement, as long as interest has been due for at least six months); Code Civil Art. 1154 (Belg.) (allowing compound interest pursuant to the parties' agreement or a judicial summons, as long as interest has been due for at least a year); Judicature Act 1908, § 87(1)(a)-(b) (N.Z.) (allowing compound interest only when payable as a matter of right); ROC Civ. C. Art. 207 (Taiwan) (prohibiting compound interest except when the parties have agreed in writing that interest may be added after a year); Cód.Com Art. 363 (Mex.) (prohibiting compound interest unless agreed upon by the parties).

[76] See O. Lando, 'The Law Applicable to the Merits of the Dispute', in Lew, *supra* note 39, at p. 101; W.L. Craig, et al., *International Chamber of Commerce Arbitration*, 2nd edn. (1990) p. 285. The above list is by no means exhaustive. Some tribunals have randomly selected a set of choice-of-law rules. See C. Croff, 'The Applicable Law in International Commercial Arbitration: Is it Still a Conflicts of Law Problem?', 16 *Int'l Law* (1982) pp. 613, 630. Other tribunals have selected a substantive law without regard to any choice-of-law rules. See V. Danilowicz, 'The Choice of Applicable Law in International Arbitration', 9 *Hastings Int'l & Comp. L. Rev.* (1985-1986) pp. 235, 268.

[77] See, e.g., Final Award in ICC Case No. 11849 of 2003, reprinted in 31 *Y.B. Com. Arb.* (2006) pp. 148, 169-170; see also Gotanda, *supra* note 5, at pp. 50-55.

[78] See *McCollough & Co.*, 11 *Iran-U.S. Cl. Trib. Rep.* (1986) p. 28 n. 21 (citing cases); Whiteman, *supra* note 45, at pp. 1975-1986 (discussing cases); J. Ralston, The Law and Procedure of International Tribunals, p. 130 (1926) (discussing cases).

[79] See, e.g., *Santa Elena, supra* note 2, at p. 200 (noting the tendency in international law "to award only simple interest … in relation to cases of injury or simple breach of contract"); *McKesson Corp. v. Iran*, 116 F. Supp. 2d 13, 41 (D.D.C. 2000) (finding that "international courts have over a period of decades followed the custom of granting only simple interest");

*Chitty on Contracts*, 2nd edn. (1994) p. 619 ("Compound interest is payable either by agreement or custom, but not otherwise."); F.A. Mann, *Further Studies in International Law* (1990) p. 378 (stating that international tribunals generally do not grant compound interest); P. Cerina, 'Interest as Damages in International Commercial Arbitration', 4 *Am. Rev. Int'l Arb.* (1993) pp. 255, 261 (assuming that the majority of arbitral tribunals do not "award compound interest in order to avoid engaging in presumably complex (and expensive) calculations and the substantial sums involved"); Knoll, *supra* note 11, at p. 306 ("The traditional, common-law rule is that prejudgment interest is not compounded.").

[80] See, e.g., Final Award in ICC Case No. 7006 of 1992, reprinted in 18 *Y.B. Com. Arb.* (1993) p. 65; *Anaconda-Iran*, 18 *Iran-U.S. Cl. Trib. Rep.* (1988) pp. 233, 238-239; *R.J. Reynolds Tobacco Co.*, 7 *Iran-U.S. C. Trib. Rep.* (1984) pp. 191-92. See also Second Interim Award in ICC Case No. 5277 of 1987, reprinted in 13 *Y.B. Com. Arb.* (1988) pp. 80, 89-90; Final Award of November 20, 1987, reprinted in 14 *Y.B. Com. Arb.* (1989) pp. 47, 68; Final Award in ICC Case No. 10377 of 2002, reprinted in *31 Y.B. Com. Arb.* (2006) pp. 72, 88-90.

[81] See, e.g., Award in ICC Case No. 2637 of 1975, reprinted in 2 *Y.B. Com. Arb.* (1977) p. 153; *LIAMCO* v. *Libyan Arab Republic*, reprinted in 6 *Y.B. Com. Arb.* (1981) p. 89; Final Award in ICC Case No. 6281 of August 26, 1989, reprinted in 15 *Y.B. Com. Arb.* (1990) p. 96; Final Award in ICC Case No. 6531 of 1991, reprinted in 17 *Y.B. Com. Arb.* (1992) p. 221.

[82] See, e.g., *AAPL* v. *Sri Lanka*, ICSID Case No. ARB/87/3, 1990, reprinted in 27 *Y.B. Com. Arb.* (1992) p. 141; *Phillips Petroleum Co. Iran* v. *Iran*, 21 *Iran-U.S. Cl. Trib. Rep.* (1989) p. 161; *McCollough & Co.*, 11 *Iran-U.S. Cl. Trib. Rep.* (1986) p. 29; Final Award in ICC Case No. 11849 of 2003, reprinted in 31 *Y.B. Com. Arb.* (2006) pp. 148, 169-170; see also A. Lowenfeld, 'The Two-Way Mirror: International Arbitration as Comparative Procedure', 7 *Mich. Y.B. Int'l Legal Stud.* (1985) p. 182.

[83] See Final Award in ICC Case No. 6230 of 1990, reprinted in 17 *Y.B. Com. Arb.* (1992) p. 164; Final Award in ICC Case No. 6162 of 1990, reprinted in 17 *Y.B. Com. Arb.* (1992) p. 153; see also *R.J. Reynolds Tobacco Co.*, 7 *Iran-U.S. Cl. Trib. Rep.* (1984) p. 191; *Starrett Hous. Corp.* v. *Iran*, 16 *Iran-U.S. Cl. Trib. Rep.* (1987) p. 199, 234-235. In fact, Marjorie Whiteman wrote in her leading treatise, *Damages in International Law*, that "there are few rules within the scope of the subject of damages in international law that are better settled than the one that compound interest is not allowable". Whiteman, *supra* note 45, at p. 1997; *Droit International Public* V, § 242 (1983) (stating that arbitral tribunals generally do not award compound interest unless its payment has been agreed to by the parties).

[84] *Santa Elena, supra* note 2; *Maffezini, supra* note 3; *Wena Hotels, supra* note 3, at p. 919. In *Metalclad Corp.* v. *United Mexican States*, the tribunal awarded the claimant a total of USD 16 685 000 for the breach of certain articles of the North American Free Trade Agreement (NAFTA). With respect to the claim for interest, the tribunal determined that an award of 6% interest, compounded annually, was appropriate because it would restore the claimant to a "reasonable approximation of the position in which it would have been if the wrongful act had not taken place". The Supreme Court of British Columbia later set aside the award of interest on the grounds that the tribunal had erred in selecting the date from which it calculated the amount of compensatory interest. The Court, however, did not discuss the award of compound interest. *Metalclad Corp.* v. *United Mexican States*, ICSID Case No. ARB(AF)/97/1, August, 30, 2000.

[85] See *Santa Elena, supra* note 2, at § 96.

[86] Ibid., at § 95.

[87] Ibid, at § 101.

[88] Ibid., at § 97.

[89] Ibid., at §§ 97-103.

[90] Ibid., at § 97.

[91] Ibid., at § 103.

[92] Ibid., at § 104.

[93] Ibid., at § 105.

[94] Ibid.

[95] Ibid., at §§ 106-107. This essentially meant that the claimant received interest at a rate of approximately 6.2291%, compounded semi-annually. This assumes a principal amount of USD 4.15 million and an accrual period of 22 years, compounded semi-annually. By contrast, an award of simple interest at a rate of 6.2291% for 22 years would have yielded USD 5.69 million. Thus, the difference between an award of simple interest and compound interest amounted to USD 6.16 million, which exceeded the award for the taking of the property at issue in the case.

[96] *Maffezini*, *supra* note 3, at § 44.

[97] Ibid., at § 83.

[98] Ibid., at § 96.

[99] Ibid.

[100] Ibid.

[101] *Wena Hotels*, *supra* note 3.

[102] Ibid.

[103] Ibid.

[104] Ibid., at p. 919.

[105] *PSEG Global*, *supra* note 1 The tribunal declined to award claimants the market value of their investment on the grounds that the BIT permits such damages only for cases of expropriation. It recognized that a number of tribunals had awarded the fair market value for non-expropriated breaches, but it distinguished those cases on the grounds that the damaged investments were in those cases in the production stage.

[106] Ibid., at pp. 341-348. Interestingly, there was no further explanation of why the LIBOR rate plus 2% was the most appropriate rate. Similarly, in *Enron Corporation Ponderosa Assets, L.P.* v. *Argentine Republic* and *Sempra Energy International* v. *Argentine Republic*, the tribunals awarded compound interest at the six-month average LIBOR rate plus 2%. However, in both cases, the tribunals ruled that interest should accrue only until the date of the award. See *Enron Corporation Ponderosa Assets, L.P.* v. *Argentine Republic*, ICSID Case No. ARB/01/3, available at: <http://www.investmentclaims.com/decisions/Enron-Award.pdf> (awarding USD 106.2 million in damages and compensation and interest "at the 6-month average LIBOR Rate plus 2 per cent for each year, or proportion thereof, [from the date that the amount of damages and compensation were determined] until the date of the dispatch of the award"); *Sempra Energy International* v. *Argentine Republic*, ICSID Case No. ARB/02/16, at p. 139, available at: <http://www.investmentclaims.com/decisions/Sempra_Energy-Award.pdf> (compensation in the amount of USD 128 250 462 and "interest at the 6-month successive LIBOR rate plus 2 per cent for each year, or proportion thereof, beginning [from the date that the amount of damages and compensation were determined] until the date of the Award" and that such "interest shall be compounded semi-annually").

[107] *Siemens A.G.*, *supra* note 2.

[108] Ibid., at § 403.

[109] Ibid., at § 396.

[110] Ibid.

[111] Ibid., at §§ 399-400.

[112] *Azurix Corp.*, *supra* note 2.

[113] Ibid., at § 440.

[114] *LG&E Energy Corp. et al.* v. *Argentine Republic*, ICSID Case No. ARB/02/1, available at: <http://www.investmentclaims.com/decisions/LG&E-Argentina-Damages_Award.pdf>.

[115] See ibid., at §§ 1-3, 108.

[116] See ibid., at § 55.

[117] See ibid., at § 56.

[118] See ibid., at § 103.

[119] *Compañía de Aguas del Aconquija S.A. and Vivendi Universal S.A.* v. *Argentine Republic*, ICSID Case No. ARB/97/3, at § 9.2.8, available at: <http://www.investmentclaims.com/decisions/Vivendi_II_Award.pdf>.

[120] Ibid., at § 11.1(i)-(v).

[121] Ibid., at § 9.2.7.

[122] Ibid., at § 9.2.8.

[123] Ibid., at §§ 9.2.4, 9.2.8.

[124] *Wena Hotels*, *supra* note 3. See also *Compañía de Aguas del Aconquija and Vivendi Universal supra* note 119, at § 9.2.2 (noting that Art. 5(2) of the BIT required that compensation be paid by a state party for lawful expropriation "bear interest, computed at an appropriate rate, until the date of payment").

[125] NAFTA Art. 1135(1).

[126] International Law Commission, Draft Articles on Responsibilities of States, Art. 38.

[127] CISG Art. 78.

[128] See generally Award in ICC Arbitration Case No. 8128 of 1995, available at: <http://cisgw3.law.pace.edu/cases/958128i1.html>; Award in Case No. SCH-4366, June 15, 1994 (Austria), available at: <http://cisgw3.law.pace.edu/cases/940615a3.html>.

[129] See Case Law on UNCITRAL Texts (CLOUT) Case No. 132, August 16, 1996, available at: <http://www.uncitral.org/uncitral/en/case_law/abstracts.html>; CLOUT Case No. 97, July 12, 1995, available at: <http://www.uncitral.org/pdf/english/clout/abstracts A_CN.9_SER.C_ABSTRACTS_7.pdf>; see also Landgericht (LG) Hamburg [Hamburg District Court], September 26, 1990, Case No. 5 O 543/88 (FRG), available at: <http://cisgw3.law.pace.edu/cases/900926g1.html>; Internationales Schiedsgericht der Bundeskammer der gewerblichen Wirtschaft [Arbital Tribunal] Vienna, June 15, 1994, Case No. SCH-4318 (Austria), available at: <http://www.unilex.info/case.cfm?pid= 1&do=case&id=56&step=Abstract; see also Mazzotta, *supra* note 4 (surveying cases).

[130] *Wena Hotels, supra* note 3, at p. 945.

[131] See generally *Santa Elena, supra* note 2 (awarding USD 4.15 million in damages and USD 11.85 million in interest); *ADC Affiliate Limited* v. *Hungary, supra* note 2 (awarding approximately USD 76 million in damages and interest at 6%, compounded monthly); *Azurix Corp., supra* note 2 (awarding USD 165 million in damages and interest at a rate of 2.44%, compounded semi-annually); *Siemens A.G., supra* note 2 (awarding approximately USD 218 million in damages and interest at a rate of 2.66%, compounded annually); *PSEG Global, supra* note 1 (awarding approximate USD 9 million in damages and interest at the applicable six-month LIBOR rate plus 2%, compounded semi-annually); *LG&E Energy Corp., supra* note 114 (awarding USD 59.9 million in damages and USD 6.5 million in compound interest).

[132] See, e.g., China International Economic and Trade Arbitration Commission (CIETAC) (PRC), Case No. Shen G2004100, April 7, 2005, available at: <http://cisgw3.law.pace.edu/cisg/wais/db/cases2/050407c1.html> (awarding buyer in a case governed by the CISG approximately USD 165 000 in damages and interest at rates of 6% and 8%); Decision of LG Freiburg, Case No. 8 O 75/02, August 22, 2002, available at: <http://cisgw3.law.pace.edu/cisg/wais/db/cases2/020822g1.html> (awarding, in a case involving the sale of a car, the purchase price under CISG Art. 81(2) and damages under CISG Art. 74 totalling EUR 14 620 and interest at the rate set forth in BGB § 288 I 2); Decision of BG St. Gallen, Case No. 3 PZ 97/18, 3 July 1997, available at: <http://cisgw3.law.pace.edu/cisg/wais/db/cases2/970703s1.html> (awarding seller in a case governed by the CISG DEM 5641.70 plus interest of 5%); Decision of Rechtbank van Koophandel [District Court] Hasselt, Case No. AR 04/601, February 25, 2004, available at: <http://cisgw3.law.pace.edu/cisg/wais/db/cases2/040225b2.html> (awarding in a case governed by the CISG EUR 34 301, which includes approximately EUR 1009 in interest at 10.5% according to the Act of August 2, 2002); CIETAC Arbitration Proceeding (*Roll aluminum and aluminum parts* case), October 30, 1991, available at: <http://cisgw3.law.pace.edu/cisg/wais/db/cases2/911030c1.html> (awarding in a case governed by the CISG USD 368 544 in damages, which included USD 25 104 in interest); see also Award of 5 April 2007, Arbitration before the Arbitration Institute of the Stockholm Chamber of Commerce between Claimant of the People's Republic of China and Respondent and Counterclaimant of Brazil, available at: <http://cisgw3.law.pace.edu/ cases/0705s5.html> (rejecting in a dispute to be resolved applying the CISG claimant's claims and awarding the respondent on counterclaims USD 648 111 and interest at a rate of 6%, compounded semi-annually). See also J. Ziegel, 'The Future of the International Sales Convention from a Common Law Perspective', 6 *N.Z. Bus. L.Q.* (2000) p. 335 (noting reported cases involving the CISG usually deal with relatively small claims).

[133] Tribunals deciding large international investment disputes must often also grapple with sophisticated legal, economic and financial issues in calculating damages, such as the discounted cash-flow method. Thus, these tribunals may be more accustomed to dealing with and more receptive to more nuanced claims for interest. See J. Gotanda, 'Recovering Lost Profits in International Disputes', 36 *Georgetown Journal of International Law* (2004) pp. 61, 88-100.

[134] See J. Gotanda, 'Compound Interest in International Disputes' (2004) Oxford U Comparative L Forum 1, at <http://www.ouclf.iuscomp.org>.

[135] See, e.g., *Petro Jamaica* v. *Ocean Logistic Co.*, Soc'y Mar. Arb. No. 3495, at *5 (1998), available at LEXIS Admiralty; *August Trading Inc.* v. *Continental Grain Co.*, Soc'y Mar. Arb. No. 3552, at *3 (1999), available at LEXIS Admiralty; see also *ADC Affiliate Limited, supra* note 2 (awarding interest at the rate agreed by the parties in the promissory note).

[136] See Final Award of November 20, 1987, reprinted in 14 *Y.B. Com. Arb.* (1989) p. 68; *R.J. Reynolds Tobacco Co.*, 7 *Iran-U.S. Cl. Trib. Rep.* (1984) p. 192.

137 See Arbitration Act 1996, § 49 (Eng.).

138 See V.V. Veeder, London Court of International Arbitration, The New 1998 LCIA Rules, Art. 26.6, 23 *Y.B. Com. Arb.* (1998) pp. 366, 385, at § 26.6 ("The Arbitral Tribunal may order that simple or compound interest shall be paid by any party on any sum awarded at such rates as the Arbitral Tribunal determines to be appropriate, without being bound by legal rates of interest imposed by any state court, in respect of any period which the Arbitral Tribunal determines to be appropriate ending not later than the date upon which the award is complied with."); Am. Arbitration Ass'n, International Arbitration Rules, Art. 28.4 (November 1, 2001), available at: <http://adr.org/index2.1.jsp?JSPssid=15747> ("A monetary award shall be in the currency or currencies of the contract unless the tribunal considers another currency more appropriate, and the tribunal may award such pre-award and post-award interest, simple or compound, as it considers appropriate, taking into consideration the contract and applicable law."); World Intellectual Property Organization Arbitration Rules, Art. 60(b) ("The Tribunal may award simple or compound interest to be paid by a party on any sum awarded against that party. It shall be free to determine the interest at such rates as it considers to be appropriate, without being bound by legal rates of interest, and shall be free to determine the period for which the interest shall be paid."); Hong Kong International Arbitration Centre, Domestic Arbitration Rules, Art. 20 (1993), available at: <http://www.hkiac.org/pdf/e_domestic.pdf> ("Unless otherwise agreed by the parties, the Arbitrator may order that compound interest be paid."); Arbitration Rules of the Singapore International Arbitration Centre, Art. 27.6 (2007) ("The Tribunal may award simple or compound interest on any sum which is the subject of the arbitration at such rates as the parties may have agreed or, in the absence of such agreement, as the Tribunal determines to be appropriate, in respect of any period which the Tribunal determines to be appropriate ending not later than the date of the award.").

139 To be entitled to such interest, the claimant would need to produce the applicable loan documents or other similar financial records. See Kizer, op cit. pp. 1299-1300; see also R.F. Lanzillotti and A.K. Esquibel, 'Measuring Damages in Commercial Litigation: Present Value of Lost Opportunities', 5 *J. Acct. Auditing & Fin.* (1989) pp. 125, 139 (recognizing that interest rate calculation should employ the claimant's borrowing cost if it had to borrow to cover its loss); Award in ICC Case Nos. 3099 and 3100 of May 30, 1979, in *Collection of ICC Arbitral Awards 1974-1995* (1990) pp. 67, 74 (awarding claimant the interest due under the contracts and the difference between the interest claimant paid to the bank and the interest due under the contracts).

140 See C. civ. Art. 1153 (Fr.); C.c. Art. 1284 (It.); *Colunga*, 722 F. Supp. 1488; *ITT Corp.*, 17 Cl. Ct. 242; *Jad Int'l Pty. Ltd.* v. *Int'l Trucks Austl. Ltd.*, 50 F.C.R. 378, 391-92 (Austl. 1994); *Wadsworth*, 1 W.L.R. 603; Dobbs, *supra* note 6, at § 3.6(2) ("When the plaintiff has in fact incurred interest costs because of the defendant's delay in paying the underlying obligation, the plaintiff may recover those costs as consequential damages, provided his proof meets the rules for recovery of consequential loss."); Hunter and Triebel, *supra* note 62, at p. 18 (stating that in Germany, although compound interest is generally prohibited, it can be given where "claimant has actually paid compound interest to his bank"); R. Kreindler, *Transnational Litigation: A Basic Primer* (1998) p. 292 (stating that "if a creditor can prove that it has actually paid a higher interest for a loan replacing the payment in dispute, then it may be able to claim such interest as damages").

141 CISG Art. 74.

142 See, e.g., *Compañía de Aguas del Aconquija and Vivendi Universal supra* note 119, at § 9.2.2.

143 See *Library of Congress* v. *Shaw*, 478 U.S. 310, 315 n. 2 (1986); C. McCormick, *Damages* (1935) § 54, pp. 207-208.

[144] See R. Brealey and S. Myers, *Principles of Corporate Finance*, 3rd edn. (1988) p. 280 (stating that if a firm chooses to invest in project net, the present value of the project would have to be higher than the firm's cost of capital or else the firm would not choose to invest in that project, and, even though it may be true that the firm might invest in a losing proposition to penetrate a market, the firm would still eventually have to exceed its opportunity cost of capital in the long run or the firm would not be profitable); Keir and Keir, *supra* note 9, at pp. 147-149 (stating that opportunity costs vary from entity to entity and in each case courts should evaluate the various opportunity costs and choose from a range of rates).

[145] See Keir and Keir, *supra* note 9, at p. 146 (stating that "opportunity cost is the benefit that is forgone when resource is not used in its next best alternative"); see also Rothschild, *supra* note 51, at p. 192 (stating that "if a judgment, years after the fact, provides only the amount of damage sustained by the claimant at the time of the incident, the claimant will have lost the opportunity to invest the amount of the damages and to earn a return on that investment").

[146] See S. Ross, et al., *Fundamentals of Corporate Finance* (1998) pp. 233-235, 402-412, 582-585 (recognizing that when funding a project, business will typically have to borrow capital or use its excess capital and, if it has temporary cash surpluses, it may invest the money in short term securities).

[147] See Brealey and Myers, *supra* note 144, at p. 279.

[148] In general, this means that it must be proved with "reasonable certainty and meet the limitations imposed by the proximate cause and *Hadley* v. *Baxendale* rules". Dobbs, *supra* note 6, at § 3.6(2) n.11.

[149] See Keir and Keir, *supra* note 9, at p. 48; see also Ross, et al., *supra* note 146, at pp. 62-63.

[150] See Ross, et al., *supra* note 146, at pp. 62-63. One commentator has argued that a claimant's opportunity cost is the same as the respondent's unsecured cost of borrowing. See Knoll, *supra* note 11, at pp. 308-311. This commentator argues that because the lost capital was invested in the respondent's business, the return to the claimant should reflect the inherent risk of the investment in the respondent and the proper way to assess this risk is to use the respondent's cost of borrowing (see ibid.). I disagree. The claimant should be awarded the amount of return adjusted or the risk it undertook by investing in the respondent's business if the claimant chose to make this investment voluntarily. However, where the respondent has breached its obligations and caused claimant to suffer a monetary loss, it seems more appropriate under the circumstances to consider that the claimant did not voluntarily agree to place its money in the respondent's business. To make the claimant whole, it should receive its lost opportunity cost, not the expected return of a forced investment.

[151] See Dobbs, *supra* note 6; Gotanda, *supra* note 134.

# 7

## The issue of interest in Middle East Laws and Islamic Law

By **Tarek Fouad A. Riad**
*Managing Partner, Kosheri, Rashed & Riad (Cairo)*
*Head of the Business and Commercial Law Department*
*of the German University in Cairo*
*Member of the Scientific Council*
*of the ICC World Business Law Institute*

This chapter briefly focuses on the issue of interest in Middle Eastern countries and the evolution and effect of this issue on the current laws of those countries, as well as the legality or illegality of certain categories of contracts that raise issues related to *Riba* (usury)[1] in the technical sense.

### RIBA (USURY)

Islamic law encourages commercial activities that are conducted among honest parties and do not violate the principles of *Sharia*. Islamic law condemns profits made by illegal or immoral means. This has resulted in the Islamic law's prohibition of usury in contracts. This issue is usually referred to as *Riba*.[2]

Islamic *Sharia* law believes that usury – *Riba* – is enrichment without justification, which upsets the balance of reciprocal benefits. Islamic scholars have defined *Riba* as "a monetary advantage without equivalent counterpart which has been stipulated in favor of one of the contracting parties on the exchange of valuables of a monetary type".[3]

As some scholars have indicated: "Riba always implies a transaction which presupposes an exchange where the equivalent of the benefits was not respected. This upsets the balance of the reciprocal obligations of the parties, and consequently the economic basis of the contract is upset." Under Islamic law, *Riba* means obtaining a gain without an equivalent return, which amounts to enrichment without justification.[4]

To sum up, the *Riba* prohibited by the *Quran* is any profit that is not obtained in a proper manner and does not represent any work but only an unwarranted gain due to luck or delay, like dramatically increasing the sum due from a debtor. As explained above, *Riba* is an unbalanced exchange of goods or money. If the money or goods exchanged are of the same amount or of an identical nature, then the goods or money exchanged should be exactly the same.

Certain Islamic scholars have tried to apply the prohibition on *Riba* strictly, but others extend the application of the prohibition not only to loans with interest but also to every kind of debt and benefit in the form of money or goods due from one person to an other.

It is important to note that *Riba* as explained above does not prohibit all increase or profit or gain. This fact is confirmed by *Quranic* verse: "But God has permitted sale and forbidden usury."[5]

This extension of the prohibition of *Riba* to interest has resulted in problems covering a variety of commercial activities in the Arab world.

In the next couple of paragraphs, I will try to show how Arab countries in the Middle East have dealt with this issue.

In accordance with Islamic law, every contract including *Riba* is *fasid*, i.e. invalid or vitiated.[6]

The prohibition of *Riba* has been interpreted by some scholars to include any interest resulting from extending credit and any banking operation or any trading of any type that includes payment of interest. Some have gone so far as to say that the theory of *Riba* are no longer limited to loans at interest but also extend to include all benefits in the form of sums of money or articles owed by one person to another and giving rise to profit for one of the parties without a corresponding advantage for the other.[7]

Certain Arab countries, such as the United Arab Emirates, Egypt, Syria, Iraq, Oman, Libya, Lebanon and Kuwait, have for a long time allowed the allocation of interest. The civil and commercial codes of these countries are influenced by Western legal theories. The codes introduced in these countries allow interest in trading and banking operations.

Therefore, if the applicable law in an arbitration is the law of one of said countries, a Western lawyer is not expected to face major problems in dealing with the issue of interest.

Article 226 of the Egyptian Civil Code allows interest on loans. In civil matters, the interest rate is 4% annually. In commercial matters, the interest rate is 5% annually, as compensation for the delay in repaying the money from the date of the judicial demand or according to the date determined by commercial custom or the parties' agreement. Article 227 of the Egyptian Civil Code allows the parties to agree to an interest rate of no more than 7%.[8] Furthermore, in certain commercial matters, Article 50 of the new Egyptian Commercial Code, enacted on May 17, 1999, allows a rate of interest equivalent to the interest rate declared by the Egyptian Central Bank, which currently stands at approximately 10% per annum.

In Articles 227 and 228, the Syrian Civil Code allows interest in a similar fashion as the Egyptian Civil Code, with the sole exception that the parties can agree to an annual interest rate of up to 9% annually.[9]

In Articles 227 and 228, the Libyan Civil Code, as initially promulgated by the Kingdom, allows for interest in a similar fashion as the Egyptian Civil Code, with the sole exception that the parties can agree to an annual interest rate of up to 10% annually.[10]

It is interesting that Arab countries that allow the application of interest in the case of a delay in repayment of amounts owed do not require the creditor to show any actual damages as a result of said delay. In accordance with the different Arab Civil Codes, the interest starts accruing under certain conditions,[11] including:

(i)   There must be an obligation to pay an amount of money such as a loan, rent or a financial due.

(ii)  The monetary obligation on which interest will start accruing could result from a contractual obligation or a statutory obligation, such as an obligation to pay alimony.

(iii) The monetary obligation should be specifically known and quantified at the time of demand. The issue is left to the judge to evaluate at the time of litigation, thus allowing interest on compensation demanded for contractual reasons or for an illicit act (delictual liability).

(iv) For interest to start accruing on the monetary obligations, there must either be a judicial demand for the principal debt in addition to interest, or the parties must have agreed on a specific date, or commercial custom dictates a specific date, or the law mentions another date. In the case of contradiction between custom and the agreement of the parties, the agreement of the parties prevails.

The Arab countries that allow interest all have a ceiling on such interest, such as 7% in Egypt, 9% in Syria and 10% in Libya. If the parties agree on a higher interest rate, this is considered a violation of public order and the penalty for such a violation is that the interest rate is reduced to the maximum allowed under the legal interest rate.[12]

Civil law in the Arab countries that allow the application of interest does not allow compound interest but allows simple interest that does not exceed the amount of the principal, provided there a no commercial customs or rules indicating otherwise and allowing compound interest and/or interest exceeding the principal, such as the case in bank loans and overdrafts.[13]

On the other hand, certain other Arab countries such as Saudi Arabia still prohibit interest, which they regard as a prohibited kind of *Riba*, and there are ongoing efforts to tailor financial transactions in such a way as not to violate this prohibition of interest.

Some types of banking operations are prohibited as a result of this strict interpretation of *Riba* in Saudi Arabia, such as:

(i) bank loans;

(ii) advances on account;

(iii) discount bills of exchange;

(iv) transfers of commercial claims for collection; and

(v) documentary credits.

Alternative banking techniques were conceived in order to conform to the prohibition of interest by *Sharia* law, including:

1.  *Mudarabat* partnership *in commendam* – one partner financing but not active);

2.  *Musharakat* partnership or association);

3.  *Murabahat* (resale with agreed margin of profit, contract between two or more persons trading with joint capital, dividing profit or loss according to agreement);

4.  *Ijara* (lease agreement); and

5.  *Ijarat wa iqtina* (lease purchase agreement).

## 1. Mudarabat[14]

*Mudarabat* is a contract of partnership between at least two parties, with one or more providing finance or capital but not active and the other party providing skills – active – with the agreement that they share the profits.[15]

According to Islamic banks, *Mudarabat* is an agreement under which the bank advances money to be utilized in a specific project in return for a prearranged percentage in the case of profits. Needless to say, there is a certain amount of risk for the bank, because if there are losses there will be no profit distribution. This also requires the bank to make sure that it is undertaking *Mudarabat* with persons who have the ability and skill to successfully run projects. Due to that risk, the bank in some cases acts as an intermediary – i.e. a paid agent – for putting the parties together in a *Mudarabat* agreement.

## 2. Musharakat[16]

*Musharakat* is a partnership in which two or more parties participate, sharing the losses and gains between them. Normally, the share of profits or losses is similar to the percentage of ownership in the capital. In *Musharakat*, all parties participate actively in the management of the project. There is a certain element of risk that the project may suffer losses instead of profits, and the choice of partners is accordingly very important.[17]

## 3. Murabahat[18]

*Murabahat* is a system commonly used by Islamic banks whereby the bank agrees to finance the purchase of certain goods, equipment, spare parts, commodities and so forth that are needed by the client and then resells them to the client at an agreed margin of profit on the original cost. In other words, this transaction can be described as a promise of sale by the bank for an agreed margin with regard to specific goods required by the client of the bank.[19]

## 4. Ijar[20]

In the system of *Ijar*, the client needs certain equipment or property, the bank buys said equipment or property and then rents it to the client in exchange for rent or periodical payments. The property or equipment is under the control and disposal of the client, who therefore bears the risk of loss as well as paying the rent. In some cases, *Ijar* includes the possibility – not the obligation – that the client may have the option to buy the equipment or property at the end of the lease. Needless to say, the element of risk in this type of transaction is greatly reduced.[21]

## 5. Ijaratwa Iqtina[22]

*Ijarat wa iqtina* is a system whereby the Islamic bank finances the acquisition of material in its own name and then rents this material to the client in return for regular, prearranged instalments that are paid into a joint account.

These instalments include a fee for the bank for undertaking this activity. After all instalments are paid, the material becomes the property of the client. Under this type of transaction – unlike in the case of *Ijar* – the client is obliged to buy whatever he has previously rented.[23]

CONCLUSION

To conclude, interest is allowed in most countries of the Middle East, with the exception of Saudi Arabia, where the Islamic banking system has established certain alternative techniques that enable it to play an important role in the different economies of the Middle East without violating Islamic *Sharia* law as interpreted in Saudi Arabia.

Arab countries that allow interest only allow simple interest that does not exceed the amount of the principal and does not require the creditor to show actual damages as a result of the delay in repayment of the amount owed.

## END NOTES

[1] Although the term *Riba* is always translated into English as "usury" or "interest", it also encompasses the concepts of "increase" or "gain" under *Sharia* law.

[2] On the issue of interest in Arab countries, see generally Nayla Comair-Obeid, *The Law of Business Contracts in the Middle East* (Kluwer Law International, 1996) pp. 40-64.

[3] On the issue of interest in Arab countries, see generally Nabil Salah, *Unlawful Gain and Legitimate Profit in Islamic Law* (Graham and Trotman, 1992) pp. 11-60.

[4] Comair-Obeid, *supra* note 2, at p. 44.

[5] Salah, *supra* note 3, at p. 17.

[6] Comair-Obeid, *supra* note 2, at p. 45.

[7] Ibid., at p. 53.

[8] On the issue of interest and related matters in Egyptian civil law, see generally the work of a great Egyptian authority on Egyptian civil law, Abd al Razzak El Sanhuri, *El Wassit Fi Shareh El Kannon El Madani* (Dar El Maaraf, Alexandria, 2004) pp. 824-864.

[9] Ibid., at p. 826.

[10] Ibid., at p. 826.

[11] Ibid., at pp. 828-831.

[12] Ibid., at pp. 843-845.

[13] Ibid., at pp. 857-864.

[14] Comair-Obeid, *supra* note 2, at pp. 179-180.

[15] Salah, *supra* note 3, at pp. 131-143.

[16] Comair-Obeid, *supra* note 2, at p. 181.

[17] Salah, *supra* note 3, at pp. 113-117.

[18] Comair-Obeid, *supra* note 2, at pp. 182-183.

[19] Salah, *supra* note 3, at pp. 117-120.

[20] Comair-Obeid, *supra* note 2, at p. 183.

[21] Salah, *supra* note 3, at p. 120.

[23] Comair-Obeid, *supra* note 2, at p. 184.

[24] Salah, *supra* note 3, at p. 122.

# 8

# A practitioner's approach to interest claims under *Sharia* Law in international arbitration

*By* **Homayoon Arfazadeh**
*Attorney at law, Python & Peter, Geneva*
*Lecturer, Geneva Graduate Institute of International
and Development Studies*

## I.   INTRODUCTION: THREE CAUTIONARY REMARKS

In this paper, I shall examine the difficulties raised by interest claims under *Sharia* law in international arbitration from the perspective of a European practitioner. As a preliminary, however, I would like to make three cautionary remarks.

First, there is no unified body of *Sharia* law. Rather, there are different schools of *Sharia* law within each tradition of Islam, notably the Sunnite and the Shiite traditions.[1] Furthermore, there seems to be plurality of opinion within each school, especially in the Shiite tradition, which ignores *Ghiyas* (analogy) as a source of *Sharia* law and places more weight on *Aghl* (reasoning) and *Ijtehad* (opinion) as dynamic sources of *Sharia* law.

Second, one should carefully distinguish between national laws that I would call "*Sharia* compatible" and *Sharia* law *per se*. The distinction is important because parties to international contracts sometimes refer to a specific school of *Sharia* law – as is increasingly done in the banking and finance industry in the Middle East and South East Asia – rather than to a *Sharia*-compatible national law as the law that should govern their contract. A *Sharia*-compatible national law remains the law of a specific state as interpreted and applied by the courts and authorities of that state. In contrast, *Sharia* law *per se* is interpreted by religious authorities and institutions that often remain independent from the state.

Third, *Sharia*-compatible finance is one of the fastest growing sectors of international banking. From Beirut and Dubai to Kuala Lumpur, all major banks are engaged in an intensive effort to develop their *Sharia* finance sector. In some instances, however, "*Sharia*" is simply a marketing brand for predominantly common law contracts drafted by English lawyers and aimed at attracting Muslim clients. The growing influence of common law in *Sharia* banking is rather paradoxical, since, historically and structurally, the civil law tradition has been more successful in melding with *Sharia* concepts and traditions.

## II.  WHAT IS *SHARIA* LAW AND HOW COULD IT BECOME RELEVANT TO INTERNATIONAL ARBITRATION?

International arbitrators can be confronted with *Sharia* law in three different ways: (1) the law applicable to the dispute is a national law that is *Sharia* compatible; (2) the parties have expressly chosen *Sharia* as the governing law of their contract; or (3) the final award may need to be enforced in a *Sharia*-compatible jurisdiction.

Faced with the growing attraction to *Sharia* law in various parts of the world, some arbitration institutions, such as the Kuala Lumpur Regional Center for Arbitration (KLRCA), have begun enacting specific rules for *Sharia* banking and finance arbitrations.[2] Parties can opt into this specific arbitration regime when drafting an arbitration clause or after a dispute has arisen.

Three provisions distinguish the KLRCA Rules for Islamic Banking and Financial Services Arbitration from the general regime that is based on the UNCITRAL arbitration rules and remain applicable to all other international arbitrations.[3] The most significant of these three is Article 33 of the KLRCA Rules, according to which arbitrators should stay the arbitration and refer disputed issues that are governed by – or concern – *Sharia* law to a *Sharia* Council for prior determination.[4] Article 33 thus supports the opinion that *Sharia* law is more about the exercise of *authority* by *Sharia* institutions than the mere application of pre-established *rules*.

As regards the focus of this paper – a claim for interest under *Sharia* law – the answer would seem straightforward and rather uncontroversial: an interest claim would be prohibited by all traditions and schools of *Sharia* law.

The prohibition of interest, however, is not the end but only the beginning of the story.

Indeed, *Sharia* law offers a broad range of alternative claims or remedies that could constitute valuable substitutes for a claim for interest. Such alternative claims can take the form of damages for late payment or late performance, claims for sharing or disgorging profits made by the defaulting party, as well as other forms of penalty as provided for by contract or custom. The main requirement, under *Sharia*, is that such financial damages need to be *proven* and cannot simply be presumed.

As we shall see below, the prohibition of interest under *Sharia* law is not incompatible with international arbitration law and/or practice; conversely, the awarding of interest by international arbitral tribunals is not necessarily incompatible with *Sharia* law.

## III. *SHARIA* PROHIBITION OF INTEREST AND PUBLIC POLICY

On the first leg of the question – is the *Sharia* prohibition of interest incompatible with international law and practice? – one could begin by mentioning recent awards, in particular form ICSID,[5] which have referred to Article 38 of the ILC Articles on State Responsibility (providing for "full recovery of damages" resulting from the breach of an international obligation) as evidence that the payment of interest – and in some instances compound interest – has become an integral part of customary international law.

Can the *Sharia* prohibition of interest be considered as contrary to customary international law and/or incompatible with international public policy?

The issue was addressed by the Swiss Federal Tribunal in an unpublished decision dismissing an appeal against an ICC arbitral award rendered in Switzerland concerning a dispute governed by Iranian law.[6] The circumstances of the case can be summarized as follows. After the 1979 revolution, Iranian law prohibited interest in compliance with the requirements of *Sharia* law as enshrined in Articles 43 and 49 of the Iranian Constitution. In 1988, however, the Iranian Guardian Council (or Constitutional Council) rendered an opinion to the effect that Iranian nationals and public entities could, notwithstanding the prohibition of interest and as matter of exception allowed by *Sharia* principles, claim and receive interest for late payment from foreign parties. Relying on the Guardian Council's opinion, the Iranian party had introduced a claim for interest over damages and late payments before the ICC arbitral tribunal. A distinguished panel of arbitrators dismissed the claim for interest based on the finding that interest had been prohibited after the 1979 revolution and that the exception provided by the Guardian Council in 1988 was discriminatory and thus contrary to international public policy, since it only applied to interest claimed by an Iranian party against a foreign party and not the other way around.[7] The Iranian party moved for a partial annulment of the final award before the Swiss Federal Tribunal, on the grounds that the refusal to award interest notwithstanding the opinion of the Guardian Council amounted to a violation of public policy as provided by Article 190(2)(e) PIL. The Swiss Federal Tribunal dismissed the request for annulment by holding that the right to receive interest is not, *per se*, a right protected by international public policy:

> "As such, the Claimant fails to indicate ... why a refusal to award late payment interest would be, per se, in contradiction with the legal order and the relevant system of values [to the public policy exception]. Furthermore, one fails to see how the question of interest would be of relevance to public policy since it is, in particular under Swiss law, a matter over which the parties can freely decide (subject to a few exceptions, such as general restrictions to the freedom of the parties, and specific restrictions destined at the prevention of abuse, in particular abusive rates), and with regard to which a waiver is admissible. Public policy does therefore not require in any manner – and the Claimant does not demonstrate the contrary – that all claims should bear interest."[8]

Yet, in another unpublished Swiss decision, an Iranian seller was successful in obtaining interest for late payment from a European buyer on the basis of Iranian law and notwithstanding the general prohibition of interest under *Sharia* law. In that case, the contract that was concluded prior to the Iranian revolution had specifically provided for 10% annual interest for any delay in the payment of the purchase price. In defence, the European company had argued the invalidity of the contractual clause providing for late payment interest under post-revolutionary Iranian law. In reply, the Iranian party invoked the exception provided by the 1988 Opinion of the Guardian Council to the effect that Iranian parties are not barred from claiming interest from their foreign debtors. The European company in turn argued that the exception was discriminatory and thus contrary to international public policy. Before the Court, however, the Iranian claimant successfully argued that the public policy exception has only a "negative" effect and should not preclude the application of foreign law, except when its application leads to concrete and effective discrimination.[9] In the instant case, the concrete result of applying the Guardian Council's opinion was to uphold the validity of a contractual clause providing for the payment of interest which, by and of itself, did not lead to any discriminatory results.

This brings me to the second leg of the question: is an international arbitral award ordering the payment of interest contrary to *Sharia* law or the public policy of a *Sharia*-compatible jurisdiction?

In my experience, parties from *Sharia*-compatible countries rarely hesitate to introduce claims *equivalent* to "interest" in the form of alternative remedies for the *compensation of effective and concrete damages* that are perfectly compatible with most schools of *Sharia* law. When *Sharia* has an impact on the case (directly as the law applicable to the merits or indirectly as the law of the possible place of the enforcement of the award), it belongs to the counsel for the parties to be creative and to justify their claim for interest under these *Sharia*-compatible alternative remedies. As stated above, such alternative remedies can consist of proven financial damages resulting from late payment or late performance or claims for sharing or disgorging profits made by the defaulting party, as well as various other forms of penalty that can be provided by contract or recognized by custom.

This is demonstrated, for instance, by an ICC arbitral award rendered in Switzerland between two Saudi parties, which, notwithstanding the general prohibition of interest or *Riba* under the applicable Saudi law, awarded the claimant interest for late payment as an alternative remedy and corresponding to the significant rate of inflation in Saudi Arabia during the relevant period.[10]

Such alternative *Sharia*-compatible remedies are also available, for instance, under Swiss law. Article 106 of the Swiss Code of Obligations (CO) provides for compensatory interest that, if proven by claimant, can go well beyond the statutory late payment interest provided by Article 104 CO (*intérêt moratoire*). Conversely, Article 423 CO allows for the disgorgement or restitution of profits when, for example, the defaulting party has drawn or obtained undue profits from cash or property withheld from the claimant in breach of contractual obligations. In some cases, the amount of restitution can well exceed the simple or even compound interest. The compensation and claims awarded on the basis of Articles 106 or 423 CO remain, in principle, perfectly compatible with *Sharia* law and enforceable in *Sharia*-compatible jurisdictions, even if the amounts awarded exceed simple or compound interest.

## IV. CONCLUSION

Notwithstanding the general prohibition of interest under *Sharia* law, a mildly creative and well-informed party could seek full recovery of its damages under the alternative remedies provided by *Sharia* law. These damages could go well beyond the simple interest awarded by, for instance, Article 104 of the Swiss Code of Obligations, and the ensuing award should in principle be recognized in all *Sharia*-compatible jurisdictions.

## END NOTES

[1] See the contribution by Tarek Fouad A. Riad in this volume: 'The Issue of Interest in Middle East Laws and Islamic Law'.

[2] KLRCA Rules for Islamic Banking and Financial Services Arbitration, available at: <http://www.rcakl.org.my/pdf/Rules%20for%20arbitration%2010.pdf>.

[3] These are:

- Article 33 which requires reference of the dispute from arbitrators to Sharia "Council" or Expert whenever the dispute raises a Sharia relevant issue ;

- Article 39 on applicable law and

- Article 18 (3) which provides that deposit and advance on costs shall be maintained on a non-interest bearing bank account.

[4] According to Rule 2, the *Sharia* "Council" is an advisory council established by the Central Bank of Malaysia and the Malaysian Securities Commission.

[5] See *Siemens A.G.* v. *Argentine Republic*, ICSID case ARB/02/8, Award, 6 February 2007.

[6] Swiss Federal Tribunal Decision 4p.267/1996 and 4p.271/1996 of November 3, 1997 in an appeal against an ICC arbitral award.

[7] In its appeal before the Swiss Federal Tribunal, the Iranian claimant had argued that the exception provided by the Guardian Council was aimed at creating equality and not discrimination between Iranian and foreign parties in international trade, since the latter continued to claim and receive interest from Iranian counterparts in foreign jurisdictions. This argument was apparently not fully developed before the Arbitral Tribunal.

[8] *"En effet, le recourant omet d'indiquer ... en quoi le refus d'allour des intérêts de retard apparaîtrait, en soi, en opposition avec l'ordre juridique et le système de valeur déterminants. On ne voit pas d'ailleurs pas en quoi la question des intérêts relèverait de l'ordre public, puisqu'il s'agit, en particulier en droit suisse, d'un point au sujet duquel les parties peuvent en principe librement disposer, (sous réserve des restrictions particulières destinées à prévenir les abus, notamment des taux abusifs), et pour lequel une renonciation est possible. L'ordre public n'exige dès lors nullement – et le recourant ne tente pas la démonstration du contraire – que toute créance porte nécessairement intérêts..."*. Ibid., at p. 9

[9] See Homayoon Arfazadeh, *Ordre Public et Arbitrage International à l'Epreuve de la Mondialisation* (2006) p. 176 et seq.

[10] Published in *YB Com. Arb.*, Vol. XXII (1997) at p. 87 et seq. The Arbitral Tribunal awarded 5% annual interest, which by chance corresponds to the statutory interest provided for by Art. 104 of the Swiss Code of Obligations. Ibid., at p. 90.

**9**

# Present-day valuation in international arbitration: a conceptual framework for awarding interest

*By* **Thierry J. Sénéchal, MBA/MPA**
*Policy Manager,*
*Banking Commission,*
*Financial Services and Insurance Commission,*
*International Chamber of Commerce*

## I. INTRODUCTION

In international arbitration, there is often a significant delay between the time when the injury occurs and the time when the decision is rendered by the arbitral tribunal. Consequently, arbitrators and parties are often confronted by the challenging question of how to deal with the passage of time and to propose with confidence a method to adjust the award to present-day value.[1] Despite the fact that an overwhelming body of international law jurisprudence supports the general proposition that the award should include an interest component, there is still considerable uncertainty concerning the calculation of interest. Consequently, the use of interest in international arbitration is often dependent on the circumstances at hand and tribunals with a wide discretion in respect of awarding interest.

In this article, we argue that, in international arbitration, the question of interest can be as important as the valuation of the loss itself. Indeed, awards of interest may in some cases exceed the principal owed because of extensive delays between the occurrence of the underlying injury and the resulting award. We strongly advocate that an international standard should be developed for awarding interest. Such a standard is required to ensure that a party is made whole after being deprived of the opportunity to earn a return on the use of its money. To help arbitrators and parties decide what interest can be reasonably and consistently applied, we introduce a conceptual framework based on a set of five principles.

## II. LACK OF A UNIVERSALLY ACCEPTED SET OF STANDARDS FOR THE CALCULATION OF INTEREST IN ARBITRATION AWARDS

There is an important body of international jurisprudence supporting the point that interest should be awarded by arbitration tribunals.[2] One can easily browse the decisions rendered by international arbitral tribunals, human rights courts, international claims commissions and settlement procedures and national courts to find out that interest has been extensively discussed in many instances. However, we should also note that many of these international tribunals have failed to adopt a standardized and uniform approach for applying interest. Not surprisingly, resolving interest claims in international arbitration is often a process fraught with uncertainty and confusion, typically leading to a set of inconsistent decisions and diverging jurisprudence concerning present-day valuation. Today, interest is still applied in many different ways under applicable arbitration rules, not to mention the fact that many of such rules are currently silent as to interest.[3]

The lack of consensus for awarding interest in international arbitration is surprising indeed. The concept of interest is not new and obscure. The finance industry, for instance, has been applying interest for centuries. It is a standard business practice in the banking sector with clearly identified calculation rules and models. Consequently, it is unclear why tribunals hearing disputes between transnational contracting parties have not been able to reach a consensus on how to award interest, i.e. on a simple or compound basis.[4]

## III. A CONCEPTUAL FRAMEWORK FOR INTEREST

In this article, we propose to develop a conceptual framework for fulfilling the arbitrators' and/or parties' goal of developing a satisfactory approach to interest. We advocate that such an approach should be clearly principles-based, internationally consistent and coherent. Such a framework is needed to act as a map to give coherence to the application of present-day valuation.

We have conducted our analysis as follows:

(a) with the objective that the conceptual framework can be applied in most instances where present-day valuation is required;

(b) under the assumption that tribunals have to keep pace with modern financial practices and standards when awarding interest;

(c) by making clear references to concepts applicable within the finance industry; and

(d) by providing options to the reader when deciding on the applicability of specific interest rates, with reference to some examples and pointing out the weaknesses of some approaches.

It is important to note that this article is written from the perspective of a valuation practitioner and not from a legal perspective. Consequently, we do not discuss situations where the parties are legally bound to a specific methodology concerning interest, usually under constraints or prohibitions from a domestic legal system. We thus aim to provide a practical approach to the concept of interest. Our main concern has been to present complex material in a manner that is readily understood.[5] The end notes provide the interested reader with additional sources of reference.

In the following figure, we provide an outline of our step-by-step conceptual framework.

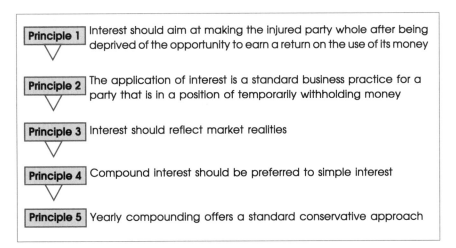

Principle 1 — Interest should aim at making the injured party whole after being deprived of the opportunity to earn a return on the use of its money

Principle 2 — The application of interest is a standard business practice for a party that is in a position of temporarily withholding money

Principle 3 — Interest should reflect market realities

Principle 4 — Compound interest should be preferred to simple interest

Principle 5 — Yearly compounding offers a standard conservative approach

**Principle 1: Interest should aim at making the injured party whole after being deprived of the opportunity to earn a return on the use of its money**

In the finance industry, it is implicit that an investment should be seen as an expenditure of money today in order to create value in the future. As such, businesses actually compare a dollar today to the promise held today to receive a dollar in one year. Indeed, the former is worth more than the latter, and this is why investment is being generated at a rate commensurate to the risk undertaken and the passage of time. When analyzing a business or investment loss, it is therefore logical to consider the loss of "return" opportunity between the time of injury and the time of award.

Under our first principle, we argue that the arbitral tribunal should always strive to place the claimant in the same position as it would have been in had no injury or loss occurred. This is why interest should be part of compensation to account for the passage of time after the date of injury. If there were no delay, a claimant would be made whole by the tribunal's award. However, abnormally lengthy delays in the payment of compensation to the injured party may lead to increased financial loss for the party suffering the loss, leading to a position of uncertainty, especially in times of monetary depreciation. In awarding interest to account for the passage of time, the tribunal rightly recognizes that the injured party is justly compensated not only for the original injury or loss but also for the passage of time between the date of injury or loss and the date of full reinstatement (i.e. final sentence or payment of the award).

Consequently, the award of interest should be generally based on what the injured party probably would have obtained if it had invested its money during the time it was deprived of this money. The failure to adjust awards to a present-day value by compensatory interest[6] would cause obvious economic harm to claimants and provide a windfall to respondents on the grounds that there is often a significant delay between the date of injury and the date of award.

**Principle 2: The application of interest is a standard business practice for a party that is in a position of temporarily withholding money**

The concept of interest is very old, dating back to the Sumerian and Egyptian cultures.[7] The Egyptians and Sumerians had also devised a specific word for interest, "*ms*", which means "to give birth". Not surprisingly, references to the concept can be found in the historical record, for example in the religious texts of the Abrahamic religions that discussed the notion of excessive interest. In ancient times, the theory of interest was a natural concept for a pastoral society. If one lends someone a herd of thirty cattle for one year, one expects to be repaid with more than thirty cattle. In the Uruk period, the practice of lending money at interest was quite developed, and a complex system for recording contractual obligations was invented. Interest is also found throughout the Middle Ages with different interpretations, and in the Renaissance era greater mobility of people facilitated the spread of the practice of borrowing of money at interest. In today's financial world, interest also reflects the price paid for borrowing money, expressed as a percentage rate over a period of time to reflect the rate of exchange of present consumption for future consumption. Interest charging is a standard practice in money markets, bond markets and option and futures markets. By far the most common form in which financial assets are lent by banks is money, but other assets may be lent to the borrower at an interest charge (i.e. shares, consumer goods, equipment, etc.), interest being considered as a "rent on money".[8]

We have argued that interest is used all over the world and that it is a standard business practice. We should make a special note regarding Islamic finance. More specifically, Islam traditionally prohibits *Riba* or the use of interest.[9] Though the term *Riba* literally means "increase", it has been variously interpreted over the recent years, sometimes as usury, more often as any kind of interest. Still, today, most of the leading Islamic finance specialists accept that time must be priced. Although they still object to the fixed, predetermined aspects of interest-based lending with its inherent risk of lender exploiting borrower, Islamic finance currently aims to replicate in Islamic form the substantive functions of modern financial instruments, markets and institutions.[10]

Overall, we can safely conclude that in most countries of the world, whether in Europe, Oceania, Asia or America, the award of interest is a standard business practice. This leads us to articulate our second principle: interest should consistently apply whenever a claimant is in a position of temporarily withholding money. It is a standard business practice to award interest to people and organizations willing to give up the temporary use of their money, and this principle should equally be applied in international arbitration and litigation.

## Principle 3: Interest should reflect market realities and be inclusive of inflation and market risk premium

In international arbitration, a tribunal reviewing a claim for interest will generally first examine all documents and circumstances giving rise to the dispute to see whether it can find an indication of an agreement, if any, concerning the application of interest. If a convention has been predetermined, we would suggest that the tribunal follow the parties' intentions and award interest in accordance with the existing convention. In the absence of a contractual interest provision, we advocate that the tribunal should strive to develop a methodology that would take into account market realities surrounding the injury.[11]

We strongly believe that the injured party is entitled to interest reflecting market realities. Consequently, we argue that the appropriate interest should equal the risk-free rate (inclusive of inflation) plus a market risk premium to account for the fact that the injured party, at the time of injury, could have invested the aforementioned resources elsewhere in order to earn a rate of return available on its market of reference.[12] Indeed, an individual or corporation investing money for repayment at a later point in time expects to be compensated for the time value of money or for not having the use of that money while it is invested.

We now provide a step-by-step framework for arriving at the most appropriate interest on a fair market basis.

*Step 1: Inflation should be included in the interest*

Prices go up every year, and we could rightly argue that a claimant will seek to be compensated, as a minimum, for that loss of purchasing power. This statement is obvious in the finance world. Without interest that is at least equal to or above the inflation rate, lenders would not be willing to lend or to temporarily give up the ability to spend and savers would be less willing to defer spending. That is why we argue that inflation should be embedded in the interest when adjusting to present-day value.

It is noted that the measure of inflation is readily available in most countries. Inflation is defined as a sustained increase in the general level of prices for goods and services. It is measured as an annual percentage increase. As inflation rises, every dollar you own buys a smaller percentage of a good or service. Let us take an example. For determining the UK inflation rate, we can refer to the UK Consumer Price Index (or CPI), which is based on a composite consumer price index showing changes in purchasing power between 1997 and today.[13] The source of information is widely available, and we can, for instance, use a composite price index for analysis of consumer price inflation, or the purchasing power of the pound, over long periods of time. The CPI is a statistical measure of a weighted average of prices of a specified set of goods and services purchased by wage earners. It is an index that tracks retail prices of a specified set of consumer goods and services, providing a measure of inflation. The CPI is a fixed-quantity price index and effectively represents a cost-of-living index. In the following graph, we show fluctuations in the CPI over the last ten years.

**UK Inflation based on Consumer Price Index**

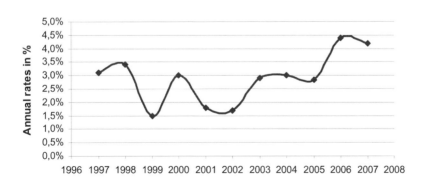

For an arbitration tribunal, the measure of inflation already provides an indication of the minimum bound for awarding interest, assuming that the parties would agree to accept the assumption of interest being equal to the inflation rate. As illustrated in the above graph, it would be easy to pick up a specific date or use an average for a determined period of time. However, we do not recommend using inflation itself as a proxy of the interest rate. One major drawback of an inflation-based method is its vulnerability to macroeconomic shocks and turbulence, i.e. devaluation and exchange rate exposures. Such turbulence can impact inflation and interest in different proportions. Furthermore, in the investment world, interest is rarely equivalent to the rate of inflation.

*Step 2: Determination of risk profile*

We now turn to the question of risk. People are either risk-adverse or risk-takers, and arbitral tribunals should recognize this fact when deciding what interest rate to apply. It is common for businesses to seek to secure different interest rates. The risk-adverse businessman will probably invest in government bonds and risk-free investments, while the risk-taking businessman will seek a higher return. When investing or placing capital into a project in China today, the investor is expecting a return based on a specific risk preference. Bear in mind that the investor always has a certain risk profile in mind when making the investment decision.

The level of political, economic and/or business risks to be undertaken by an individual investor is indeed a matter of preference. It is clear that the investor will want to be compensated for the risks undertaken in making the investment, Therefore, the investor should not only be compensated for inflation risks but also for systematic and regulatory risks. Such risks include the possibility of default or the inability to fulfil the originally agreed upon terms. In international arbitration, it is important for the tribunal to account for the underlying risk profile of the assets that form the object of the dispute. For instance, when computing an interest rate for a business loss, the tribunal will have to determine the risk profile of the investment. It should be noted that rational investors would usually not invest at a rate below the risk-free rate available in the market.

As a minimum, the rate of interest to be used for adjusting the award to present-day value should be equal to or above the risk-free rate. This rate represents the interest an investor would expect from an absolutely risk-free investment over a specified period of time. It usually includes inflation. Consequently, the risk-free rate is the minimum return an investor expects for any investment, since he or she would not bear any risk unless the potential rate of return is greater than the risk-free rate.

For a transnational commercial dispute, we advocate the use of an interest rate that reflects market realities. The rationale for using such an approach is based on the assumption that businesses will generally tend to demand an extra payoff above the risk-free rate for investing in assets with some level of risk. The *raison d'être* of businesses is to seek higher returns based on their risk profile. Incorporated investors and businesses will not usually invest at the risk-free rate. In international arbitration, arbitrators and parties should recognize that the claimant will seek to maximize profits and earn incremental returns on its investments that are proportional to the amount of additional risk those investments add to its portfolio.

### Step 3: The cost of capital or borrowing cost as a proxy for interest

Some experts or lawyers may be tempted to argue that the appropriate interest rate for adjusting an award to present-day value could be derived from the claimant's cost of capital or internal borrowing rate. It would be theoretically correct to assume that the award of interest can be envisaged on such a basis. However, we do not recommend using the cost of capital or the internal borrowing rate for adjusting an award to present-day value unless the claimant demonstrates in a credible manner how to arrive at such an opportunity cost.

The cost of capital is defined as the return that needs to be earned by a firm in order for the financial markets to be prepared to invest in that firm's security. It represents a measure used for discounting investment cash flows on specific projects and for pricing products. While it would be theoretically accurate to award interest on a cost of capital basis, it is problematic from a practical standpoint. In practice, it may be very difficult for a claimant to demonstrate how it arrived at such a cost of capital. The cost of capital can be difficult to derive because it is based on too many assumptions, including the fact that financial markets are dominated by rational, risk-averse investors seeking to maximize satisfaction from return on their investment and that markets are efficient, frictionless and without imperfections like transaction costs, taxes and restrictions on borrowing and short-selling.

In addition, the cost of capital model usually assumes that investors base their judgment on a common time horizon. As a result, the cost of capital approach can be costly to determine and may well lead to a "battle of the experts".

The claimant or respondent's borrowing rate may be used to derive the interest, but such a rate based on the costs of borrowing may be difficult to derive and may rely heavily on judgment. Indeed, it can be challenging to estimate the borrowing rate or cost of debt for a particular company. The "total debt" ratio of a firm is defined as the ratio of short-term and long-term debt, finance leases and preferred stock to the value of the firm (market capitalization plus book value of debt). In other words, the cost of debt is equivalent to the risk-free rate plus a margin that reflects the credit and market risk of the debt issued by a company. This market risk of debt is often difficult to estimate and depends on many assumptions and variables that could lead to arbitrary results.

Three methods can be proposed to derive the cost of borrowing:

- **Method 1:** The first method consists of taking into account the observed interest margins payable over the risk-free rate over the years, averaging them and adding them to the risk-free rates in each year that debt finance is raised. However, this is not so straightforward, because it is indeed cumbersome to apply a series of different risk-free rates to individual borrowings according to the years in which they are made.

- **Method 2:** The second method consists of finding the cost of debt capital based on bond ratings for each of the selected firms. Then the cost of debt can be found by assuming an average debt profile for the company under review and obtaining an average rating. The average rating is indeed difficult to estimate in some cases, and when information is lacking (i.e. because the firm is not publicly traded) it is necessary to estimate the borrowing spreads by comparing corporate issues of similar standing.

- **Method 3:** An intuitive – but not absolutely accurate – method consists of obtaining the ratio of finance charges over the total (or net) debt for similar individual firms over a period of time and then obtaining a weighted average.

    However, this method can only give a crude approximation of the borrowing rate. Using book value for finance charges is a risky business, especially when firms are involved in "creative accounting". Furthermore, such a measure does not differentiate between short-term and long term debt and does not take into account the different risk-free rates in each year that debt finance is raised. Interest charges on zero-coupon bonds would also not appear on the balance sheets of the firms.

In summary, we recommend using an approach that reflects market realities. The cost of borrowing or the cost of capital should only be used when the injured party can persuasively derive such a cost under a set of tested assumptions and using reliable data.

## Principle 4: Compound interest should be preferred to simple interest

One of the most difficult issues confronting an arbitral tribunal is whether to award simple or compound interest. Compound interest differs from simple interest in that the principal balance grows by the amount of interest earned in past periods depending on the stated compounding period (see below). Compound interest is sometimes referred to as the capitalization of interest or as "interest on interest". This type of interest computation is determined on the principal and any interest earned over a period of time. In the simple interest scenario, the interest that accrues each period is not added to the base that is used to calculate interest in future periods. Let us take an example. We want to calculate the interest on EUR 1 000 000 at 5% interest per year for a period of ten years. The formula that we will use for this is the simple interest formula, or:

$$I = Prt$$

Where:

(a) **P** is the principal amount: EUR 1 000 000
(b) **r** is the interest rate: 5% per year or, in decimal form, $5/100 = 0.05$
(c) **t** is the time involved: a 10-year time period

To calculate the simple interest, we multiply EUR 1 000 000 × 0.05 × 10 to find that the interest is EUR 500 000. We can provide an illustration by adjusting an award of EUR 1 000 000 according to different time and interest rate scenarios (on a yearly compounding basis).

*(in EUR)*

| Rate/Time period | 5% | 8% | 12% | 15% |
|---|---|---|---|---|
| 5 years | 1 276 282 | 1 469 328 | 1 790 848 | 2 011 357 |
| 10 years | 1 628 895 | 2 158 925 | 3 105 848 | 4 045 558 |
| 15 years | 2 078 928 | 3 172 169 | 5 473 566 | 8 137 062 |
| 20 years | 2 653 298 | 4 801 021 | 9 646 293 | 16 366 537 |

All other things being equal, compound interest has a larger effect as the time period increases and as the interest rate increases. For instance, over a 10-year time period, the difference between a 5% interest rate and a 15% interest rate is quite significant, i.e. a rise from EUR 1.6 million to EUR 4 million. Consequently, the compounding will have a greater impact at high interest rates and longer periods of time.

There is no real international consensus in international arbitration as to whether or not interest should be awarded on a simple or compound basis. Still, in the finance world, compound interest is the international standard applied in most time value applications. Indeed, the adoption of compound interest reflects the majority of commercial realities, in that a loss of value incurred by a company that is active in normal trading operations implies the loss of the use of that value. Not recognizing this reality would lead to awarding a windfall to the respondent.

## Principle 5: Yearly compounding offers a standard and conservative approach

The choice of the compounding period is crucial. The shorter the compounding period, the faster the principal amount will grow. All other things being equal, compound interest also has a larger effect as the time period and the interest rate increase. To illustrate, the following table shows the final principal amount of an initial investment amount of EUR 1 000 000 after 10 years, at an annual 5% interest rate, with the given compounding periods.

| Periodic compounding P(1 + r/n)Yn (in EUR) | | | | | | |
|---|---|---|---|---|---|---|
| 1 | 2 | 4 | 12 | 52 | 365 | Pe$^{Yr}$ |
| Yearly | Semi-annually | Quarterly | Monthly | Weekly | Daily | Continuous |
| 1 628 895 | 1 638 616 | 1 643 619 | 1 647 009 | 1 648 325 | 1 648 665 | 1 648 721 |

Now, let us use a rate of 15% to demonstrate the effects of rate sensitivity over a principal amount of EUR 1 000 000.

| Periodic compounding P(1 + r/n)Yn (in EUR) | | | | | | |
|---|---|---|---|---|---|---|
| 1 | 2 | 4 | 12 | 52 | 365 | Pe$^{Yr}$ |
| Yearly | Semi-annually | Quarterly | Monthly | Weekly | Daily | Continuous |
| 4045 558 | 4247 851 | 4360 379 | 4440 213 | 4472 022 | 4480 308 | 4481 689 |

There are no prescribed standards for choosing one particular compounding period over another[14] (annually, quarterly, monthly or daily are the most common options). The compounding period usually depends on the financial products chosen by the client. For many products, interest is calculated on a quarterly basis (on March 31, June 30, September 30 and December 31). Other compounding periods are used at the client's request (as a special condition, for example, a compounding period of one year).

For some special products, such as forfaiting transactions or bank-to bank loans, interest is calculated on a semi-annual basis, and in the case of short-term finance even for an exact period (e.g. 90 days).[15] We can easily conclude that, after looking at banking usage, a standard compounding period does not clearly emerge.

We can even complicate the issue further by mentioning the following practices related to compounding:

- Bonds are often compounded on a yearly or semi-annual basis. Corporate bonds are most frequently payable on a semi-annual basis. The amount of interest paid (every six months) is the disclosed interest rate divided by two (multiplied by the principal), the yearly compounded rate being higher than the disclosed rate.

- Mortgage loans generally refer to semi-annual compounding, but sometimes a monthly compounding basis is used (e.g. in the US market).

- Most financial institutions worldwide award interest on a daily (and sometimes bi-monthly) compounded basis for money on deposit.

- Continuous compounding is not widely used. In financial engineering, the valuation of derivatives may use continuous compounding, which is the limit as the compounding period approaches zero. The shorter the compounding period, the faster the principal amount will grow. Different options are available (annually, quarterly, monthly or daily are the most common options).

Different practices can be also applied in different countries. Some countries require financial institutions to have most of their interests on an annual basis, with banks then using several types of interest periods. For instance, for letters of credit and letters of guarantee, compounding could be done quarterly in advance after the first quarter. For loans, the compounding period could be "monthly past the month". It is also noted that interest rates for loans could be calculated on a daily balance and applied monthly. This would obviously result in a compounding effect based on the monthly cycle.

We conclude that there are no prescribed standards for choosing one particular compounding period over another. On the conservative side, we suggest using the yearly approach. Furthermore, the yearly compounding period is implicit in using average annual returns on the market. Clearly, the continuous compounding approach should be banned as it is rarely used. (In financial engineering, the valuation of derivatives may use continuous compounding, which is the limit as the compounding period approaches zero.)

## IV. CONCLUSION

We have argued that, when arbitral tribunals award interest in international arbitration, they should seek to fully compensate the aggrieved party for the loss of the use of money. Indeed, the award of interest should be a significant element in full compensation to reflect the lapse of time between the original injury and the decision of the arbitral tribunal. Notwithstanding the well-established acceptance of interest as a component of compensation, its application often remains an issue subject to the wide discretion of tribunals. This is partly due to the fact that no standardized approach has been developed and accepted by the arbitral community.

We have advocated following existing business practices in regard to the application of interest. Based on the analysis provided in the previous pages, the following are arguments that may be suggested to adjust awards to present-day values:

- Under the first principle, we have argued that interest should aim at making the injured party whole after being deprived of the opportunity to earn a return on the use of its money. A failure to adjust values to the present day would be contrary to well-established international law principles that compensation must be full.

- Under the second principle, we have argued that a failure to adjust values for the passage of time would also be inconsistent with the practice of most of the major modern financial systems. If no adjustment is made for the passage of time, we may conclude that the injured party would be unjustly affected by the lack of opportunity to receive compensation for the temporary withholding of its money.

- Under the third principle, we have clearly stated that the injured party as a corporate entity is entitled to an interest reflecting market realities. We have highlighted that a pure inflation-based approach is flawed for the following reasons: (1) inflation is a monetary phenomenon not related to interest rate policy only (in fact, inflation is influenced by the relative elasticity of different variables, including wages, prices and interest rates); (2) consumer price indices that measure the price of a selection of goods purchased are not always representative; and (3) inflation in itself does not account for the time value of money. As such, international arbitrators should strive to award interest at a fair market rate, taking into account the notion of risk. We have argued that the cost of capital could be used as a proxy but that it can be difficult to determine in some situations, i.e. for non-listed companies and for some regions of the world. We have concluded that we would prefer to use a market-based approach that reflects the fact that investors generally tend to demand an extra payoff above the risk-free rate for investing in assets with some level of risk.

- Under the fourth principle, we have advocated the use of compound interest over simple interest. Although we must admit that there is a line of arbitral authority that has generally awarded simple interest, we strongly advocate reverting to compounding, which is the standard in the financial community. In addition, the usually long delays between the time of injury and the time of the award justify the use of compound interest.

- Under the fifth principle, we have concluded that there are no convergent standards for choosing the compounding period but advocated that yearly compounding seems to be a conservative basis.

In international arbitration, the charging of compensatory interest is logical. A failure to adjust values between the date of the loss and the date of the award would be contrary to the well-established international principle that compensation must be full. This article presents a conceptual framework for assessing compensatory interest in accordance with financial standards and market realities.

## END NOTES

[1] A fundamental question has to be asked regarding the exact date of loss and the date on which interest ceases to accrue, but we leave this issue for another article.

[2] See, e.g., J. Gotanda, 'Awarding Interest in International Arbitration', *American Journal of International Law* (1996).

[3] We have to admit that statutes in many jurisdictions could clearly specify the applicable interest rate on court judgments. However, in this chapter, we only refer to a conceptual framework to be applied to international arbitration and do not make references to specific national laws that would govern the application of interest.

[4] See, e.g., J. Gotanda, 'Compound Interest in International Disputes', Oxford University Comparative Law Forum (2004). This paper provides a thorough analysis of the notion and application of compounded interest.

[5] This chapter does not provide a case study. For a concrete example of how to derive interest rates, see T. Sénéchal, 'Time Value of Money: A Case Study', 4(6) *Transnational Dispute Management* (2007).

[6] It should be clarified that we distinguish between the use of compensatory ("prejudgment" or "pre-award") interest – the interest that is used to account for the lapse of time between the original injury and the arbitral award – and the use of moratory interest, often referred to as "post-judgment" or "post-award interest" because it is related to the delay in acting upon the judgment or award. In this chapter, the main concern is to provide an overview of the use of compensation interest.

[7] See, e.g., S. Homer and S. Richard, *A History of Interest Rates* (New Brunswick, Rutgers University Press, 1991).

[8] See, e.g., S.G. Kellison, *The Theory of Interest* (Homewood, R.D. Irwin Inc., 1970).

[9] A presentation on Islamic finance was provided by Fakihah Azahari at the ICC Banking Commission meeting of April 2007 in Singapore. The details of this presentation can be obtained from the author of this chapter.

[10] See, e.g., M. El-Gamal, *Islamic Finance: Law, Economics and Practice* (Cambridge University Press, 2006).

[11] We do not make references to the constraints that may be imposed by relevant national laws, and we admit that the tribunal may be obliged to apply domestic conventions about choosing an interest rate. This is particularly true for domestic arbitration. See also, e.g., J.M. Colon and M.S. Knoll, 'Prejudgment Interest in International Arbitration', 4(6) *Transnational Dispute Management* (2007).

[12] In this chapter, we do not aim at discussing the impact of foreign currency exchange rates. Still, in a few words, we would like to suggest the following rule. When the parties do not operate in the same market and currency, we recommend computing the loss in the claimant's currency (assuming that the loss is claimed for the claimant's country of operation in which the harm is done), applying an interest rate from that country or market and converting the final award into the appropriate destination currency only at the end.

[13] The UK CPI is based on both official and unofficial sources. In our case, it replaces previous long-run inflation indices produced by the Office for National Statistics, the Bank of England and the House of Commons Library.

[14] The author requested members of the ICC Banking Commission to provide input on the issue of compounding. From the responses provided, it is clear that there exists a great divergence of opinions and practices worldwide. The ICC Banking Commission comprises about 500 members from more than 65 countries. The Commission is thus representative of the finance industry.

[15] This is based on a discussion with Monika Houštecká, Head of the Trade Finance Department, Èeská Spoøitelna, Czech Republic.

# Concluding remarks

*By* **Filip De Ly**
*Co-editor,*
*Professor of Law, Erasmus University Rotterdam*
*Member of the Governing Council*
*of the ICC Institute of World Business Law*

## I. INTRODUCTION

Arbitration proceedings are very often aimed at obtaining monetary awards as a contractual remedy. However, other remedies may also be pursued in any such proceedings.[1] The objective of the 27th Annual Meeting of the ICC Institute of World Business Law was to pay attention to some of these other remedies.

The topic is to a large extent novel and raises difficult issues. Traditionally, remedies may substantially differ from one jurisdiction to another. For instance, specific performance meets much more resistance in common law jurisdictions than it does in civil law.[2] Also, some jurisdictions have remedies that are unfamiliar or unknown to others, such as the *astreinte* of French law and the law of the Benelux countries.[3] These differences not only create problems in international relations but also pose challenges as soon as international arbitration is involved. This book attempts to shed some light on some of these delicate issues. Rather than embark on a comprehensive overview of awards other than monetary awards providing direct relief for breach of contract, the editors have preferred to focus on some specific issues such as interest,[4] contractual remedies (such as liquidated damages clauses) and provisional and auxiliary remedies. In this regard, they could rely on the expertise of the contributors who also met demanding deadlines and without whom the publication of this volume in the Dossiers of the ICC Institute of World Business Law simply would not have been possible.

These concluding observations will not attempt to summarize the various contributions but will merely identify a number of threads that can be found throughout this book and which relate to party autonomy (Part II), the impact of the applicable law (Part III) and arbitrator autonomy (Part IV).

## II. PARTY AUTONOMY

Parties to a contract may already at the stages of negotiations and contract drafting provide for some contractual clauses dealing with remedies. This relates primarily to clauses providing for a predetermination of contractual damages in the case of liquidated damages or even, to the extent permitted by the applicable law, incentives to perform absent which penalties may become payable, as is the case with penalty clauses.[5] Other examples are interest clauses in international commercial contracts, in which the parties may regulate interest issues including the interest rate, simple or compound interest, a notification requirement or the dates from and until which interest will accrue. Any such clauses are manifestations of party autonomy regarding contractual remedies.

Remedies may not only stem directly from contractual clauses but may be incorporated into contracts by virtue of an arbitration clause referring disputes to institutional arbitration. To the extent that arbitration rules contain provisions regarding remedies (for instance, regarding interest, interim relief[6] or the possibility for arbitrators to award a judicial penalty (*astreinte*)), any such institutional rules have become contractual terms by reference and are indirect manifestations of party autonomy regarding remedies.

Party autonomy in relation to remedies has features of its own as well as limitations. As contractual terms, any such remedies may be subject to interpretation as is the case with liquidated damages clauses when the contractual clause does not explicitly state whether the contractual remedy is of an exclusive nature or when an interest clause is unclear as to whether interest is to be simple or compounded. As to its limitations, contractual remedies are subject to mandatory rules of the governing law as is the case with the prohibition on penalty clauses in most common law jurisdictions, the prohibition on excessive penalties in some civil law countries or the mandatory control over penalties in other civil law systems.[7]

Moreover, limitations on party autonomy may follow from their characterization in accordance with the applicable law. Some remedies may pertain to procedural law bringing them outside the scope of party autonomy, which may imply that any contractual provisions regarding any such remedies may be considered to be null and void or unenforceable. The latter raises the question as to the impact of procedural law on remedies available in international commercial arbitration, which will be discussed in the following section.

## III. REMEDIES AND APPLICABLE LAW

The broad range of remedies discussed in this book raise questions as to their proper characterization, which may determine the law to be applied to any such remedy. Both aspects will be discussed below.

### 1. Characterization of remedies

Characterization has hardly been analyzed in relation to international commercial arbitration. If one were to makes a comparison with domestic courts, characterization may be operated in accordance with the *lex fori*, the *lex causae* or autonomously, with conflict of laws having a clear preference for characterization according to the local law of the court unless there is uniform law that may indicate a more autonomous approach. In his 1963 Hague lectures, Goldman already questioned this approach in relation to international commercial arbitration and advocated the opinion that domestic conceptions of characterization should not lead arbitrators, since there is no *lex fori* in international arbitration.[8]

However, the proper approach to characterization in international arbitration is only relevant to the extent that the characterization in the legal systems involved differs.[9] Some remedies, such as liquidated damages or penalty clauses or the obligation to pay interest (as opposed to most other interest issues), are likely not to raise characterization questions as most legal systems will characterize them as contractual remedies. But many of the other remedies discussed in this volume might create true conflicts between competing rules of the law governing the contract, the procedural rules of the place of arbitration and – in relation to interest – the law of the contract currency.

This book gives many such examples.[10] Are judicial penalties in Sweden to ensure compliance with procedural instructions or orders available when the place of arbitration is Stockholm (and, if so, is it further required that the dispute is somehow connected to Sweden other than as the place of arbitration?) or only when the law applicable to the contract is Swedish? Are judicial penalties available as to substantive remedies in France or the Benelux when the place of arbitration is in these countries (also if, but for the location, no other connections exist) or does it depend on the governing law? Is specific performance possible in England (eventually through the courts) on the basis that the seat is in London or on the basis of a governing law other than English law authorizing specific performance on terms more favourable than English law? Is the interest rate, the possibility of awarding compound interest or the calculation of the interest period to be derived from the law of the seat, from the law governing the merits of the case or from the law of the contract currency?

Furthermore, these questions may arise not only in arbitration proceedings on the merits but also in interim relief proceedings. This raises yet another question, namely: does interim relief warrant different answers?

An answer to these questions would exceed the scope of this concluding chapter but some general observations can be made. First, as Goldman already pointed out in 1963, the analogy between domestic courts and international arbitration fails for a number of reasons, certainly when the place of arbitration has been chosen for reasons of neutrality and is otherwise unconnected to the merits of the dispute. This implies that domestic notions of the law of the seat of the arbitration should not automatically be transposed to arbitration. Second, in view of the contractual origins of arbitration, the law applicable to the merits has a stronger claim to be applied to merits issues, while the choice of a seat may be interpreted as extending only to procedural (and not to merits) issues. This implies that contractual remedies and interest issues by and large fall outside the scope of the procedural law of the seat. Third, a preference for merits issues to be governed by the law applicable to the contract does not exclude the consideration of alternative characterizations, such as autonomous characterizations or, for interest issues, the law of the contract currency.

Fourth, an arbitrator should be cautious not to impose a remedy available under the governing law that would raise setting-aside problems at the place of arbitration. Fifth, in interim relief proceedings, time constraints may prevent an elaborate debate and deliberation on these issues. As a consequence, the discretionary nature of decisions in any such proceedings on the basis of balancing the interests of the parties and the preservation of the *status quo* between the parties will be decisive.

The most difficult characterization issues arise where a substantive remedy is sought that is available at the seat but not in the governing law. This is the case in relation to the French and Benelux judicial penalty (*astreinte*). In these countries, the judicial penalty has a mixed nature. First, it has a judicial function, as judges and arbitrators are authorized to award, by way of an auxiliary and ancillary order to an order for specific performance or an injunction, a certain monetary sum to be forfeited to the creditor in case of non-compliance with the order or the injunction. Second, the judicial penalty clearly has a merits aspect in that it provides an incentive for compliance with a contractual obligation. Under a purely procedural characterization, one may be tempted to accept this remedy in international arbitration since it is available at the seat. However, the judicial penalty also has a contractual function and thus conflicts with any such remedy not available under the law governing the merits. However, since the remedy is available at the seat and the parties may have chosen the seat, they may be deemed to have accepted this mixed remedy in addition to remedies available under the law governing the merits. The issue is thus primarily restricted to cases where the seat is not determined by the parties but, for instance, by the institution administering the case or by the arbitral tribunal and where the question arises whether any such determination of the seat also implies that remedies available there but not under the law governing the contract can be sought. This question remains unsolved and raises problems primarily at the enforcement stage if the judicial penalty contributes to enforcement in the country of the governing law.

## 2. Applicable law

After characterization, the arbitral tribunal will need to determine the applicable law. In this regard, the traditional conflict of laws method pointing to domestic law by virtue of a conflict rule has gradually lost its predominance and is competing with other methods that may equally provide the applicable rules.

First, uniform law is becoming increasingly relevant worldwide as well as at a regional level (such as in the European Union), and its influence is specifically felt on interest issues.[11] In the case of sales contracts, for instance, the 1980 Vienna Convention on the International Sale of Goods (CISG) may be applicable. The CISG entitles the seller to payment of interest under Article 78 but fails to deal with other interest issues that raise delicate questions relating to interest periods and rates. Similarly, under the laws of the member states of the European Union, commercial receivables are subject to the interest rate of the European Central Bank plus 7% by virtue of the EU Collection Directive.[12] For procedural issues, however, uniform law is by and large lacking, with the exception of the Benelux Uniform Act on Judicial Penalties, which was annexed to the Convention of November 26, 1973 between Belgium, The Netherlands and Luxembourg and has been incorporated into the codes of civil procedure of these countries. Regarding the future, it is worth mentioning the revision of the UNCITRAL Model Law on International Commercial Arbitration[13] with regard to interim relief, as states adopting legislation based on this revision will provide a uniform basis for arbitral tribunals to grant interim relief.

Second, the question of the applicable law is also less relevant to the extent that issues relating to remedies or interest are governed by contractual provisions or by the incorporation of arbitration rules, which will often pre-empt the applicable law to the extent that any such law is of a non-mandatory character. This is highly relevant in relation to international commercial arbitration, since the arbitration laws in numerous countries – as well as international arbitration rules – provide that an arbitral tribunal should first apply the contractual provisions, which reduces the impact of the applicable law.

Its relevance is thus limited to situations where the contract is silent on remedies (for instance, on remedies in interim relief proceedings) or interest, where there is uncertainty as to the interpretation of contractual clauses or where mandatory law is involved.

Last but not least, questions regarding the applicable law are just different in international commercial arbitration than in domestic court litigation. Since the 1960s, international commercial arbitration in many jurisdictions has departed from the application of the conflict of laws of the place of arbitration in relation to merits issues (including, for the purposes of this discussion, interest). Arbitral tribunals are authorized to apply the conflict rules they consider appropriate (indirect approach) or, as in France and The Netherlands, the substantive rules they consider appropriate (direct approach). In relation to procedural issues, arbitration laws and rules often give arbitral tribunals large discretionary powers to conduct the proceedings, subject to minimal procedural safeguards such as due process, equality of arms and good administration of justice. This implies that domestic rules of civil procedure at the seat of arbitration that apply to domestic court proceedings do not automatically apply to international commercial arbitrations seated in any such country. Thus, procedural issues regarding remedies do not necessarily apply to arbitration, granting arbitrators a lot of autonomy in relation to various issues that will be discussed below.

## IV. ARBITRATOR AUTONOMY

Absent party autonomy, the question arises whether arbitral tribunals need to fall back on the applicable law as domestic courts would do or whether and to what extent they are authorized to exercise their own autonomy in framing remedies and awarding interest.

To answer this question, merits issues are clearly distinguishable from mere procedural issues, which will require a proper characterization by the arbitral tribunal as set forth in section III.1 above. If the characterization process leads to an issue being considered as a merits issue, the arbitral tribunal will be bound by a choice of law operated by the parties.

Absent any such choice of law provision in the contract or during the arbitral proceedings, the arbitral tribunal will, under many arbitration laws or arbitration rules, enjoy broad discretion to either determine the applicable law by virtue of a conflict rule or directly apply an appropriate substantive rule. Even if a conflict rule is to be applied under the indirect approach, this will not necessarily imply that domestic rules are to be applied, because the question will then arise whether any such domestic rule applies in an arbitration context. Even if domestic rules apply, they may still entrust an arbitral tribunal, like a domestic court, with broad discretionary powers, as for instance regarding *quantum* issues. These factors contribute to arbitrators having a lot of autonomy to decide merits issues, absent a choice of law or applicable mandatory rules. The contributions on interest in this volume confirm these propositions and argue for broad discretionary powers in deciding on interest issues, by and large irrespective of domestic law.[14] On the other hand, some contributions have drawn attention to the possible impact of mandatory rules prohibiting interest altogether or only compound interest.[15]

A procedural characterization of remedies raises somewhat different questions, since arbitrator autonomy has not been explicitly recognized to the same extent as in relation to merits issues. Although arbitrator autonomy is generally recognized for case management purposes relating to the handling of the proceedings, it is still unclear whether this autonomy also extends to other issues, such as remedies, or whether a territorial approach is to be followed, under which remedies need to follow or be consistent with the curial law of the seat of the arbitration. Sometimes, the curial law provides the answer, as in the case of Articles 1051(1) and 1056 of the Dutch Code of Civil Procedure, which refer back to the powers of domestic courts in interim relief proceedings or with regard to awarding judicial penalties and thus determine the authority of arbitral tribunals in relation thereto by reference to the similar powers of domestic courts. In the absence of an explicit authorization by the curial law, the question remains whether and to what extent arbitrators have autonomy regarding remedies that are to be characterized as procedural. An answer needs to be found at different levels. First, the arbitral tribunal needs to have authority to grant a remedy requested by a party that would exclude remedies against third parties or imply some coercion on a party to the arbitration.[16]

In practice, arbitral tribunals are aware of these limits to their powers, and problems will rarely occur in relation to these limitations. Second, the exercise of arbitrator autonomy, for reasons of efficiency, needs to be scrutinized against the arbitration law of the place of arbitration to see whether it prohibits any such exercise,[17] since the courts at the seat might be called upon to set aside the award granting certain remedies. If no explicit or implied prohibition stems from the arbitration law at the seat, it is submitted that arbitral tribunals enjoy autonomy to frame remedies based on their inherent powers to conduct the proceedings and to give appropriate relief at the outcome of these proceedings, provided certain minimal requirements are met. These requirements relate first to the parties' procedural autonomy, in that the arbitral tribunal should not order remedies that fall outside the scope of the submission to arbitration. Also, any remedy should not come as a surprise to the parties, since it might violate due process, and the arbitral tribunal may be advised to raise the remedies issue timely in the course of the proceedings. Finally, any remedy should not violate procedural public policy at the seat, although any such violation is not to be deduced from the mere fact that the remedy is unknown in court litigation at the seat.[18]

## END NOTES

[1] M. Moses, *The Principles and Practice of International Commercial Arbitration* (Cambridge University Press, 2008) pp. 186-188.

[2] For instance, Art. 10(2) of the 1980 Rome Convention on the Law Applicable to Contractual Obligations provides that, in relation to the manner of performance and the steps to be taken in the event of defective performance, regard shall be had to the law of the country in which performance takes place. This provision is to be replaced by identical wording in Art. 12(2) of the Rome I Regulation expected to be adopted in the spring of 2008 and to enter into effect in the fall of 2009.

[3] For the position under Swiss law, see J.C. Landrove and J.J. Greuter, 'The civil *astreinte* as an incentive measure in litigation and international arbitration practice in Switzerland: is there a need for incorporation?', in C. Chappuis, B. Foëx and T.K. Graziano (eds.), *L'harmonisation internationale du droit* (Zurich, Schulthess, 2007) pp. 536-549; L. Lévy, 'Les astreintes et l'arbitrage international en Suisse', 21 *ASA Bull.* (2001) p. 21.

[4] See also B. Chappuis, *Le moment du dommage: Analyse du rôle du temps de la détermination et la réparation du dommage* (Zurich, Schulthess, 2007) pp. 363-379.

[5] See the contribution of Ms Dimolitsa in this volume.

[6] For an overview of arbitration rules regarding interim relief, see the contribution of Messrs Beechey and Kenny in this volume.

[7] M. Fontaine and F. De Ly., *Drafting International Contracts: An Analysis of Contract Clauses* (Ardsley, Transnational, 2006) pp. 342-346.

[8] B. Goldman, 'Les conflits de lois dans l'arbitrage international de droit privé', *Recueil des Cours*, Vol. 109 (1963-II) p. 422.

[9] Conflict scholars refer to this situation as a true conflict (as opposed to false conflicts).

[10] For a more extensive discussion on judicial penalties, see the contribution of Mr Mourre in this volume.

[11] See the contribution of Professor Giardina in this volume.

[12] Art. 3 of Directive 2000/35/EC of 29 June 2000 on combating late payment in commercial transactions, *OJ* L 200, August 8, 2000, p. 35.

[13] UN General Assembly Resolution 61/33 dated December 18, 2006, available at: <http://www.uncitral.org>.

[14] See the contributions of Professor Gotanda and Mr Sénéchal in this volume. In a joint publication published after the 27th Annual Meeting of the ICC World Business Law Institute, both argued for the determination of interest rates at a market rate of return with compound interest on an annual basis. See J. Gotanda and T. Sénéchal, 'Interest as damages', Villanova Public Law and Legal Theory Working Paper Series (April 2008), available at: <http://ssrn.com/abstract=1116382>.

[15] See the contributions of Messrs Riad and Arfazadeh in this volume.

[16] See Landrove and Greuter, *supra* note 3, at pp. 537-539.

[17] On the English position, see the contribution of Mr Veeder in this volume.

[18] For a Swiss perspective, see Landrove and Greuter, *supra* note 3, at pp. 539-541. J.J., *l.c.*, 539-541.

# Key-words index

# B

# C

# D

# E

# F

# G

# H

# I

## J

## K

## L

# M

# N

## R

# V

# W

# ICC at a glance

ICC is the world business organization, a representative body that speaks with authority on behalf of enterprises from all sectors in every part of the world.

The fundamental mission of ICC is to promote trade and investment across frontiers and help business corporations meet the challenges and opportunities of globalization. Its conviction that trade is a powerful force for peace and prosperity dates from the organization's origins early in the last century. The small group of far-sighted business leaders who founded ICC called themselves "the merchants of peace".

ICC has three main activities: rules-setting, arbitration and policy. Because its member companies and associations are themselves engaged in international business, ICC has unrivalled authority in making rules that govern the conduct of business across borders. Although these rules are voluntary, they are observed in countless thousands of transactions every day and have become part of the fabric of international trade.

ICC also provides essential services, foremost among them the ICC International Court of Arbitration, the world's leading arbitral institution. Another service is the World Chambers Federation, ICC's worldwide network of chambers of commerce, fostering interaction and exchange of chamber best practice.

Business leaders and experts drawn from the ICC membership establish the business stance on broad issues of trade and investment policy as well as on vital technical and sectoral subjects. These include financial services, information technologies, telecommunications, marketing ethics, the environment, transportation, competition law and intellectual property, among others.

ICC enjoys a close working relationship with the United Nations and other intergovernmental organizations, including the World Trade Organization and the G8.

ICC was founded in 1919. Today it groups hundreds of thousands of member companies and associations from over 130 countries. National committees work with their members to address the concerns of business in their countries and convey to their governments the business views formulated by ICC.

# Some ICC specialized divisions

- ICC International Court of Arbitration (Paris)
- ICC International Centre for Expertise (Paris)
- ICC World Chambers Federation (Paris)
- ICC Institute of World Business Law (Paris)
- ICC Centre for Maritime Co-operation (London)
- ICC Commercial Crime Services (London)
- ICC Services (*ICC affiliate*, Paris)

## • Publications

ICC Publications Department is committed to offering the best resources on business and trade for the international community.

The content of ICC publications is derived from the work of ICC commissions, institutions and individual international experts. The specialized list covers a range of topics including international banking, international trade reference and terms (Incoterms), law and arbitration, counterfeiting and fraud, model commercial contracts and environmental issues.

## • Events

ICC's programme of conferences and seminars is the essential channel for passing on the world business organization's expertise to a wider audience.

ICC Events, a Department of ICC Services, spotlights policy issues of direct concern to business such as banking techniques and practices, e-business, IT and telecoms, piracy and counterfeiting.

ICC Events also runs training courses on international arbitration and negotiating international contracts for business-people, corporate counsel, lawyers and legal practitioners involved in international trade.

# Source products for global business

ICC's specialized list of publications covers a range of topics including international banking, international trade reference and terms (Incoterms), law and arbitration, counterfeiting and fraud, model commercial contracts and environmental issues.

ICC products are available from ICC national committees, which exist in over 80 countries around the world. Contact details for a national committee in your country are available at **www.iccwbo.org**

You may also order ICC products online from the ICC Business Bookstore at **www.iccbooks.com**

**ICC Services**
**Publications Department**
38 Cours Albert 1er
75008 Paris – France
Tel     +33 (0)1 4953 2923
Fax     +33 (0)1 4953 2902
E-mail  pub@iccwbo.org